1965

Yale Studies in English

Benjamin Christie Nangle, Editor

Volume 142

Published with aid from the foundation

established in memory of Philip Hamilton McMillan

of the class of 1894, Yale College

ALVIN KERNAN

THE CANKERED MUSE

Satire of the

English Renaissance

New Haven and London · Yale University Press

© 1959 by Yale University Press, Inc.

Set in Baskerville type and
printed in the United States of America by
Vail-Ballou Press, Inc., Binghamton, New York;
reprinted by The Carl Purington Rollins Printing-Office
of the Yale University Press, New Haven, Connecticut.

First published, November 1959
Second printing, January 1962

Library of Congress catalog card number: 59–12815

The Philip Hamilton McMillan

Memorial Publication Fund

The present volume is the fifty-sixth work published by the Yale University Press on The Philip Hamilton McMillan Memorial Publication Fund. This Foundation was established December 12, 1922, by a gift to Yale University in pursuance of a pledge announced on Alumni University Day in February, 1922, of a fund of $100,000 bequeathed to James Thayer McMillan and Alexis Caswell Angell, as Trustees, by Mrs. Elizabeth Anderson McMillan, of Detroit, to be devoted by them to the establishment of a memorial in honor of her husband.

He was born in Detroit, Michigan, December 28, 1872, prepared for college at Phillips Academy, Andover, and was graduated from Yale in the Class of 1894. As an undergraduate he was a leader in many of the college activities of his day, and within a brief period of his graduation was called upon to assume heavy responsibilities in the management and direction of numerous business enterprises in Detroit, where he was also a Trustee of the Young Men's Christian Association and of Grace Hospital. His untimely death, from heart disease, on October 4, 1919, deprived his city of one of its leading citizens and his University of one of its most loyal sons.

PREFACE

The pages which follow first advance a critical proposition, that satire is a distinct artistic genre with a number of marked characteristics, and then make use of that proposition to describe the complex and seemingly disparate mass of prose, poetry, and drama which is English satire of the late Renaissance. Although the critical theory necessarily comes first here, it originally derived from an attempt to understand one part of English Renaissance satire, the plays of John Marston. This in turn led on to an examination of the Elizabethan conventions and theories of nondramatic satire. During the course of this work it became clear that the difficulty which Elizabethan satire presents for a modern reader is simply a crucial instance of our difficulties in reading all satire, and that no meaningful statement can be made about Marston's satiric productions or those of his contemporaries unless it is based in turn on a complete theory of satire.

The problem thus became to define the genre, for it immediately appeared that despite the long and distinguished history of satire in the West we have no comprehensive critical treatment of it, only partial discussions such as Horace's occasional comments in his *Sermones,* Dryden's "A Discourse Concerning the Original and Progress of Satire," and, somewhat obliquely, Freud's "Wit and Its Relation to the Unconscious." However, there has been, as I shall attempt to show, a tacit definition of satire running just below the surface of various criticisms of specific satires and satiric authors.

Somewhat surprisingly, Elizabethan satire, with all its disorder, confusions, and artistic clumsiness, proved for a number of reasons to be remarkably suggestive to someone interested in the problem of "what is satire?" The enormous amount of satire written between approximately 1590 and 1640 makes it possible to establish and define a tradition with certainty and observe its growth and change. The authors, like most Elizabethan writers, were extremely self-conscious and frequently discussed their chosen form, stopping to point out what they were doing and why they were doing it. The few formal critics of the day, such as Lodge and Puttenham, were interested enough in satire to spare it a little time in their attempts to write complete poetics. Elizabethan satire fortunately stands distinctly between two other well-defined periods of satire, the medieval and the neoclassical, and the contrast forces certain questions about the ways in which satires can differ and the ways, if any, in which they always remain the same. Elizabethan satire had one great and thoroughly honest author, Ben Jonson, and great satire always makes clear the tendencies and possibilities which are barely perceptible in the minor works of the genre. Finally, and by far most importantly, satire was not confined to the printed page, but after it had taken its peculiar Elizabethan form in poetry it was carried over complete into the theater, and there a number of its peculiarities are explained. But the dramatists went beyond mere repetition of the devices of formal verse satire and conducted in a number of plays an explicit inquiry into the very nature of satire itself: its psychological origins, its relation to the world it claims to mirror faithfully, and its ultimate usefulness. The explanation of satire offered in this book really derives from plays such as *Timon of Athens*, *Troilus and Cressida*, *The Malcontent*, *King Lear*, and *The Duchess of Malfi*, where probing questions are asked about satire, not considered merely as a literary form, but as a basic attitude toward life which eventuates in those gestures and works we call satiric.

While the substance of this book remains a reading of Elizabethan satire, that satire is itself offered as but one chapter in the true history of the genre satire, one mutation of the fundamental energies and the characteristic expressive forms of the satiric approach to life. The emphasis is on the critical proposition made about satire, and I have therefore not stopped to quarrel with other critics about minor points of interpretation, nor have I lingered over a number of problems usually discussed in treatments of Elizabethan satire: e.g. "Is Hall's claim to be the first English satirist justified?" "How serious was the Hall-Marston quarrel or the War of the Theaters?" "Did Ben Jonson wait until 1599 and the prohibition of the further printing of satires to translate formal satire to the stage?" These questions have been competently treated at length elsewhere, and I have indicated in notes where the relevant material is to be found. Finally, in order to keep my argument uncluttered I have selected my illustrative material rather rigorously. No point is made, I hope, without substantive evidence, but I have felt it unnecessary to quote every line in Elizabethan satire which supports a particular interpretation, or to deal with every play in which a satirist appears.

The foundation of this book, a study of the plays of John Marston, was submitted as a doctoral dissertation at Yale, and my thanks are due Charles Prouty, the director, for his encouragement and help. Many of my friends have listened patiently to my awkward attempts to explain what I was trying to do, and to them my thanks; but I owe particular debts to Talbot Donaldson, Martin Price, Aubrey Williams and Adam Parry, all of whom read parts of my manuscript and offered helpful criticism. To the readers of the manuscript for the Yale Studies in English, Davis Harding and Eugene Waith, I am indebted for a great number of helpful suggestions and criticisms of both content and style. Benjamin Nangle, editor of the Yale Studies in English, carefully went over the proofs and has saved me from a great number of inaccuracies and inelegancies. The section on *Histriomastix* in Chapter 4 is a reduced version of an article printed in *The Modern Language Quarterly,* June 1958, which the editors have graciously given me permission to reprint.

I am indebted to the Fund for Young Scholars for assistance in the publication of the book. Finally, I should like to offer this book as a formal expression of my gratitude to my wife, who after seeing it in many drafts and foul papers would no doubt settle just to get it out of the house.

A. K.

New Haven, March 1959

CONTENTS

CHAPTER 1

A THEORY OF SATIRE

"There was in our time a certain parasite, Golias by name, notorious alike for his intemperance and wantonness . . . a tolerable scholar, but without morals or discipline . . . who did vomit forth against the Pope and the Roman curia a succession of famous pieces, as adroit as they were preposterous, as imprudent as they were impudent." [1] These lines, written in the early thirteenth century by the historian Giraldus Cambrensis, contain a fundamental error: there was no such person as "Golias." There were, however, a number of satiric poems, written in the twelfth and thirteenth centuries by anonymous poets, which were purportedly the work of one Bishop Golias, a sprightly, irreverent, devil-may-care figure who divided his time between laughing at the clergy and praising the pleasures of the flesh. But Golias himself was the purely poetic creation of those poets called the goliards or *ordo vagorum*, the wandering, witty clerics of the late medieval period, who refused to attach themselves to any benefice or to submit to any strict rule. For them Golias, whose name seems to derive from Latin *gula*, throat and gluttony, became "a kind of eponymous hero," [2] and under the cover of this *persona*

1. Giraldus Cambrensis, *Speculum Ecclesiae,* in *Works,* ed. J. S. Brewer (London, 1873), *4,* 291–2. The translation is from Helen Waddell's *The Wandering Scholars* (London, John Constable, 1927), p. 160.
2. G. F. Whicher, *The Goliard Poets* (Norfolk, Conn., New Directions, 1949), p. 3. The etymology of "Golias" is still a matter of dispute; alternate

the poets flaunted their own unorthodox wit and wrote
their mocking attacks on a world where people like Giraldus took themselves far too seriously.

Giraldus was a historian and he read the goliardic satires
as documents, pieces of reporting, making no allowance for
their pronounced artistic qualities of obliquity, exaggeration, and irony. The satiric mask of Bishop Golias was for
the historian the direct reflection of an actual living person
whose discreditable character, revealed by his manner of
writing, explained the "preposterous," i.e. historically un-
true, nature of his attacks on the church. While Giraldus'
particular confusion is evident, his general approaches to
satire have tenaciously remained the dominant ones down
to our own time. The character who delivers the satiric attack is still identified as the author, the biographical
method; and the picture of the world given in satire is taken
as an attempt to portray the "actual" world, the historical
method. These methods have been applied with varying
degrees of sophistication, but even at their best they inevitably lead us to such unanswerable questions as, "Was
first-century Rome as completely debased as Juvenal painted
it?" or "Did Swift hate mankind as extravagantly as Gulliver hated the Yahoos?" Our attention is thus directed
away from the satiric work itself and toward some second
object, the personality of the author or the contemporary
social scene. In this way satire is denied the independence
of artistic status and made a biographical and historical
document, while the criticism of satire degenerates into
discussion of an author's moral character and the economic
and social conditions of his time.

Curiously enough, the authors of satires have encouraged
this response to their works, for of all the major literary
genres satire has traditionally made most pretense of being

---

suggestions are *"guliar,"* to deceive, and "Goliath." See J. M. Manly, "The
Familia Goliae," *Modern Philology,* 5 (1907), 201–9.

realistic. The man who after reading *Gulliver's Travels* tried to find Lilliput on the map may have been a fool, but he was led on by Swift's elaborate apparatus of verisimilitude. Elsewhere the game is not so apparent, and the satirist always assures us most seriously that he alone describes the world as it actually *is*, he deals in "deeds and language such as men do use," he has "stoop'd to truth," his subject is "quidquid agunt homines." He argues that other literary kinds—epic, romance, love poetry—are mere lies which avoid the truth about mankind, and he delights in mocking these genres and parodying them. He emphasizes his own dedication to truth by the use of straightforward language, even slang at times, and fills his work with references to contemporary customs, places, names. He will proudly call attention to the absence from his writing of the usual ornaments of poetry and raise the question, as Horace does in the fourth satire of his first book of *Sermones,* whether on the basis of realism, rough diction, and crude meter satire is even entitled to the name of poetry? Pietro Aretino's boast, which owes a good deal to Horace, is typical of the satirist's proud claim to downright truth without any fancy decoration:

> Caesar and Homer, I have stolen your bays!
> Though not a poet or an emperor;
> My style has been my star, in a manner, for
> I speak the truth, don't deal in lying praise.
> I am Aretino, censor of the ways
> Of the lofty world, prophet-ambassador
> Of truth and smiling virtue.[3]

In short, the satirist makes every effort to repudiate the Muse and to emphasize the down-to-earth quality of himself and his work, but the very vigor of these efforts and

3. *The Works of Aretino,* trans. Samuel Putnam (Chicago, P. Covici, 1926), 2, 273.

their continuous appearance in satire suggest that they are themselves stylistic devices used in a perfectly conventional manner to establish the character and tone traditionally thought appropriate for the satiric genre. Paradoxically, the claim to have no style is itself a trick of style employed by nearly every satirist, and his realistic touches are themselves satiric conventions. In point of fact, the claims to blunt, straightforward, and unskilled honesty made by the satirist are so patently false as to be outrageous, for in practice he is always an extremely clever poetic strategist and manipulator of language who possesses an incredibly copious and colorful vocabulary and an almost limitless arsenal of rhetorical devices. This paradox of the artless artist, innate in satire, has usually been solved either by ignoring all evidences of art and taking the satirist's word for it that he is a truthful, unskilled fellow driven to write by his indignation; or by noting his techniques of exaggeration and dismissing his presentation of himself as a plain man dedicated to truth as a mere pose designed to cover some such sinister intention as blackening the names of his enemies or passing off smut and scandal as truth in order to sell his book. Every major writer of satire has been praised by some critics for his fearless determination to tell the truth about his world and damned by others for a twisted, unstable, prurient liar whose works no careful father should allow his children to open.

This dilemma has been created by the biographical and historical methods of criticism, and to solve it we need to approach satire in the way we do other poetry—as an art; that is, not a direct report of the poet's feelings and the literal incidents which aroused those feelings, but a construct of symbols—situations, scenes, characters, language —put together to express some particular vision of the world. The individual parts must be seen in terms of their function in the total poem and not judged by reference to things outside the poem such as the medical history of the author or the social scene in which he wrote.

There have been in recent years a number of discussions of the art of satire, but these have focused somewhat narrowly on the satirist's use of linguistic devices and his ability to contrive incidental effects. We have been shown that he is a master of irony, caricature, disabling imagery, the unexpected thrust of wit, anticlimax, burlesque, and invective.[4] He seems to be a man with an immense supply of rhetorical tools which he uses in rapid succession to belabor his victims. On the rare occasions when attempts have been made to show that the art of satire extends beyond the manipulation of language, the emphasis has still fallen on isolated effects. Mary Claire Randolph, for example, points out that within formal verse satire we find "miniature dramas, sententious proverbs and quotable maxims, beast fables (often reduced to animal metaphors), brief sermons, sharp diatribes, series of vignettes, swiftly sketched but painstakingly built up satiric 'characters' or portraits, figure-processions, little fictions and apologues, visions, apostrophes and invocations to abstractions. This bewildering array of devices suggests the diverse origins of satire and the appropriateness of its name '*satura*,' or 'medley.' " [5] Demonstrations of the satirist's skillful handling of language and management of single effects have made suspect the once popular examination question, "Is Satire Art?" but we are still left with a satirist who is only an artist manqué, a contriver of farragoes rather than articulated wholes.[6]

4. See, for example, David Worcester, *The Art of Satire*, Cambridge, Mass., 1940.

5. "The Structural Design of Formal Verse Satire," *Philological Quarterly*, *21* (1942), 373.

6. There are a number of recent critical studies, however, in which the coherence of entire satires has been demonstrated. See, for example, Aubrey Williams, *Pope's Dunciad. A Study of Its Meaning*, London, 1955; and W. S. Anderson, "Studies in Book I of Juvenal," *Yale Classical Studies, 15* (1957), 33–90.

What is required is a more comprehensive method of describing satire which will not limit our investigations to linguistic analysis or the location of single effects but will instead include all the major elements of composition used in the form. An adequate set of terms will permit us to see individual satires as entities and thus make it possible for us to grasp the relationship of one satire to others, and ultimately to define satire with some exactitude. Historical and biographical critics have focused on what are certainly the two most striking aspects of satire, the picture of the society which is presented as a literal rendering of the *hic et nunc,* and the elusive speaker who is sometimes merely identified as "I" and sometimes given a name. In historical terms the picture of society is identified always as Rome, London, Hollywood, or some other specific place, and in biographical terms the speaker becomes Swift, Juvenal, Fielding, or some other specific author. If, however, we translate the historical and biographical terms into the dramatic terms which they readily suggest, a number of the dilemmas seemingly inherent in satire become comprehensible. Using the terms of drama, the picture of society drawn by the satirist becomes the "scene," and the voice we "hear" becomes the satiric "hero." Since the chief character of satire always lacks so signally the qualities which we associate with heroism, it will be better to refer to him simply as the "satirist," and from this point on when the word "satirist" is used it refers to the chief character—whether named, identified as "I," or the anonymous voice that tells the tale—in a satiric work. The author will be designated by other terms. The adoption of two dramatic terms, scene and satirist, entails the use of a third, "plot," for wherever we have characters in a setting there is always movement, or attempted movement, in some direction.

Satire is, like comedy and tragedy, a very ancient form which appears to have its roots in primitive ritual activities such as formulaic curses and the magical blasting of personal and tribal enemies; [7] and just as we find tragic and comic attitudes outside art, so we find that the attitudes expressed in satire are also felt and expressed by individuals in various extraliterary ways ranging from the sneer to the street-corner tirade. But satire, although critics have always regarded it as a minor form, has long been established as a recognizable literary genre with its own traditions and conventions. The protean nature of satire has interfered with any precise definition of its conventions, but since by general agreement works as surfacely diverse as Jeremiah's bitter denunciation of his sinful people, *Gulliver's Travels, The Praise of Folly, The Clouds* and *The Threepenny Opera* have been identified as satires, then it would follow that they share some quality which we take to be characteristic of satire. For most of us satire is synonymous with attack, particularly the savage variety, but there are attacks which are not satires—Ahab's bitter descriptions of Moby Dick, for example—and so satire must be a definite kind of attack. That is, there must be specific groupings, roles, tones, patterns, which we implicitly recognize as characteristic of satire, and these I propose to describe in terms of scene, character, and plot.

THE SCENE OF SATIRE

The scene of satire is always disorderly and crowded, packed to the very point of bursting. The deformed faces of depravity, stupidity, greed, venality, ignorance, and maliciousness group closely together for a moment, stare boldly out

7. Inquiry into the magical origins of satire was begun by F. N. Robinson, "Satirists and Enchanters in Early Irish Literature" in *Studies in the History of Religion Presented to Crawford Howell Toy*, ed. D. G. Lyon and G. F. Moore (New York, 1912), pp. 95–130. See also Mary Claire Randolph, "Celtic Smiths and Satirists: Partners in Sorcery," *Journal of English Literary History, 8* (1941), 127–59; and R. C. Elliott, "The Satirist and Society," *ELH, 21* (1954), 237–48.

at us, break up, and another tight knot of figures collects, stroking full stomachs, looking vacantly into space, nervously smiling at the great, proudly displaying jewels and figures, clinking moneybags, slyly fingering new-bought fashions. The scene is equally choked with things: ostentatious buildings and statuary, chariots, sedan-chairs, clothes, books, food, horses, dildoes, luxurious furnishings, gin bottles, wigs. Pick up any major satiric work and open it at random and the immediate effect is one of disorderly profusion. The sheer dirty weight, without reason or conscious purpose, of people and their vulgar possessions threatens to overwhelm the world in Trimalchio's banquet room, the streets of Juvenal's Rome, Langland's "felde ful of folke," Eleanor Rumming's Tavern, Bartholomew Fair, the City as the Dunces set off for Westminster, Don Juan's London streets that "boil over with their scum," and before the Hollywood theater where the vast mob of yokels gathers to see the "movie stars" in Nathanael West's *The Day of the Locust*. Everywhere the satirist turns he finds idiocy, foolishness, depravity, and dirt. "Auriculas asini quis non habet?" [8] (Who is there who has not the ears of an ass?) shouts "Persius," and "Juvenal's" exclamation, "It is difficult *not* to write satire," (difficile est saturam non scribere) expresses the satirist's sense of a world where vice is so omnipresent and so arrant that it cannot be avoided. It is no accident that most satire is set in the city, particularly in the metropolis with a polyglot people.

In satiric painting this quality of dense, turbulent weight is even more immediately striking. The human stupidity and malice concentrated in the faces of Hieronymus Bosch's Dutch burghers crowd in a shapeless, suffocating mass which threatens to overwhelm and obliterate the face of Christ in

8. Persius, Satire I, 121. All translations of Persius and Juvenal are from *Juvenal and Persius*, ed. and trans. G. G. Ramsay, Loeb Classical Library, London, 1930.

The Carrying of the Cross; and in Bosch's surrealistic pictures such as *The Temptation of Saint Anthony* where human nastiness is given fantastic form, the typical density of the satiric scene finds expression in a vast multitude of small, grotesque monsters who work madly and aimlessly around the praying saint. Hogarth's satiric drawings, e.g. *Gin Lane,* are always crowded with debris and a host of rotting things, human, animal and vegetable. In Reginald Marsh's *Coney Island* vulgarity, vanity, lust, and animality combine to create a writhing mass of flesh and human litter which nearly blots out the sea, the sky, and the sand. In the occasional instances where the literary satirist uses a painting image to heighten the visual impact of his scene, the qualities of density, multiplicity, and disorder are always stressed. Henry Savile, in his "Advice to a Painter to draw the Duke by" begins his instructions on satiric composition by saying,

> Spread a large canvass, Painter, to containe
> The great assembly and the numerous traine,
> Who all in triumph shall about him sitte
> Abhoring wisdome and dispising witt.
>
> *(lines 1–4)* [9]

The chief character in Nathanael West's *The Day of the Locust* is a young painter who is attempting to get on canvas the same horrified and fearful perception of a world gone mad expressed by the book as a whole. The painter's vision is apocalyptic, and his picture, "The Burning of Los Angeles," makes concrete those forces which lie behind all satiric scenes. "Across the top, parallel with the frame, he

9. Printed in *The Poems and Letters of Andrew Marvell,* ed. H. H. Margoliouth (Oxford Univ. Press, 1927), *1,* 197. The "advice to a painter" became a popular satiric technique in the late 17th century. For a good example see Andrew Marvell's "The Last Instructions to a Painter," where he prescribes such a vast number of scenes, objects, and persons that the compositional techniques of even a painter such as Bosch would be strained to include them all in a single canvas.

had drawn the burning city, a great bonfire of architectural styles, ranging from Egyptian to Cape Cod colonial. Through the center, winding from left to right, was a long hill street and down it, spilling into the middle foreground, came the mob carrying baseball bats and torches. For the faces of its members he was using the innumerable sketches he had made of the people who had come to California to die. . . . In the lower foreground, men and women fled wildly before the vanguard of the crusading mob." [1]

The men and women who flee before the mob in "The Burning of Los Angeles," while they are not morally attractive, do represent the only virtues possible in such a world: courage, vitality, intelligence. But their position on the canvas suggests that they are about to be obliterated, and this is typical of the satiric scene. Somewhere in his dense knots of ugly flesh the satiric author or painter usually inserts a hint of an ideal which is either threatened with imminent destruction or is already dead. Humanity, what man is capable of achieving, is reflected in the lovely human faces of Bosch's tortured Christ and his St. Anthony, both about to be destroyed by the monstrosities which surround and press inward on them. Far above and in the distance behind *Gin Lane* rises a church steeple, but the three balls of the pawnbroker, in the form of a cross, dominate the immediate scene of squalor and filth. In Daumier's *Articles Placed in Evidence,* one of a series of satires on the French legal system, only the feet of Christ nailed to the cross show in a picture which hangs behind three bored and stupid judges presiding at a murder trial. Juvenal manages in his satires to refer in a variety of ways to the sturdy independence and moral vigor of the old Romans of the Republic; Celia retains her virtue, somewhat woodenly, in Volpone's palace; Pope can still talk to Arbuthnot; and a copy of Shakespeare still exists and is read by one man in the desert of the *Brave New World.*

1. (New York, New Directions, 1950), pp. 165–6.

Although there is always at least a suggestion of some kind of humane ideal in satire—it may in the blackest type of satire exist only as the unnamed opposite of the idiocy and villainy portrayed—this ideal is never heavily stressed, for in the satirist's vision of the world decency is forever in a precarious position near the edge of extinction, and the world is about to pass into eternal darkness. Consequently, every effort is made to emphasize the destroying ugliness and power of vice. The author of satire always portrays the grotesque and distorted, and concentrates to an obsessive degree on the flesh. Northrop Frye remarks that "genius seems to have led practically every great satirist to become what the world calls obscene," [2] and it is certainly true that the most unpleasant details appearing in literature are to be found in satire: Juvenal's pathic who tells us in explicit and revolting terms about his relationship with his patron, the descriptions of the excrementary functions of the Yahoos, Trimalchio's purge in *The Satyricon,* Rochester's pictures of the amorous pleasantries of King Charles and his mistresses. The satiric painter cannot be so frank, but he too seems to be fascinated by the flesh, particularly fat and the sagging, graying skin. His subjects if they are young and healthy are always gross and seem to reek of sweat, while if they are old they are either bursting the seams of their clothes or horribly cadaverous. If the satirist is more delicate than in the examples mentioned above, his characters still seem always indecently carnal; man is caught in his animal functions of eating, drinking, lusting, displaying his body, copulating, evacuating, scratching. He is riddled with hideous and deforming diseases, most often venereal: the bone-ache, falling hair, a decayed nose, ulcerous teeth, boils, scurf. Gross, sodden, rotting matter is the substance of the satiric scene and any trace of the beautiful or the spiritual is always in danger of being destroyed by the weight of this mere "stuff."

2. *Anatomy of Criticism* (Princeton Univ. Press, 1957), p. 235.

The faces peering out at us from the crowded satiric
scene seldom have normal features but are grotesquely distorted by the vices they mirror. Stupidity, lust, pride, greed,
hatred, and envy are revealed in exaggerated facial linea-
ments, gestures, bodies, and postures. We seem in satire always to be at the extreme: the bore never goes away, but
prattles on without end; the flatterer says *any* outrageous
thing to the vain man, who believes *all* that is said; the
miser wants absolutely *all* the wealth in the world; the fop
literally smothers himself under a mass of fantastic clothes;
the blockhead can be persuaded to do *anything;* the politician actually sells his mother for advancement. From the
"realistic" forms of satire where there is still some degree
of resemblance to actual humanity and where man's bestiality, smallness of mind, and mechanistic responses to ap-
petite are suggested by metaphors, it is but a step to more
obviously symbolic types of satire where the metaphors are
given substantial form. Men *are* fantastic monsters, part
rodent and part machine, in Bosch's surrealistic paintings;
the ordinary worker *is* a robot in *R.U.R.;* citizens *are* horses
and pigs in *Animal Farm;* and humans *are* Lilliputians and
Yahoos in *Gulliver's Travels.*

The more "realistic" kinds of satire are always just on the
verge of falling over into the overtly symbolic mode, despite
the satiric claims to literal truthfulness, and it would be
possible to classify satire according to the degree of realism
to which it pretends. Working from the point of extreme
realism we would begin with satires such as those of
Juvenal, or Pope's *Imitations of Horace,* and pass, with the
degree of realism progressively diminishing through such
works as *The Alchemist, The Adding Machine,* and *The
Birds* to beast fables such as "The Nun's Priest's Tale"
where literal imitation of the human scene has very nearly
disappeared. Criticism has, however, traditionally distinguished, under various names, only two main types of

satire: formal verse satire and Menippean satire. The term
Menippean originally referred to those satires which were
written in a mixture of verse and prose, but it has gradually
come to include any satiric work obviously written in the
third person or, to put it another way, where the attack is
managed under cover of a fable. Dryden—who prefers the
alternate term Varronian—cites as examples Petronius'
Satyricon, some of Lucian's dialogues, *The Golden Ass, The
Praise of Folly,* and his own *Absalom and Achitophel.*[3] In
the traditional scheme all works short of extreme realism
would then be classified as Menippean. Formal verse satire,
a loosely defined term at best, has been used to designate
those satires written in verse where the author appears to
speak in his own person without the use of any continuous
narrative, preferring to describe bits and pieces of the world
which has stung him into writing. Works falling in our
scale at the extreme realistic end would be in the category
of formal verse satire: the collections of satires of Juvenal,
Hall, Marston, Boileau, Rochester, some of Horace's *Sermones,* Byron's *English Bards and Scotch Reviewers,* and
Gay's *Trivia.* While I should prefer to drop the word
"verse" from the term formal verse satire to allow the in-
clusion of works such as Philip Wylie's *Generation of
Vipers* which obviously belong in this category, the terms
formal and Menippean are useful because as employed
today they make a meaningful differentiation of species
within the genus satire. But they are confusing if used too
rigidly to make something approaching an absolute distinction between two species of satire, for the scene of formal satire, despite the attempts of the author to make it
appear a piece of reporting, is as much a selection of significant and interrelated details, a symbolic world, as is the
scene of the beast fable where men are transformed into

3. "A Discourse Concerning the Original and Progress of Satire," in
Essays of John Dryden, ed. W. P. Ker (Oxford Univ. Press, 1925), 2, 66–7.

animals living in the forest or the barnyard. The qualities we have isolated as characteristic of the satiric scene, density, disorder, grossness, rot, and a hint of an ideal, are present in both formal and Menippean satire; they are simply made concrete in different terms.

There is, of course, a great deal of variation in the scenes of individual satires: the Rome of Horace is not identical with that of Juvenal, and the Londons of Ben Jonson and Alexander Pope are considerably different. Every author of satire is free to stress the elements of the scene which appear most important to him, but beneath the divergencies of the surface the satiric scene remains fundamentally the same picture of a dense and grotesque world of decaying matter moving without form in response only to physical forces and denying the humane ideal which once molded the crowd into a society and the collection of buildings into a city.

THE SATIRIST

Somewhere in the midst of the satiric scene or standing before it directing our attention to instances of folly and vulgarity and shaping our responses with his language, we usually find a satirist. In some cases he remains completely anonymous, merely a speaking voice who tells us nothing directly of himself, e.g. the narrator in *Nightmare Abbey* or in most satiric novels. In formal satire where the satirist is usually identified as "I," or may even be given the author's name as in "An Epistle to Dr. Arbuthnot," he begins to emerge from the shadows of anonymity, and, while his back is still turned to us, he speaks of himself from time to time, giving us hints of his origins and his character. One step further and the satirist acquires a name—Colin Clout, Pierce Penilesse—and a more complete personality. At this stage it may become fairly obvious that the satirist has an unsavory character himself, and we may begin to wonder if the author is not mocking his own creation while using him to attack others, e.g. Erasmus' use of Folly in *The Praise of Folly,* or Swift's manipulation of the "Modest Proposer" and Lemuel Gulliver.[4] Here too we must place various satirists appearing in plays who are even more unpleasant than the characters they attack: Jonson's Macilente, Shakespeare's Thersites, and Webster's Bosola. Finally, the satirist disappears altogether and we are left with only the fools and the villains who are allowed to expose and punish one another. Examples of this type of satire usually come from the theater (Jonson's *Volpone* or Aristophanes' *The Birds*), although a determined novelist may manage to keep his narration neutral enough to prevent any suggestion of a definite personality existing behind the events of the tale.

We might at this point sharpen our distinction between formal and Menippean satire somewhat and say that in formal satire the satirist is stressed and dominates the scene, while in Menippean satire the scene is stressed and absorbs the satirist, to some degree or altogether. Obviously, in the case of works occupying the middle range (such as *Gulliver's Travels*) the decision as to whether they are formal or Menippean becomes an extremely nice question: is Gulliver to be considered a part of the scene or a satirist describing and defining it? A distinction made on the basis of the extent to which the satirist is featured is useful for describing various subtypes of satire, but, again, it must not be allowed to obscure our perception of the basic unity of satire. The satirist must be regarded as but one poetic device used by the author to express his satiric vision, a device which can be dispensed with or varied to suit his purpose. We can expect, however, that if satire is a true genre then whenever

4. For a discussion of Swift's creation and handling of his satirists see Martin Price, *Swift's Rhetorical Art.* Yale Studies in English, *123* (New Haven, 1953), pp. 57–102.

the satirist does appear, whether he remains anonymous, is identified as "I," or is given a name, he will share certain basic characteristics with all other satirists. This basic character will be dictated by his function in the satiric work and established by tradition. The biographical critics of satire have insisted that each satirist is either an exact image of his creator or at least his spokesman, but, ironically enough, their writings tend to confirm the idea of a basic satiric character, for whether they are describing Juvenal, Pope, Byron, Swift or Philip Wylie they seem always to be talking about the same proud, fiery, intolerant, irascible man whom no one would want for a neighbor. There are, of course, considerable differences between the satirists created by different authors at different times, and these will be taken up in more detail shortly, but it should be possible to define in very general terms the essential satirist, those traits, attitudes, passions, which every author of satire brings together, stressing some and repressing others, and gives concrete expression to in the language, actions, and body of his particular satirist.

Every satirist is something of a Jekyll and Hyde; he has both a public and a private personality. The public personality is the one he exposes to the world, the face which he admits to and, indeed, insists on as a true image of his very nature.[5] The chief features of this personality have already been suggested in the opening pages of this chapter, and we need deal with them only briefly. Very simply, the satirist always presents himself as a blunt, honest man with no nonsense about him. This pose is established in a number of traditional ways. The satirist usually calls attention

5. The manner in which Pope employs this "public personality" in his satires is discussed by Maynard Mack, "The Muse of Satire," *Yale Review 41* (1951–52), 80–92; who points out that in creating this type of persona the satiric author is following Aristotle's advice to the rhetorician to establish with his audience a character which will lend credence to what he has to say.

to his simple style and his preference for plain terms which express plain truth. St. Jerome, who is in fact no amateur in rhetoric, longs for "the ocean of eloquent Cicero" and the "rushing torrents of Demosthenes" [6] to express the absolute depravity of a priest who has used the cave where Christ was born as a place of assignation. When advised to abandon satire and "tell of the feats of Caesar," "Horace" says humbly, "Would that I could, good father, but my strength fails me. Not everyone can paint ranks bristling with lances, or Gauls falling with spear-heads shattered, or wounded Parthian slipping from his horse." [7] Joseph Hall in his *Virgidemiae* tells us that his satires are "but packe-staffe plaine uttring what thing they ment." [8] Professions of this kind are one of the commonplaces of satire, but they need not always be given direct statement. The satirist may suggest that his own style is simple, and therefore truthful, simply by mocking the pretentious styles and pompous jargon of his contemporaries, as Juvenal does in his first satire; or he may employ slang and other idiomatic terms to refer to himself while using the terms of eloquence for his adversaries as Philip Wylie does in the introduction to his *Generation of Vipers.*

The pose of simplicity is frequently reinforced by references to humble but honest origins. The typical medieval satirist assumes the mask of the humble plowman working hard in the fields to support his family, close to Nature and to God. "Pope," in "An Epistle to Dr. Arbuthnot," paints a charming picture of his early years, his retirement from

6. "Calling a Lecherous Priest to Repent," in *The Satirical Letters of St. Jerome,* trans. Paul Carroll (Chicago, Gateway, 1956), p. 115.

7. *Sermones,* II.i.12–15. All translations of Horace are from *Horace, Satires, Epistles and Ars Poetica,* ed. and trans. H. R. Fairclough, Loeb Classical Library, London, 1926.

8. III, Prologue, 4. All citations of *Virgidemiae* in my text are to *The Collected Poems of Joseph Hall,* ed. Arnold Davenport, Liverpool Univ. Press, 1949.

the busy world, his mild acceptance of insults, and his father who "held it for a rule / It was a Sin to call our Neigh-
bour fool," while the "harmless Mother thought no Wife
a Whore." [9] Somehow the satirist seems always to come
from a world of pastoral innocence and kindness: he is the
prophet come down from the hills to the cities of the plain;
the gawky farm-boy, shepherd, or plowman come to the
big city; or the scholar, nurtured at the university, abroad
in the cruel world.

The satirist's moral code, which is too traditional and
too straightforward to be called a philosophy, suits his rural
background. "Enough for me, if I can uphold the rule our
fathers have handed down, and if, so long as you need a
guardian, I can keep your health and name from harm," [1]
says "Horace's" father, and the words are a good description
of the moral ideals of all satirists. Metaphysics, elaborate
ethics, theories of redemption through suffering, these are
all beyond the satirist. He views life in social terms and
exhorts his audience to return to the ways of their fathers,
to live with fortitude, reason, chastity, honor, justice, simplicity, the virtues which make for the good life and the
good society. A Christian satirist will usually add repentance
and humility before God to the list of pagan virtues, but
he too takes these for granted and does not bother with
speculations about their ultimate validity.

But mildness and simplicity do not suffice to make a
satirist. He must not only shake his head at what he sees,
he must attack it, and with vigor, if there is to be any satire.
Where other men passively accept the "mortifying sight
of slavery, folly and baseness" among which they are "forced
to live," or rage inwardly and ineffectively, the satirist re-

9. Lines 382–4. All citations of Pope in my text are to the Twickenham
Edition of the Poems of Alexander Pope, Vol. *4, Imitations of Horace,* ed.
John Butt, London, Methuen, 1939.
1. *Sermones,* I.iv.116–19.

sponds with that "perfect rage and resentment"[2] of which Swift speaks, and cries out with Juvenal,

Si natura negat, facit indignatio versum.
(Though nature says no, indignation forms my verses.)

(I, 79)

Or with Pope,

> Ask you what Provocation I have had?
> The strong Antipathy of Good to Bad.[3]

The degree of indignation varies with the man, and the satiric conventions of his time; it ranges from Horace's ironically mild "quid faciam" when faced with the corruption of Rome to the *saeva indignatio* of Juvenal and the violence of Elizabethan satire where, as John Marston puts it, with characteristic exaggeration:

> Unlesse the Destin's adamantine band
> Should tye my teeth, I cannot chuse but bite.[4]

This violent indignation is, of course, somewhat at variance with the pose of the mild, honest man, and the satirist always presents his raging at a wicked world as a compulsion. Things are so bad, vice so arrant, the world so overwhelmingly wicked that even a plain man like the satirist who prefers to live in peace is forced to attack the vice of mankind.

But what his passion forces him to do, his reason assents to, for the satirist views the world pessimistically and sees

2. These quotations are from a passage in Swift's letter to Pope, June 1, 1728, in *The Correspondence of Jonathan Swift*, ed. F. E. Ball (London, G. Bell, 1910–14), *4*, 34.

3. "Epilogue to the Satires, Dialogue II," pp. 197–8. Hereafter referred to as "Dialogue II."

4. *The Scourge of Villanie* (1598–9), Satire VIII, p. 82. Hereafter referred to as *The Scourge*. All citations of *The Scourge* are to the facsimile edition of G. B. Harrison, Bodley Head Quartos, *13*, London, 1925. Since the lines are unnumbered, references are given to satire and page numbers.

little hope for reform unless violent methods are used to bring mankind to its senses. His melancholy views on the prospects for the world are best understood by contrast with the situation in tragedy and comedy. Satire shares with comedy the knowledge that fools and foolishness have gotten out of hand, but it lacks the characteristic balance of comedy and the tone of amused tolerance which derive from the underlying certainty in comedy that right reason *is* ultimately the way of the world. Fools in comedy only need to be given enough rope and they will hang themselves, for Nature operates to restore the balance. While watching the fools in their foolishness the comic hero—Philinte, Millamant, Falstaff, or Shaw's St. Joan—can remain relatively detached and good-humored because of the deep conviction that "normality" will reassert itself.

Such consolation is denied the satirist, who typically believes that there is no pattern of reason left in the world. If Nature once operated or society functioned to maintain a reasonable world, the sheer idiocy of mankind has long since thwarted the great plan:

> each Ape,
> That can but spy the shadow of his shape,
> That can no sooner ken what's vertuous,
> But will avoyd it, and be vicious.
>
> (*The Scourge*, IV, p. 43)

The satirist's despair of man and society, which he builds up with direct statement and catalogues of human depravity, extends to the very operation of the cosmos itself. "With a goose-quill and a bottle of ink," says Aretino, "I mock myself of the universe." [5] The powers divine and human that once kept man virtuous and society healthy seem no longer operative to the satirist, the flow of grace has been stopped by "the slime that from our soules doe

5. *Works, 1*, 17.

flow." [6] If the satirist does not choose merely to relieve his
pain by mockery, he regards himself and his satire, all other
forces having withdrawn, as the only method of correction
left, the last hope of mankind. Swift tells us that "the reason that satire was first introduced into the world" was to
control those "whom neither religion, nor natural virtue,
nor fear of punishment were able to keep within the bounds
of their duty." [7] "Pope" is

> proud to see
> Men, not afraid of God, afraid of me:
> Safe from the Bar, the Pulpit, and the Throne,
> Yet touch'd and sham'd by *Ridicule* alone.
>
> ("Dialogue II," lines 208–11)

The author of satire may believe, as Pope and Swift clearly
did, that God still exists, but when he assumes the mask
of the satirist he acts as if God and Nature were withdrawn
and he stood alone in the lunatic world to stay its progressive degeneration. For this reason comic detachment and
ease are impossible for the satirist. He is convinced that the
fate of the world depends solely on him, and this gives rise
to the heroic postures he frequently assumes. He becomes
the only champion of virtue who dares to speak the truth
in a world where the false insolently maintains itself as the
real.

Satire shares this darkly serious view of the world with
tragedy—thus the resemblance of the satiric and tragic
scenes—and both satirist and tragic hero suffer an agonized
compulsion to appraise the ills of the world and cure them
by naming them. Every tragic hero has pronounced satiric
tendencies, but he also has additional dimensions; chief
among these are his ability to ponder and to change under
pressure. The satirist, however, is not so complex. He sees

6. *The Scourge*, VII, p. 76.
7. "The Examiner," No. 39, in *The Prose Works of Jonathan Swift*, ed.
Temple Scott (London, G. Bell, 1902), *9*, 253.

the world as a battlefield between a definite, clearly understood good, which he represents, and an equally clear-cut
evil. No ambiguities, no doubts about himself, no sense
of mystery trouble him, and he retains always his monolithic
certainty. Since these differences in character control the
directions taken by the satiric and tragic plots, they will be
discussed more fully later.

This is, very roughly, the public character of the satirist.
Now it would be nonsense to argue, as the biographical
critic does, that all authors of satire are straightforward,
honest, pessimistic, indignant men who dislike ostentatious
rhetoric, come from the country, and have simple moral
codes. Each of these traditional qualities is a function of
satire itself, and not primarily an attribute of the man who
writes the satire. The typical satirist we have described is
brought into being by the necessities of satire. If the attack
on vice is to be effective, the character who delivers it must
appear the moral opposite of the world he condemns; he
must be fervent, he must be horrified at what he sees, and
he must be able to distinguish between vice and virtue
without any philosophical shillyshallying about "what is
right and what is wrong?" The traditional character of the
satirist enables him to perform each of these acts.

If the satirist remained as simple and coherent as his
public personality, then his character would give little difficulty. He might appear too uncomplicated to deal with an
extremely complicated world, but he would be fully understandable. There is always, however, a darker side to his
nature, a private personality which the author may or may
not allow his satirist to discuss openly, and this personality
is, like the public personality, consequent upon the satirist's
functions in satire. As a result of his violent attacks on vice
he acquires a number of unpleasant characteristics which
make suspect his pose of a simple lover of plain truth.
These characteristics are best described as a series of closely

related tensions. The most obvious tension results from the satirist's categorical contention that he is showing us the world and man as they actually are. Writers of epic, love poetry, or pastoral are, the satirist assures us, merely writing fiction. Only the satirist truly has for his subject "quidquid agunt homines." The lines from Joseph Hall's *Virgidemiae* (1598) are a typical instance of the satiric boast:

> For in this smoothing age who durst indite,
> Hath made his pen an hyred Parasite,
> To claw the back of him that beastly lives,
> And pranck base men in proud Superlatives.
>
>   .   .   .   .   .
>
> Goe daring Muse on with thy thankless taske,
> And do the ugly face of vice unmaske:
>
>   .   .   .   .   .
>
> Truth be thy speed, and Truth thy Patron bee.
> (I, Prologue, lines 9–24)

But in no art form is the complexity of human existence so obviously scanted as in satire. The satirist is out to persuade us that vice is both ugly and rampant, and in order to do so he deliberately distorts, excludes, and slants. We never find characters in satire, only caricature: Swift's Yahoos, Juvenal's Romans, Pope's Dunces, Philip Wylie's Moms. The dilemma is inescapable, for the satirist is caught between the conflicting necessities of the claim to truth and the need to make vice appear as ugly and dangerous as possible. Whenever the author of satire allows his satirist to admit his inconsistency, his argument will be that distortion of literal reality is necessary in order to get at the truth. Philip Wylie tells us that he is attempting in *Generation of Vipers* to break through certain ancient dogmatic faiths, and then goes on, "The effort involves a considerable diversion of thought from normal channels and I have

twirled a rather elaborate kaleidoscope, to divert it." [8]
Wylie's kaleidoscope becomes "squint-eyed sight" in Marston's satirist's attempt to explain his outrageous exaggeration:

> Who would imagine that such squint-eyed sight
> Could strike the world's deformities so right? [9]

This distortion of reality in an attempt to make vice
as ugly and ridiculous as it truly is always requires a considerable amount of rhetorical skill, but, as we have seen,
in order to establish his credibility the satirist must present
himself as a plain, outspoken man who calls a spade a spade.
In fact he then turns out to be the most cunning of rheto-
ricians, highly skilled in all the tricks of persuasion. As a
result we have the curious spectacle of the most artful of
writers pretending, like Chaucer's Franklin to whom
"colours of rethoryk been . . . queynte," to be rude and
artless.

There is an old saying that "he who sups with the devil
needs a long spoon," and it appears that the satirist has
never had a long enough spoon. Inevitably when he dips
into the devil's broth in order, he says, to show us how
filthy it really is, he gets splattered. In order to attack vice
effectively, the satirist must portray it in detail and profusion, and he must explore the nastiest activities of the
human animal and describe them in the revolting terms
"Pope," for example, uses in the following passage:

> Let Courtly Wits to Wits afford supply,
> As Hog to Hog in huts of *Westphaly;*
> If one, thro' Nature's Bounty or his Lord's,

---

8. (New York, Rinehart, 1942), p. xiv.

9. *The Metamorphosis of Pigmalions Image And Certaine Satyres,* (1598),
Satire II, lines 37–8. Hereafter cited as *Pigmalion.* All citations of *Pigmalion*
in my text are to *The Works of John Marston,* ed. A. H. Bullen (Boston,
John Nimmo, 1887), Vol. 3.

Has what the frugal, dirty soil affords,
From him the next receives it, thick or thin,
As pure a Mess almost as it came in;
The blessed Benefit, not there confin'd,
Drops to the third who nuzzles close behind;
From tail to mouth, they feed, and they carouse;
The last, full fairly gives it to the *House*.

("Dialogue ii," lines 171–80)

The *adversarius* speaks for all of us when he answers, "This filthy Similie, this beastly Line, / Quite turns my Stomach"; and Pope's answer is the standard defense of the satirist, "So does Flatt'ry mine." At times the satirist will go beyond mere prurience and appear pathological in his unending revelations of human nastiness and his paraded disgust with the ordure of the world. Trapped by his need for making sin appear hideous he seems always to be seeking out and thoroughly enjoying the kind of filth which he claims to be attacking. And at the same time that he opens himself to the charge of being a literary Peeping Tom, he also makes it possible to charge him with sensationalism, for the more effectively he builds up catalogues of human vice, the more it will appear that he is merely purveying salacious material to satisfy the meaner appetites of his audience.

The satirist's probity is further compromised by the necessary strength and vigor of his attack on his victims. He denounces them for being intemperate and unreasonable, and the very violence of his denunciations proclaims him equally unreasonable and intemperate. St. Jerome in his satiric letters takes his contemporaries to task for their unchristian behavior, but his own bitter attacks—as he remembers from time to time—violate the fundamental tenet of the Christian religion, charity. Juvenal's satirist adheres to some loose variety of Stoicism, but his fiery indignation stands in direct contrast to the Stoic ideals of passionless calm and stern endurance of misfortune, and he is forced

to explain that though Nature, the principle of right reason operating through the universe, forbids his satiric out-
bursts, indignation insists upon them: "si natura negat,
facit indignatio versum." But the satirist's sharp tongue
involves him in even more unpleasant contradictions than
mere philosophical confusion. He believes that the case
of man and society is desperate, and he applies appropriate
therapeutic treatments: the whip, the scalpel, the strappado,
the emetic, the burning acid.[1] But each of these cruel methods of treatment suggests that the man who uses them exclusively enjoys his work. The more powerfully the satirist
swings his scourge—and he usually does so with considerable
gusto—the more he will appear to have a marked sadistic
tendency.

The necessary straightforwardness of his attacks on vice
always opens the satirist to accusations of being proud. As
the satirist passes a succession of absolute moral judgments
on his fellow men, he inevitably becomes an egoistic monster bursting with his own righteousness and completely
devoid of any sympathy for his victims or doubts about his
own moral status. "Byron" in *English Bards and Scotch Reviewers* admits that,

> Every Brother Rake will smile to see
> That miracle, a Moralist in me.
>
> (lines 699–700) [2]

"Horace's" adversarius speaks to him about the same question (I.ii.25–7), "When you look over your own sins, your
eyes are rheumy and daubed with ointment; why, when you
view the failings of your friends, are you as keen of sight
as an eagle?"

1. The traditional use of this type of imagery in satire is discussed by
Mary Claire Randolph, "The Medical Concept in English Renaissance
Satiric Theory: Its Possible Relationships and Implications," *Studies in
Philology, 38* (1941), 125–57.
2. *Works,* ed. E. H. Coleridge (London, J. Murray, 1905), Vol. *1.*

All but a few critics [3] of satire have unerringly sought out and concentrated on these weak spots in the satirist's character, his private personality. Thomas Love Peacock, we are told, "showed himself rather obstinately blind to many of the higher aspects of life in general." [4] *Don Juan* consists of "the beastly utterances of a man who had lost all sense of decency," [5] and William Blackwood was struck with horror by "the vile, heartless, and cold-blooded way in which this fiend [Byron] attempted to degrade every tender and sacred feeling of the human heart." [6] Another critic informs us that John Marston "exhibits an insane delight in raking the cesspits of vice . . . and feels the same pleasure in drawing attention to [evil] . . . that boys experience in chalking up newly-discovered verbiage of obscenity." [7] Speaking of the same author, Thomas Warton pontificates: "The satirist who too freely indulges himself in the display of that licentiousness which he means to proscribe, absolutely defeats his own design. He inflames those passions which he professes to suppress, gratifies the depravations of a prurient curiosity, and seduces innocent minds to an acquaintance with ideas which they might never have known." [8] "Pope," it is argued, "finds himself unable to re-settle the equilibrium in his nervous system until he has taken out his revenge by an extra kicking administered

3. Maynard Mack, "The Muse of Satire," and John Holloway, "The Well-Filled Dish: An Analysis of Swift's Satire," *Hudson Review, 9* (1956), 20–37, call attention to the division that exists between the author of satire and the personality he assumes in order to perform his critical function.

4. George Saintsbury, *English Prose*, ed. Henry Craik (New York, 1896), *5*, 286.

5. Harriet Beecher Stowe, *Lady Byron Vindicated* (Boston, 1870), p. 62.

6. From a letter quoted by F. H. C. Oliphant in *William Blackwood and His Sons* (New York, 1897), *1*, 381.

7. J. Le Gay Brereton, *Writings on Elizabethan Drama* (Melbourne Univ. Press, 1948), p. 43.

8. *The History of English Poetry* (London, 1778–81), sec. 65.

to some old mendicant or vagrant lying in a ditch." [9]

All of the defects of character noted by these critics are unhesitatingly assigned to the authors, and while it is true that some of the greatest satiric authors have not been the most stable of men, the fact seems to have been missed that many of the characteristics confidently attributed to them derive from the very nature of satire itself. Anyone who writes vigorous satire will inevitably appear to share these traits. If, however, we accept the strange, twisted, contradictory satirist as a fictitious character created in order to achieve the satiric end, the exposure of vice and depravity, then we can direct our attention to the ways in which the authors of great satire manipulate their satirists and exploit them in a thoroughly dramatic fashion. Juvenal's stern, impoverished, decayed noble who stamps about the streets of Rome suffering indignities at the hands of the noveaux riches, and bursting with indignation and sophistic rhetoric; Skelton's crude, rustic, straightforward, unlearned countryman whose simple piety mocks the sophisticated churchmen; John Marston's biting, snarling, despairing, contradictory malcontent who noses into all the filth of Elizabethan London and becomes nearly incoherent with rage while denouncing it on the street corners; Swift's bumbling, credulous, prideful Gulliver voyaging from one misunderstood adventure to the next and finally filled with proud disdain for the human animal, the Yahoo—all these are satiric personae.

I have described in the preceding pages a basic satiric persona, and no doubt the reader has by now thought of a number of cases where some of the qualities I have called characteristic are so attenuated that they nearly cease to exist. Savagery, despair, hate, pride, intransigeance, prurience, and sadism may be innate in satire, but Horace,

9. Thomas DeQuincey, "Lord Carlisle on Pope" in *The Collected Writings of Thomas DeQuincey*, ed. David Masson (Edinburgh, 1890), *11*, 126–7.

Chaucer, Erasmus, and, to a lesser degree, Ben Jonson, all
manage to soften or find out more acceptable variations of
these unpleasant traits by avoiding the extreme forms of
indignation and the more shocking varieties of vice. They
stress the public personality of the satirist. Their kind of
satire verges on the comic, and their satirists, without los-
ing their cutting-edge, exude good humor, easy laughter,
urbanity. In Jonson's words, they "sport with human follies,
not with crimes," and Horace's phrase "ridentem dicere
verum" characterizes their method.

On the other hand there is an even larger group of satiric
writers who seem to delight in stressing every extravagant
attitude and every contradiction in the satiric character.
Juvenal, Swift, Pope, Byron, Marston, Rochester, Marvell,
all create satirists who lash out with violence, are filled with
outrage, and seek out the vilest of men. When Horace goes
for a walk he encounters a bore, when Juvenal walks *he*
encounters a cast-off pathic. These bitter works are characterized by Juvenal's saeva indignatio, and they seem always to be on the threshold of tragedy. The works of these
authors have provided a majority of my examples for the
simple reason that such writers, by carrying to the extreme
the private personality of the satirist, bring into relief the
tendencies of all satire, tendencies which are repressed in
the gentler types.

Horace and Juvenal thus provide us with the two extremes of the satirist, and while it seems likely that the
personality of the author has some connection with the type
of satirist he creates, other factors are more important in
molding the satiric figure. The radical characteristics are
always necessarily present, but just as each age forges its
own typical verse forms or its architectural style, so, allowing for minor differences resulting from the different personalities of the authors involved, each age creates its own
satirist who is distinguished from the satirists of the pre-

ceding age and the following. Bishop Golias, Piers Plowman, Thersites, the Pope of the *Imitations of Horace* are
all related figures, but they are different in many ways, and
each is a defining example of the standard satiric character
of his age. Changes in satirists seem to come about in con-
junction with major shifts in thought, and perhaps the
best way of describing this process is to say that the satirist
is always an amalgamation of the basic characteristics which
develop whenever satire is written and of the ethos of a
particular age. It is possible to distinguish a distinctive
satiric figure in each of the major periods of our literature,
and in later chapters I shall discuss in some detail the
medieval satirist and the Renaissance satirist.

THE SATIRIC PLOT

If we take plot to mean, as it ordinarily does, "what happens," or to put it in a more useful way, a series of events
which constitute a change, then the most striking quality
of satire is the absence of plot. We seem at the conclusion
of satire to be always at very nearly the same point where
we began. The scenery and the faces may have changed outwardly, but fundamentally we are looking at the same
world, and the same fools, and the same satirist we met
at the opening of the work. Juvenal begins in his first satire
by belaboring a variety of transgressors: the eunuch who
has married, the matron who has exposed her breasts and
entered the arena, and the former barber who has become
one of the richest and most powerful men in Rome; fifteen
satires later he is viciously attacking the army, and the
brutality with which the soldiers treat civilians. Presumably the eunuch is still married and the barber more prosperous than ever. The scene is still as crowded with fools
and villains, and the same forces of luxury, money, and
foreign ideas which perverted traditional Roman virtue

inside the city have infected the barracks. The satirist is still as indignant, as brave, as skillful, and as certain of himself as ever. His method is still the direct attack despite the fact that in fifteen satires he has not achieved a single result. What is true of formal satire is almost equally true of Menippean varieties, although there usually is more movement when the satire is carried by a fable. Trimalchio is as rich and gross as ever at the end of the description of his banquet; the "Big-enders" and the "Little-enders" come to no recognition of their foolishness in *Gulliver's Travels;* Colin Clout ends his song still complaining about prelates whose ease and power have not been disturbed in the slightest by an attack which Colin knows from the outset will only result in those he is attacking calling him a prating "losel . . . with a wide wesaunt!" Whenever satire does have a plot which eventuates in a change, it is not a true change but simply intensification of the original condition. After a number of adventures Gulliver becomes a more unpleasant kind of simpleton; during the course of *The Dunciad* dullness seeps into every part of London just as the slime from the Fleet ditch pollutes the river; absolutism stamps out the last trace of individualism in *1984,* and the hero is left drinking ersatz gin, crying maudlin tears, and adoring the face of Big Brother on the telescreen.

The normal "plot" of satire would then appear to be a stasis in which the two opposing forces, the satirist on one hand and the fools on the other, are locked in their respective attitudes without any possibility of either dialectical movement or the simple triumph of good over evil. Whatever movement there is, is not plot in the true sense of change but mere intensification of the unpleasant situation with which satire opens. It is here that one of the basic differences between satire and the other major literary genres, tragedy and comedy, becomes evident, for in both the latter kinds the developing plot is very close to being the absolute heart of the form. Perhaps the essence of comedy is that things somehow do "turn out all right." Usually they do so in a rather miraculous, unexpected, and fairly painless manner. An unknown will is discovered, a rich uncle returns from the West Indies, the boy and girl turn out not to be brother and sister after all. The deus ex machina may be anathema in tragedy, but it is a vital part of comedy. In tragedy the progression of events, both psychic and external, leads inevitably to adjustment and change, but for a time it is not unusual for the tragic hero to lock himself in the rigid attitude of the satirist and strive "in his little world of man to out-scorn / The to-and-fro-conflicting wind and rain." Both satirist and tragic hero cry out that they are men "more sinn'd against than sinning," and try to oppose the course of evil with the lash of scorn and vituperation: e.g. Oedipus' attack on superstition and prophecy which he mockingly calls "bird-lore," Hamlet's description of the world as an "unweeded garden," or Lear's magnificent explosions that relieve the unendurable pressure in his heart. But the tragic hero *learns* that evil is too powerful to be opposed in this way, and as he suffers the consequences of his stand he passes on into knowledge that evil is a part of the fabric of the world, not mere depravity or bad manners; and with this recognition he is forced on to see his own involvement in the mixed world and accept the extraordinarily heavy price he must pay to achieve an end which is only dimly perceived.

The tragic plot has been described as a continuing rhythm of "purpose, passion and perception," [1] in which the tragic hero does something (purpose), is forced to endure the consequences of his act (passion), and then as a result of his suffering comes to a new understanding (perception), which constitutes the basis of a new purpose. The rhythm

1. The terms are Francis Fergusson's and form the basis of his discussion of drama in *The Idea of a Theater,* Princeton Univ. Press, 1949.

of satire, however, lacks the crucial act of perception which permits development and forward movement. Instead, the satirist alternates endlessly between his purpose and the passion which it brings on. His characteristic purpose is to cleanse society of its impurities, to heal its sicknesses; and his tools are crude ones: the surgeon's knife, the whip, the purge, the rack, the flood, and the holocaust, all typical metaphors of satire. He employs irony, sarcasm, caricature, and even plain vituperation with great vigor, determined to beat the sots into reason or cut away the infected parts of society; but the job is always too much for him. The massive weight of stupidity, bestiality, greed, and cunning, which is his scene, resists his uttermost efforts, and so he suffers frustration and the agonized sense that evil multiplies faster than it can be corrected or even catalogued. But suffering brings no change in him: his methods, his sense of his own righteousness, and his understanding of evil remain the same. His feelings of futility lead him not to revaluation of his methods and his enemies but to the belief that he simply needs to apply the lash more vigorously, and he doubles his efforts. This constant movement without change forms the basis of satire, and while we may be only half aware of the pattern as we read, it, more than any other element, creates the tone of pessimism inherent in the genre.

English literature contains, of course, a great many poems, plays, and novels with pronounced satiric qualities, which do have a developing plot where movement results in metamorphosis. Ben Jonson's plays usually result in the unmasking and punishment of the fools; Webster's *The Duchess of Malfi* and a number of other Jacobean tragedies are heavily satiric but usually arrive at a much diminished tragic recognition; *Pride and Prejudice* has some of the deftest satire ever written—and one of the finest satirists, Mr. Bennett—but "good sense" and "warm hearts" bring an ending of tolerance and adjustment. Shaw in his plays belabors the English middle class with true satiric delight, but the "life force" works through his satire to bring about comic change in a play like *Man and Superman,* and tragic change, at least for a moment, in *Saint Joan.* Pure satire is far rarer than the mixed kinds in which after a time the satiric stasis is broken and the characters, both satirists and fools, are swept forward into the miraculous transformations of comedy or the cruel dialectic of tragedy.

CONCLUSIONS

Exact definition of any literary genre is perhaps an impossibility, but the terms I have used to describe satire are broad enough to allow for its considerable diversities without permitting the idea of the genre to disappear either in the multitude of different techniques of presentation which have been used to convey satire, or in the mass of shadowy, borderline cases where satire seems inextricably mixed with comedy or tragedy. It would seem that the basic impulse or "sense of life" which lies behind all satire finds concrete expression in a wide variety of ways. In life itself it appears without mediation in the sneer and in the sarcastic remark, or it will be sharpened and organized somewhat in the lampoon, the exposé, and the political cartoon. At this point it passes over into art where it appears in epigrams, "characters," pasquinades, "dictionaries," parodies, and a host of other minor types. But it is in the major satiric works of the literary tradition extending from classical antiquity to the present day, in the pure satires of Horace, Juvenal, Persius, the goliardic poets, Skelton, Marston, Pope, Swift, Byron, that we get the full expression of the satiric sense of life and the development of innate tendencies which are only suggested by the minor examples of the genre. These works exist in a variety of modes extending from the extreme realism of formal satire to the extreme symbolism of the beast fable, and may be presented in poem, play, essay, or novel.

But no matter what the mode of presentation, the elements of satire which I have distinguished remain fairly constant. The scene is always crowded, disorderly, grotesque; the satirist, in those satires where he appears, is always indignant, dedicated to truth, pessimistic, and caught in a series of unpleasant contradictions incumbent on practicing his trade; the plot always takes the pattern of purpose followed by passion, but fails to develop beyond this point. For purposes of discussion I have treated scene, plot, and satirist as distinct from one another, while in any given satire where all are present they interact and reinforce one another to form a composite whole. Take, for example, the well-known tendency of satire to pass rapidly from one subject to another without lingering for very many lines on any single fool or particular piece of foolishness. We can consider this quality, which has earned satire the reputation of being fragmentary, as an attribute of the scene contributing to the effect of a disordered world in which there is a limitless amount of depravity. Or in formal satire, where the scene is described for us by the satirist and has no being in its own right, these rapid transitions reflect the character of the satirist and suggest his sense of urgency, his zeal, and his unwillingness to ponder any situation or investigate it thoroughly. Or we may see this same fragmentary quality as a function of the plot, demonstrating the continuous movement that never brings about change.

The theory of satire offered in this chapter is no doubt rough, and certainly incomplete. Each of the various elements discussed could be developed and refined a great deal by consideration of a larger number of satires than are dealt with here and by more curious examination of scene, satirist, and plot. But the theory I have outlined is a valuable working perspective which permits us to approach satire as literary critics examining a piece of literature made up of symbolic and interacting parts. The testing ground for the theory is English satire of the Renaissance, particularly of that period between approximately 1590 and 1615 when a distinctly nonmedieval type of satire appeared, although the shift in thought which worked the change had been taking place for a good many years before it transformed satire. Before we turn to an examination of this satire we must look briefly at some of the satiric poetry and critical theories with which every Renaissance English author of satire was familiar.

CHAPTER 2

THE BACKGROUND OF ENGLISH
RENAISSANCE SATIRE

In recent years there has been an increasing tendency to regard satire as a formal variety of poetry, and students of neoclassical satire particularly have searched for the "art" of the genre. As yet, however, Renaissance satire has not been approached in this way—perhaps because it is cruder than the polished works of Dryden, Pope, and Swift—and the usual extraneous explanations have instead been applied. One critic writing on Elizabethan satire assures us that "The significant sources of satire are not literary or philosophical: they are social and economic. For the understanding of satire, and the response to it, we need not so much an acquaintance with models and conventions, or an understanding of ideas and principles, as a knowledge of the social milieu from which the satire sprang." [1] Another theory frequently put forward is that the Elizabethan satiric authors were simply attempting to satisfy the new middle-class taste for sensational pictures of a wicked world.[2] Or we are told that the writing of formal satire had by the end of the sixteenth century become very modish and that it was written solely by young courtiers

1. Hallett Smith, *Elizabethan Poetry* (Cambridge, Harvard Univ. Press, 1952), p. 194.
2. See, for example, John Peter, *Complaint and Satire in Early English Literature* (Oxford Univ. Press, 1956), p. 170.

who hoped to establish a reputation for cleverness which would aid in the struggle for favor at Elizabeth's court.[3]

But by far the most persistent approach to this poetry has been the familiar biographical one of identifying author and speaker, particularly in the case of John Marston, who has received more attention than any other Elizabethan writer of formal satire. Speaking of Marston's early satiric work, one critic tells us that it reveals a personality [Marston's] in which "native instability . . . has been exaggerated to the point of incoherence."[4] The majority of the criticisms of Marston's plays are based on the same popular idea: that his poetic satires, which he wrote before his plays, are an absolute expression of his own nature and views. Working on this assumption the critics have concluded that when one of the characters in Marston's plays speaks in the tone and manner found in his verse satire and bursts forth with a vicious denunciation of men and their world, this is the voice of Marston himself breaking through his character into the play and usually doing violence to both dramatic structure and characterization. O. J. Campbell explains the unsatisfactory nature of one of Marston's dramatic characters, Feliche, in this way: "Marston obviously could not resist the impulse to push Feliche aside and to appear himself, under thin disguise, in his own familiar part of Juvenalian satirist. By so doing he showed that he had not yet learned to tame his satiric spirit to the indirect and impersonal methods of drama."[5]

All of these approaches to Elizabethan satire are correct to some extent. It is certainly true that the evils against which

3. John Wilcox, "Informal Publication of Late Sixteenth-Century Verse Satire," *Huntington Library Quarterly, 13* (1949–50), 191–200.

4. Peter, p. 174. Any number of examples could be given here, but for a particularly striking recent instance see Samuel Schoenbaum, "The Precarious Balance of John Marston," *PMLA, 67* (1952), 1069–78.

5. *Comicall Satyre and Shakespeare's "Troilus and Cressida"* (San Marino, Huntington Library, 1938), p. 146.

the satirists cried out were, with a few exceptions, genuine problems in Tudor and Stuart England. Usury, rack-renting, land enclosures, the growth of London, soldiers discharged from the Lowland wars, and the vast increase of personal fortunes are all dealt with in both the satires of the time and in various nonliterary documents such as petitions to the Crown and acts of Parliament. Furthermore, the writing of formal satire clearly was a fashionable affair toward the end of the sixteenth century, for the authors make every effort to disclaim any connection with native satire and to stress their classical correctness, their learning, and their unconcern for being read by the vulgar. The amount of sensational "Sunday supplement" material in these satires suggests an attempt to satisfy an audience avid for the lurid details of sin in the new Sodom. We can even say with reasonable surety that John Marston, Thomas Nashe, Ben Jonson, and other writers of satire shared fiery, quarrelsome personalities with the satirists they created.

But whatever literal truth and personal expression there may be in these satires is mixed with a great deal of art. For every Elizabethan author who followed Sir Philip Sidney's advice to himself, to "look in thy heart and write" —and Sidney is actually employing a rhetorical device here —there were dozens of young writers who looked anywhere but in their hearts; they looked instead to the literary productions of Rome, to the latest poetic fashions, to the various types of themes written in grammar school, to the successful works of their English and Continental predecessors. For most Elizabethan authors literary composition was a reworking of themes already treated by older writers in the styles established as appropriate to the given subject. "Decorum" was the governing term of criticism. The best of the Elizabethan poets, of course, simply built on these conventions, but the inferior writers imitated their models and one another's works so successfully that vast numbers of sonnets and pastorals, for example, are very nearly indistinguishable.

Satire, too, had its conventions, some of them explicitly stated, others simply taken for granted. These latter can be discovered only by examining the actual satires with which the Elizabethans were familiar and noting the ways in which they consistently imitated their models. But in order to see the new Renaissance satire distinctly, it is first necessary to know the tradition against which the authors were reacting, the kind of satire they were extremely conscious of *not* writing, and it is to this that we must first turn, using our dramatic terms to describe its peculiarities.

NATIVE ENGLISH SATIRE: THE MASK OF THE PLOWMAN

Until approximately the middle of the fourteenth century goliardic and Anglo-Norman satire, roguish, witty, and filled with a spirit of gaiety, predominated in England. But during the preceding century—the dating of the poems is problematical—a native satiric tradition written in English began to take form and became by the late fourteenth century, a time of quickening religious and social protest, the primary mode of satiric expression. These "Songs on Evil Times" differ greatly in tone from their gayer predecessors. "The old familiar note of undisguised fun, the impish delight in personal taunt and abuse akin to the careless schoolboy spirit, has . . . vanished away. In its place are notes of solemn indignation, bitterness and pessimism. If the new satirist ever laughs at all, it is with a fierce, mocking laughter, that bursts out suddenly without warning here and there, filled often with the spirit of mad exasperation and a reckless despair." [6]

6. G. R. Owst, *Literature and Pulpit in Medieval England* (Cambridge Univ. Press, 1933), p. 216.

This "new satirist" was created to express the particular
values of his times, values which if recognized at all in
earlier periods were not vital to the *vir bonus*. In the late
fourteenth century Juvenal's satirist filled with indignation and rhetorical tricks would have been considered a
monster—although by concentrating only on his *sententiae*
medieval scholars made the Roman satirist "moral Juvenal"
—and Bishop Golias would have been thought no more
than a light, frivolous fool—Chaucer's Miller is described
as "a janglere and goliardeys." What was required was a
figure who, while he would inevitably retain some of the
unpleasant characteristics innate in the satirist, would sym-
bolize the new ethical ideals of the period. The fourteenth
century was a time of quickening social protest and the
beginning of the long political and religious struggles which
were eventually to lead first to reformation and then to
revolution, and the new satire was from the beginning
closely tied to these movements. But a word of caution is
required here. No satirist ever led anyone to the barricades.
What we call "progress" is of no interest to him, for he
is always a conservative who calls not for experimentation
and social change but for a return to the time-tested virtues
and the "good old ways" which have been perverted or
abandoned by greedy man. In point of fact, of course, the
Golden Age to which the satirist refers probably never
existed, and the virtues he calls time-tested and traditional
have probably never been put into practice. For this reason
the satirist is always that paradoxical creature, the conservative revolutionary—paradox seems to be his natural in-
heritance. The medieval satirist is no exception to this
general rule, and while his satires may have been the voice
of forces which led to profound, and from the satirist's point
of view undesirable, changes, in his work he is always a
radical—in the original sense of that word—who hopes for
a return to the fundamental ideals of Christianity and the

stable, hierarchical social structure which we think of as characteristic of the Middle Ages, the social structure described in Passus VI of the B text of *Piers Plowman.*

It is these values which by redirecting and modifying the original impulses of the satiric character molded the medieval satirist. He had to embody the basic Christian ethos personified by Christ and stated with simplicity and clarity by the Lord in Isaiah: "But to this man will I look, even to him that is poor and of a contrite spirit, and trembleth at my word" (66:2). The Lord's association of poverty and humility was well suited to the requirements of medieval satire, for these writings were not only an expression of revivified Christianity but a social protest as well, a protest made from the bottom by the economic victims of a society which only pretended to be organized on Christian principles.

Simple piety, humility, honest poverty, these are the qualities forced on the medieval satirist, and they are doubtless the most incongruous imaginable with the fiery, proud, flamboyant creature who emerges naturally in satire. To fulfill these new requirements a unique satiric spokesman was created during the fourteenth century. The peasant had heretofore been treated with contempt in literature, but now the idealized figure of the simple plowman began to be used to champion the Christian social ideals.[7] At times he stands merely in silent and anonymous contrast to the depraved members of the old order as Chaucer's plowman "Lyvynge in pees and parfit charitee" does to the Summoner, the Friar, and other corrupt figures. In Langland's poem the plowman acquires a name, a good, common country name, Piers, and becomes "a universalizing of the English rural way of living, the life which all readers of the poem would understand and in terms of which they could

7. See Owst, ch. 9, "A Literary Echo of the Social Gospel," for a complete discussion of the use of the plowman in satires and sermons.

establish a common idiom with its author.[8] While Piers is not yet a satirist in any final sense, but rather a seeker of truth and the right way, his voice lifts from time to time with true satiric anger born of near despair.

It was inevitable that Piers Plowman should become the basic medieval satirist, for here was a figure already associated with religious and social protest who had the characteristics needed for attacking vice and foolishness.[9] Piers does not appear by name, of course, in the majority of medieval satires, but even in those cases where the speaker remains anonymous the Piers characteristics are evident: a plain man with plain morals addressing plain people in plain terms on plain matters. Piers Plowman is simply the most popular name for the medieval satirist, and although in the course of time the figure acquired many names he remained the same type. Colin Blowbol, Cock Lorel, Roderick Mors, Colin Clout, Jack Napes, and Jack Upland are all satiric personae who, as their plain, country names suggest, are proliferations of the Piers type. We shall meet this same phenomenon again in late Elizabethan satire where the basic satyr figure receives such various names as Pasquil, Don Kinsayder, Jaques, Macilente, Bosola, and Thersites.

The character of Piers as satirist is drawn clearly and succinctly in the anonymous *I Playne Piers* (printed 1550?),

> I playne Piers which can not flatter
> A plowe man men me call
> My speche is fowlle / yet mark the matter
> Howe thynges may hap to fall. (Sig. A1ᵛ)

---

8. Derek Traversi, "Piers Plowman," in *The Age of Chaucer*, ed. Boris Ford (Baltimore, Pelican Books, 1954), p. 132.

9. The full history of the Piers Plowman tradition is traced by Helen C. White, *Social Criticism in Popular Religious Literature of the Sixteenth Century*, (New York, 1944), ch. 1.

The pose of honesty and straightforwardness found in all satire is here carried to the extreme. Piers is primarily "playne" as befits his rustic background. He speaks truth by concentrating on "the matter" and paying little attention to poetic expression: "my speche is fowle." Wherever we encounter Piers we find that he is at pains to establish in a number of ways this character of the plain, unlettered, commonsensical rustic, speaking bare truth. His frequent use of the alliterative verse form, which by the fifteenth century was highly unsophisticated, and doggerel rhythms suggest his association with older ways of thought. His language is usually crude, flat, and bare of elaborate tropes. He always stresses his literary and moral naïveté, and refers to his life of hard, honest work on the land:

> "Sir," quod he, "I am an hyne;
> For I am wont to go to the plow,
> And erne my mete yer that I dyne.
> To swete and swinke I make avow,
> My wyf and children therwith to fynd,
> And servë god, and I wist how;
> But we lewd men ben full[y] blynd." [1]

Piers's morals are appropriately simple, and he usually reduces true religion to the basic tenets of Christianity as stated in the Creed. From these grounds he criticizes the wealthy and the hypocritical, particularly those churchmen who are busily engaged in leading pleasant lives and feathering their own nests rather than in fulfilling their vows. But he will turn on the members of any social class, even the king, who are failing to play their proper role in the Christian society. His satiric attacks are no more subtle than his character or his verse, and he usually delivers them in such forthright terms as "Such pryde tofore God doth stink."

1. "The Plowman's Tale," in *The Complete Works of Geoffrey Chaucer,* ed. W. W. Skeat (Oxford Univ. Press, 1897), Suppl. Vol., 148.

It may be objected here that the qualities I am describing as the conventions of medieval satire are not the result of any conscious effort on the authors' parts but the inevitable outcome of their own moral preoccupations and artistic clumsiness. This is the biographical argument enlarged sufficiently to identify a group of authors with a group of satirists, and the answer to it is to point to the tradition. A good many of the medieval satirists were no doubt dull, humble, and plain, but whenever the first-rate writers wrote satire they too tended to sound very much like their more earnest fellows. Chaucer in "The General Prologue" of *The Canterbury Tales*,[2] Skelton in *Colin Clout,* and Langland in *Piers Plowman* all wear some variation of the mask of the plain, guileless, humble man; "Chaucer," Colin, and Long Will reveal how much can be done with the basic satirist when an imaginative artist uses him. In inferior satires of the late Elizabethan and Jacobean periods, such as *Tyro's Roring Megge* (1598) or Richard Johnson's *Look on Me London, I Am an Honest Englishman, Ripping up the Bowels of Mischiefe, Lurking in the Sub-urbs and Precincts* (1613), the authors, though as artless and clumsy as any satiric writers of the fifteenth century, have abandoned the pose of plainness and try, as their titles indicate, to create the furious, vicious satirist who by that time had been established as appropriate for satire. And by the eighteenth century the second-rate satiric authors, who were no doubt as bumbling as their medieval counterparts, produce satirists who bear little resemblance to either Piers or his Elizabethan cousin but are weak imitations of the urbane, witty figures developed by Pope and Dryden.

It is obvious that the chief effect of the revitalized Chris-

2. E. Talbot Donaldson, "Chaucer the Pilgrim," *PMLA, 69* (1954), 928–36, has an excellent description of the character Chaucer creates here and his relationship to the author. While the Chaucer of "The General Prologue" is not the usual rustic and is used in a far more sophisticated manner than is ordinarily the case, his connection with the traditional satirist is still clear.

tian ethos on the character of the satirist was to repress his more colorful qualities and control his rampant individualism. But even the humble plowman when he engages in satire is to some degree subject to charges of pride, sadism, and intemperance. If he attacks vice effectively, i.e. with vigor and skill, then his pose of plainness, "lewdness," and simple piety is in danger of being questioned. The medieval solution of this continuing problem of satire was to diminish even further the satiric character by concentrating on the satiric scene. For example, in "The Plowman's Tale," the satirist, after lamenting the sad state of the world, swears that he is so unlearned that he cannot preach, but it just so happens that he knows by heart a sermon which he proceeds to repeat for us. And in "The Creed of Piers Plowman" the satirist, who in this case is searching for Piers, maintains the pose of a poor, simple man by going in turn to representatives of each of the religious orders and asking them for guidance. Each of the friars attacks all orders but his own and reveals at the same time his own defects. At the end the humble Piers gives us the true creed. By allowing the attacks to be delivered by other figures while he remains simply a humble listener or a reciter of others' words, the plowman avoids taint.

This tendency to shift the focus from the satirist to the scene is evident in some form in most medieval satire. The gluttonous clerics, overdressed and unfaithful women, brutal nobles, cunning lawyers, ignorant doctors, immoral foreigners, and personifications of the Seven Deadly Sins who make up the "felde ful of folke," the basic scene of medieval satire, are regularly presented within a frame of some kind: a dream, prophecy, pilgrimage, vision, quest, mirror, arraignment, will, or sea voyage. These devices all de-emphasize the satirist himself and direct our attention to the symbolic scene of human folly and vice. In this respect medieval satire is but one instance of the general rule that whenever an age sees human character in terms of humility, mildness, simplicity, or other qualities which tend to suppress or make meaningless the expression of individualism, then the satiric scene rather than the satirist will be emphasized. In our own age the profoundly pessimistic view that the individual is helpless in the midst of the amoral forces of nature, history, and society has been reflected in the concentration on scene in our satire. *Brave New World, Decline and Fall, 1984, The Day of the Locust,* for example, have chief characters who are not fearless champions of truth and virtue but ineffectual observers nearly submerged in a scene where vice and ignorance are all-powerful.

The plowman tradition continued through the sixteenth century and into the early seventeenth—the majority of the texts we have in which Piers is the satirist were printed about the middle of the sixteenth century, when religious and social issues were again boiling. But as time passed Piers and his satiric cousins began to undergo various changes. John Skelton continued to employ the plowman's mask, and in "Colin Clout," a name coined to suggest rusticity and plainness, he makes use of the old argument of "lewdness,"

> For though my rhyme be ragged,
> Tattered and jagged
> Rudely rain-beaten,
> Rusty and moth-eaten,
> If ye take well therewith,
> It hath in it some pith.[3]

Colin's morality is simple and open, "Flee / from worldly vanity," and his satiric methods equally crude and direct. His rhythms, the Skeltonics, were, an Elizabethan classicist

3. *The Complete Poems of John Skelton,* ed. Philip Henderson (London, J. M. Dent, 1948), p. 251.

tells us, "measures pleasing only to the popular ear." [4]
But the pose of simplicity is more complex in Skelton than
in his predecessors. When Colin stands gaping at the rich
tapestries depicting scenes of pagan mythology, which the
clerics hang on their walls,

> With dame Diana naked;
> How lusty Venus quakéd,
> And how Cupid shakéd
> His dart, and bent his bow
> For to shoot a crow
> At her tirly tirlow;
> And how Paris of Troy
> Dancéd a lege de moy,
>
> .   .   .   .   .
>
> With Triumphs of Caesar,
> And of Pompeius' war,
>
> (pp. 277–8)

he appears to be no more than a gaping yokel translating
the stories of antiquity into his own provincial terms and
country rhythms. But there is a new edge to this, for Colin
is very slyly making an invidious comparison of the honest
countryman and the Christian monks who "let down fall /
Their churches cathedrall" and ignore the poor while they
spend their money on rich hangings celebrating not Christian truth but pagan lies. Furthermore, Skelton's distinctive
hurtling rhythms, and the intensity with which he hammers
at a victim relieve his satire of the typical medieval drone
and give it a flavor of Juvenal's saeva indignatio. In the
long run, however, the intense person who wore a gorgeous
cloak embroidered with the letter "C" (for Calliope), covered his own character with the conventional mask of Piers.

Throughout most of the sixteenth century, authors of

4. George Puttenham, "*The Art of English Poesy* (1589) in *Elizabethan
Critical Essays,* ed. Gregory Smith (Oxford Univ. Press, 1904), 2, 87.

satire continued to work in the satiric tradition established
in the fourteenth. Latimer in his "Second Sermon Before
Edward VI" (1549) could still hold up the plowman as the
ideal Christian in contrast to the wicked young gentlemen
of London, and as late as 1621, long after the fashion in
satire had changed, John Taylor in his *Superbiae Flagellum*
identifies himself as a humble waterman and praises the
plowman:

> The painfull Plowmans paines doe never cease,
> For he must pay his Rent, or lose his lease.
>
> (Sig. Ci^v)

Even when the sixteenth-century author clearly thinks of
himself as drawing on the classical rather than the native
tradition, his writings will often appear to owe more to
Langland and Barclay than to Juvenal or Horace. George
Gascoigne, for example, in his satiric poem, *The Steele
Glas* (1576), writes in an obviously rhetorical and polished
manner, and he opens his "Satyra" with an attack on
amorous poetry that is reminiscent of the opening attacks of
Juvenal and Persius on the epic bombast of their time. But
the medieval framework, the "mirror," is still employed,
and in the end Gascoigne sets up an ideal very close to that
of Piers Plowman:

> But foure estates, to serve eche country Soyle,
> The King, the Knight, the Pesant, & the Priest.
> The King should care for al the subjectes still,
> The knight should fight, for to defende the same,
> The Pesant he, should labor for their ease,
> And Priests shuld pray, for them & for themselves.
>
> (lines 298–303)

Interestingly enough, the various attacks on vice made by
Puritan writers in the latter part of the century are much
closer to classical satire in spirit than are "literary" satires
like *The Steele Glas*. In such writings as Stephen Gosson's

The Schoole of Abuse (1579) and Philip Stubbes' *The Anatomie of Abuses* (1583) we find the "realism," the vividness, the interest in sins of the flesh, and the powerful indignation which are alien to the humble plowman. Gosson brings the Elizabethan theater to life and condemns it roundly:

> In our assemblies at playes in *London,* you shall see suche heaving, and shooving, suche ytching and shouldring, too sitte by women; Suche care for their garments, that they bee not trode on: Such eyes to their lappes, that no chippes light in them: Such pillowes to ther backes, that they take no hurte: Such masking in their eares, I knowe not what: Such giving them Pippins to passe the time: Suche playing at foote Saunt without Cardes: Such ticking, such toying, such smiling, such winking, and such manning them home, when the sportes are ended.[5]

But in the last decade of the century the humble Piers Plowman gave way to a new satirist. The completeness of the transformation is apparent in Thomas Nashe's, *Pierce Penilesse His Supplication to the Divell* (1592). Nashe uses Piers's name, and he organizes his satire around the Seven Deadly Sins, but there is very little of the plodding medieval humility left. Instead we have fantastic, soaring rhetoric, vivid and obviously exaggerated pictures of sin, and a Piers who now is a poverty-stricken scholar. Out of disappointment and anger he turns on the world, "Whereupon (in a malecontent humor) I accused my fortune, raild on my patrones, bit my pen, rent my papers, and ragde in all points like a mad man. . . . I resolved in verse to paint forth my passion." [6] He groans with envy, like Juvenal, that

5. *The Schoole of Abuse,* ed. Edward Arber (London, 1869), p. 35.
6. *Works, 1,* 157. All citations of Nashe in my text are to the edition of R. B. McKerrow, 5 vols., London, Sidgwick & Jackson, 1910.

his social, moral, and mental inferiors prosper, those who "write a Treatise of *Tom Thumme*, or the exployts of *Untrusse*," while the good scholar and poet is not appreciated. But in the process of attacking others Pierce reveals that gambling and improvidence have brought him to this state. The reason for his writing satire is, he tells us, using a most unpleasant metaphor, not the humble corrective purpose of Piers the Plowman but sheer anger and desire to hurt the fools who have prospered: "I determined to clawe Avarice by the elbowe, till his full belly gave mee a full hande, and lette him bloud with my penne (if it might be) in the veyne of liberalities." He reveals the true satiric delight in causing pain when he launches an attack on the younger Harvey and commands him, "off with thy gowne and untrusse, for I meane to lash thee mightily," and after scourging him mightily indeed, Pierce exclaims with smug self-satisfaction in both his morals and his rhetoric, "Have I not an indifferent pretty vayne in Spurgalling an Asse?"

The same pattern of development can be observed in another satiric persona created somewhat later than Piers. In 1501 an ancient and mutilated statue was set up in Rome and given the name of *Pasquino* or *Pasquillo*—Pasquill was thought to be the name of a schoolmaster living across the street from where the statue was found. On St. Mark's Day the statue was costumed and became the subject of orations by humanist scholars, but gradually the practice began of attaching anonymous satires to the statue, and these satires were attributed to Pasquin. Another statue was unearthed about the same time on the Campus Martius (*a foro Martius*) and became Marforio, or Mavortius, the companion of Pasquin. A pasquinade then became a dialogue in which Marforio played the adversarius to Pasquin.

Pasquil was introduced to England by Sir Thomas Elyot in his *Pasquil the Playne* (1533), and despite Pasquil's humanist associations and his connection with the biting

Italian cinquecento satire, Elyot transforms him into something very close to the still dominant Piers figure. He is now
Plain Pasquill who attacks vice with earnestness and humility and describes his style and his origins in the typical
manner: "Sens plainnes in speking is of wise men comended
/ and diverse do abhorre longe prohemes of Rhetoricke: I
have sette out this mery treatise, wherein plainnes and
flateri do come in trial in such wise as none honest man will
be therewith offended. . . . Pasquille is an olde Romane /
but by longe sittinge in the strete, and heringe market men
chat / he is become rude and homely." [7] Pasquil stresses his
plainness, simplicity, and good will, using as the basis for
his criticism of others his gentle honesty: "I have professed
from my chyldehode never to speak in ernest to my mayster
or frende, contrarye to that, that I thynke."

Having been anglicized by Elyot, Pasquil became an
alternate satiric persona during the sixteenth century, and
in such works as the anonymous *Pasquin in a Trance* (1566)
he retained the traditional humility and plainness. But the
mutation of the satiric persona which we have observed taking place in the Piers figure also affected Pasquil, and when
we encounter him next he is furiously engaged in exchang-
ing blows with Martin Marprelate. The titles of the various
pamphlets, sometimes ascribed to Thomas Nashe, in which
Pasquil appears in this "war" suggest the change: *The Return of the Renowned Cavaliero Pasquill of England, from
the Other Side of the Seas, and His Meeting with Marforius
at London upon the Royall Exchange* (1589) and *A Coun-
tercuffe Given to Martin Junior by the Venturous, Hardie,
and Renowned Pasquill of England, Cavaliero* (1589). Plain
Pasquil become Cavalier Pasquil, speaks with joy of biting
others, and advertises his book with, "If my breath be so
hote that I burne my mouth, suppose I was printed by
Pepper Allie."

7. Sigs. Ai^v–Aii^R.

But it remained for Nicholas Breton to complete the transformation of Plain Pasquil to Biting Pasquil. In *Pasquils Madde-Cappe* (1600), the first of a long series of pasquinades, the change is immediately suggested by the deliberately insolent tone of the preface: "What you are that reade this I know not, and how you like it I greatly care not." [8] No longer does Pasquil write out of a humble desire for correction, but rather from a diseased hatred of the world. In the introductory verses by Maphorious to *Pasquils Fooles-Cap* (1600) we are told that the work is the result of a diseased mental condition variously described as a "fit," "franzy," "Madding fit," and "humor." Maphorious adds that in writing this piece Pasquil's "meaning was, to please none but himselfe." Similarly in *Melancholicke Humors* (1600) the satire is said to have resulted from these conditions: "Pasquil having been long in his dumpes . . . hath brought forth the fruites of a fewe Melancholicke Humours; which chiefly he commendeth to spirits of his own nature, full of melancholy, and as nere Bedlem as Moorgate: a figure in the fields, to be easily deciphered." [9]

Breton's Pasquil and Nashe's Pierce are but two examples of the new Renaissance satirist, and the transformation of plain Piers and plain Pasquil into these malcontent, arrogant, ostentatious figures is one outward sign of the general shift in thought we call the English Renaissance.[1] The ultimate reasons for the change in satirists are buried deep in the complex causes of the Renaissance itself and are beyond the scope of this work. The concept of satire reflected

8. In *The Works in Verse & Prose of Nicholas Breton,* ed. A. B. Grosart (London. 1879), *1,* 4.

9. P. 5. The attribution to Breton of this and other Pasquil poems printed in Grosart's volume is doubtful, but it is the most complete collection of English pasquinades printed.

1. There is an excellent description of the Renaissance style in fools and practical jokes in Jacob Burckhardt, *The Civilization of the Renaissance in Italy,* Pt. II, ch. 2, "Modern Wit and Satire."

in the new satirist also found expression in critical theory and the choice of new satiric models, and we must turn to these briefly.

ELIZABETHAN CRITICAL THEORIES OF SATIRE

Satire has always been considered a minor genre, and Renaissance critics usually devote only a few lines to it before passing on to the more serious matters of tragedy, comedy, and the heroic poem. But all of the numerous critics, both Italian and English, who wrote "Poetics" in imitation of Aristotle during the sixteenth century do deal with satire, however briefly, and they are generally in agreement on major points. Their collective opinions about the origins and nature of satiric writing constitute a theory of satire and, implicitly, a prescription for writing it.

The use of the word "satire" (*satyr* was the Elizabethan spelling) to denote a form of writing first occurs in English in Alexander Barclay's *The Shyp of Folys of the Worlde* (1509), where he says, "This present Boke myght have ben callyd nat inconvenyently the Satyr (that is to say) the reprehencion of foulysshnes." [2] Here, then, at the beginning of the century we have the relatively simple view which equates satire with any attack on foolishness. But later Elizabethan critics derived an expanded theory of satire from the discussion of the genre included in the history of comedy and tragedy written by Aelius Donatus, a fourth-century grammarian, and prefixed regularly to the editions of Terence read in all Elizabethan grammar schools. Donatus says that satire descended from the *vetus comoedia* which was repressed because of its scandalous attacks on personalities. The dramatic type that succeeded was, according to Donatus, the satyr play, in which actors assumed the character of satyrs and under this mask attacked in-

2. Ed. T. H. Jameson (London, 1874), *1*, 17.

dividuals in the rough, savage fashion befitting such woodland creatures. Because of its excesses the satyr play in turn gave way to the New Comedy in which identifiable individuals were no longer attacked. The idea that poetic satire had its origin in a dramatic form distinguished for its viciousness of attack and spoken by rough satyrs was the basis for nearly all Elizabethan theories of satire. Here, for example, is a typical early definition: "A satire is a Poesie, rebuking vices sharply, not regarding anye persones. . . . [It] is very railing, onely ordained to rebuke vice. . . . The Satires had their name of uplandyshe Goddes, that were rude, lassivious and wanton of behavior." [3]

In this manner the association was made between poetic satire and satyrs. At least a few of the Elizabethans, however, were aware that there were other etymological possibilities, but their alternative derivations also tended to affirm the qualities of roughness and bitterness which they believed to be inherent in satire. Thomas Drant in his translation of the first two satires of Horace in 1566 offers in a prefatory poem the possibilities that the word "satyr" may be related to the Arabic word for spear, to satyrs, to the planet Saturn, and to the Latin adjective *satur* meaning full or charged with a mixture.[4] But the majority of Elizabethan critics accepted without question the connection of satyrs and satire. Specifically acknowledging his indebtedness to Donatus, Thomas Lodge in his *Defence of Poetry* (1579) says that drama began originally in tragedy which was

3. Thomas Langley, *An Abridgemente of the Notable Works of Polidore Vergile* (1570), sigs. cii–ciii.

4. Drant's poem is reprinted and discussed by Mary Claire Randolph, "Thomas Drant's Definition of Satire, 1566," *Notes and Queries, 180* (1941), 416–18. John Weever in his *Faunus and Melliflora* (1600) offers another etymology. The poem is an extremely interesting allegorical history of satire which tells the story of two lovers who angered Diana. She in revenge caused their first child to be a satyr and the foe of love. The child was called a satyr, Weever explains jokingly, because he "satisfide her ires."

written to praise the gods. But as time advanced the form
was changed to deal with the fortunes of exiles, the decay
of countries, and the fall of princes. "Yet," Lodge goes on,
"not content with this, they presented the lives of Satyers,
so that they might wiselye, under the abuse of that name,
discover the follies of many theyr folish fellow citisens. And
those monsters were then as our parasites are now adayes:
suche as with pleasure reprehended abuse." [5]

George Puttenham in *The Arte of English Poesie* (1589)
gives a more detailed view of the origin of satire and carries his discussion of the form into the area of nondramatic
writing. He differs from Lodge in regarding the satyr play,
not tragedy, as the archetypal dramatic form, which arose,
as did comedy and tragedy in his view, as a corrective for
the vices of men. "And the first and most bitter invective
against vice and vicious men was the *Satyre:* which to th'
intent their bitternesse should breede none ill will . . .
they made wise as if the gods of the woods, whom they called
Satyres or *Silvanes,* should appeare and recite those verses
of rebuke." [6] Puttenham then simply transfers the qualities
he believes to be present in the satyr plays to satiric poetry.
"There was yet another kind of Poet, who intended to taxe
the common abuses and vice of the people in rough and
bitter speaches, and their invectives were called *Satyres,*
and themselves *Satyricques:* such were *Lucilius, Iuvenall,*
and *Persius* among the Latines, & with us he that wrote the
booke called Piers plowman." [7]

These are the major pronouncements on satire made by
the Elizabethan critics, and the practitioners of the form
testify to the orthodoxy of the view that satire was an attack
on vice delivered by a satyr. Joseph Hall, for example, in
"His Defiance to Envie" which precedes his collection of
satires, *Virgidemiae,* says,

5. *Elizabethan Critical Essays, 1,* 80.
6. Ibid., 2, 32.
7. Ibid., 2, 27.

> The ruder *Satyre* should goe rag'd and bare:
> And show his rougher and his hairy hide.
>
> (lines 76–7)

In his *Seven Satyres* (1598), William Rankins constructs a pastoral world from which the satyr satirist emerges to view the affairs of men.

> From woods, to wood and mad conceited men,
> That with the Moone participate their minde,
> I leave my hollow vast desertfull den,
> To tell them the derision of their kinde.
>
> (I, lines 1–4) [8]

At the beginning of one of his satires, illustrated with a picture of a shaggy, fierce satyr, George Wither says,

> Though in shape I seeme a Man,
> Yet a Satyr wilde I am;
> Bred in Woods and Desert places,
> Where men seldome shew their faces;
> Rough and hayrie like a Goate,
> Clothed with Dame Natures coate. [9]

It is most important to note here that both authors and critics take it for granted that in satire the writer *assumes* the mask of the satyr either to avoid ill will or to discover folly more effectively. Satire was commonly thought, following on Donatus, to derive from a play where actors *took the part* of satyrs and attacked their victims in a rough and savage fashion. Lodge speaks of how the ancients played the part of satyrs "so that they might wisely, *under the abuse of that name* discover the follies of many" (my italics). Puttenham tells us that the actors in satyr plays *"made wise as if* they were the gods of the woods" (my italics). And each of the quotations from Elizabethan satire shows clearly that

---

8. Ed. A. Davenport, Liverpool Univ. Press, 1948.

9. "Vices Executioner: or the Satyrs Selfe-description of Himselfe," in *The Workes of Master George Wither* (London, 1620), p. 307, lines 1–6.

the authors are consciously constructing the satyr persona to deliver attacks on fools and folly.

Out of the association of satyrs and satire the Elizabethans derived their theories of the decorum of satire. Since satire was thought to deal exclusively with the foolishness of men, it followed that the subject matter was base and required treatment in a base style. In *Mother Hubberd's Tale,* for example, Spenser, using a classical criterion in a medieval form of satire, tells us at the outset,

> No Muses aide me needes heretoo to call:
> Base is the style, and matter meane withall.
>
> (lines 43-4) [1]

And Bishop Hall, suggesting that he has used a higher style at times than decorum required, addresses his satiric Muse in the following manner,

> And if thou canst not thine high flight remit,
> So as it mought a lowly Satyre fit,
> Let lowly Satyres rise aloft to thee:
> Truth be thy speed, and Truth thy Patron bee.
>
> (I, Prologue, 21-4)

Furthermore, since satire was thought of as being spoken by rough, crude, wanton satyrs, it followed that the style and matter should be appropriate to these creatures. Specifically this seems to have meant harsh meters, coarse language, and frank descriptions of the most unattractive kinds of vice.

This conception of satiric decorum coincided with the Elizabethan estimation of the style of the Roman satirists. Here is Nashe on the subject. *"Horace, Perseus, Iuvenall,* my poore iudgment lendeth you plentifull allowance of applause: yet had you, with the *Phrigian* melodie that stirreth men up to battalle and furie, mixt the *Dorian* tune, that favoreth mirth and pleasure, your unsugred pilles (however excellently medicinable) would not have beene so harsh in

1. *Spenser's Minor Poems,* ed. E. de Sélincourt, Oxford Univ. Press, 1910.

the swallowing." [2] And in *The Mirrour for Magistrates* we find,

> Be rough in ryme, and then they say you rayle,
> Though Iuuenal be so, that makes no matter.[3]

Then too, when the Elizabethans looked at *Piers the Plowman* and other Piers poems they found the rough verse and plain language of the "lewd" tradition and concluded that their theory of satiric decorum was universally true. The result was the standard identification of Piers as an English satirist much like the Romans and their English imitators. "As *Horace, Lucilius, Iuuenall, Persius* & *Lucullus* are the best for Satyre among the Latines; so with us in the same faculty these are chiefe, *Piers Plowman, Lodge, Hall* of Imanuel Colledge in Cambridge; the Authour of *Pigmalions Image and certaine Satyrs;* the Author of Skialetheia." [4]

Further support for this decorum of satire was derived from the satires of Pietro Aretino, the best known of the Italian satirists, to judge from the frequency with which the Elizabethans referred to him, who in his verse, and perhaps in life, was as rough, coarse, and lascivious as any imaginable satyr. The scurrility of his satires was such, in fact, that he was able to support himself for the last thirty years of his life by blackmail, so great was the fear among people of wealth and position of being the subject of his pen. Nashe, in the person of Jack Wilton, speaks of Aretino in eulogistic terms which showed the qualities for which he was noted:

> Before I goe anie further, let me speake a word or two of this *Aretine*. It was one of the wittiest knaves that

2. "Strange Newes, Of the Intercepting of Certaine Letters," in *Works, 1,* 284–5.
3. Ed. Lily B. Campbell (Cambridge Univ. Press, 1938), p. 347. "How Collingbourne was cruelly executed for making a foolishe rime," lines 8–9.
4. Francis Meres, *Palladis Tamia*, ed. D. C. Allen, Scholars' Facsimilies and Reprints (New York, 1938), p. 283ᵛ.

ever God made. . . . His pen was sharp pointed lyke a poinyard; no leafe he wrote on but was lyke a burning glasse to set on fire all his readers. With more than musket shot did he charge his quill, where hee meant to inveigh. No houre but hee sent a whole legion of devils into some heard of swine or other. . . . His sight pearst like lightning into the entrailes of all abuses. . . . He was no timerous servile flatterer of the commonwealth wherein he lived. His tongue & invention were foreborne; what they thought they would confidently utter. Princes hee spard not, that in the least point transgrest.[5]

The belief that low style was appropriate for satire acquired a rather curious corollary. The Elizabethans believed that a genuine satire was obscure. "The obscurity arising from the difficult and glancing allusions, the sudden and abrupt transitions of thought, the unexpected insertion of conversation not clearly divided between the speakers, and the highly-coloured rhetoric in the satires of Juvenal and Persius, was taken as characteristic of the form itself." [6] Hall gives direct utterance to this idea in attempting to answer the charge leveled at him, no doubt by some pedant priding himself on his exact knowledge of classical decorum, that his satires are,

> But packe-staffe plaine uttring what thing they ment:
> Contrarie to the Roman ancients,
> Whose wordes were short, & darksome was their sence;
> Who reads one line of their harsh poesies,
> Thrise must he take his winde, & breath him thrise.
>
> (III, Prologue, 4–8)

There appears to have been a minor critical squabble on this matter, possibly because obscurity conflicted to some

5. "The Unfortunate Traveler," *Works*, 2, 264–5.
6. Davenport, *Collected Poems of Joseph Hall*, p. xxv.

degree with the frank and fearless attitude which the satirist cultivated. John Marston, who could be as "darksome" as needful, takes exception to the doctrine of obscurity in a passage worth quoting in full since it makes several interesting points about satire in general.

> Know I hate to affect too much obscurity, & harshness, because they profit no sence. To note vices, so that no man can vnderstand them, is as fond, as the French execution in picture. Yet there are some, (too many) that think nothing good, that is so curteous, as to come with in their reach. Tearming all Satyres (bastard) which are not palpable darke, and so rough writ, that the hearing of them reade, would set a mans teeth on edge. For whose vnseasoned pallate I wrote the first Satyre in some places too obscure, in all places mislyking. . . . *Persius* is crabby, because antient, & his ierks, (being particularly giuen to priuate customes of his time) dusky. Iuuenall (vpon the like occasion) seemes to our iudgement, gloomy. Yet both of them goe a good seemely pace, not stumbling, shufling. *Chaucer* is hard even to our vnderstandings: who knowes not the reason? how much more those old Satyres which expresse themselues in terms, that breathed not long euen in theyr dayes. But had we then liued, the vnderstanding of them had been nothing hard. I will not deny there is a seemely decorum to be obserued, and a peculier kinde of speech for a Satyres lips, which I can willinglier conceaue, then dare to prescribe; yet let me haue the substance rough, not the shadow. I cannot, nay I will not delude your sight with mists: yet I dare defend my plainnes gainst the veriuyce face, of the crabbed'st Satyrist that euer stuttered.[7]

7. *The Scourge*, pp. 9–10. For a general discussion of cultivated obscurity see Arnold Stein, "Donne's Obscurity and the Elizabethan Tradition," *ELH, 13* (1946), 98–118.

The Elizabethan definition of satire as it appears in formal pronouncements amounts to little more than, "a poem in which the author playing the part of the satyr attacks vice in the crude, elliptic, harsh language which befits his assumed character and his low subject matter." Decorum is the guiding critical principle, and the definition turns on the connection of satyr with satire. For the scientific etymologist this is all nonsense, of course, for it is by now well established that "satire" derives ultimately from Latin "satur," meaning full of different things. In fact, the Elizabethans were woefully mistaken in every one of their assumptions about satyrs. The Greek satyr plays, to judge from the two extant examples, were not satiric in the usual sense, but comic versions of the tragic stories which they followed, and the satyrs who appear in them are not at all harsh and bitter but a group of mischievous clowns. Furthermore, the Elizabethans pictured the satyr as half-man and half-goat with a long tail—this curious creature appears on the title-pages of many Elizabethan satires and was still used by Hogarth in 1726 in his frontispiece for *Hudibras*— but the Greek satyr was no more than a very shaggy man whose only animal qualities appeared in his features.

But historical naïveté is not necessarily critical naïveté, and we are not entitled to dismiss the Elizabethan theories of satire as mere nonsense because they are historically inaccurate. Mistaken or doubtful etymologies frequently state truths of another order, as does the Middle English adjective "abhominable" or our own doubtful tracing of the word "tragedy" (i.e. "goat song") to the ancient sacrifice of a scapegoat. The identification of satire and satyr, despite the fact that the Elizabethans present it as historical truth, must be understood as a critical proposition about satire which gathers up and focuses the Renaissance critical understanding of satire as a rough, savage poem in which the attack on vice is delivered by a fictional character possessing the traits required to make him effective in his work. Seen in this light the satyr theory is far more sophisticated, artistically at least, than our own theory which locates the origin of the word "satire" in a word meaning "filled with many different things" and then makes heterogeneity the distinguishing quality of satire.

It may well be that critics like Lodge and Puttenham thought they were writing a literal history of satire, but the crucial point is that their "facts" obviously must have fitted their own understanding of the satires, chiefly the classics, with which they were familiar. And satire was for them dramatic: it originated in the drama; attacks on vice were delivered by a man playing the part of the satyr, and his speech conformed to his character. The choice of the satyr as the chief actor, with emphasis on his savagery, lasciviousness, and delight in reprehending vice, reflects both the Renaissance preference for classical rather than medieval satire and a new ethos in which humility and simplicity were no longer the ideals. The "new" critical theory of satire provides us with one further lead. In all Renaissance discussions of satire little or nothing is ever said about the satiric scene; instead of spending time describing the vices which are to be lashed and the manner in which they are to be presented, critics and authors, with only rare exceptions, concentrate all their attention on the satyr-satirist. His character controls every part of satire, and all the other portions are adjusted to suit him. The fools described are the type of fools he would "naturally" select, and the language used to describe them is the language he would "naturally" use. This is a direct reversal of the situation in medieval satire, where the satirist is repressed and the scene featured, and suggests that our investigation of Elizabethan satire should center on the satirist.

JUVENAL, "PRINCE OF SATYRISTS" [8]

It was standard practice for the Elizabethans to include the writer of "the booke called Piers plowman" in their lists of great satirists, probably to add dignity to the tradition of English letters; but when the Elizabethans began about 1590 to write a new type of satire, they turned away from the native tradition and found their models among the Roman satires.[9] Bishop Hall, who claims to be the first English satirist, tells us that the only modern satires he had been able to see were those of Ariosto and "one base french Satyre," and explains that "in want of more late and familiar presidents I am constrained thus farre of to / imitate" my "Roman predecessors."[1] In practice this seems to have meant, most often, imitating Juvenal, although the authors of the new satire were thoroughly familiar with Horace, Persius, and the epigrammatist Martial, and frequently borrowed from them. In concentrating our discussion on Juvenal's satires we shall not, however, be slighting Horace, who was also a major influence, since to describe the formal characteristics of Juvenalian satire is to describe those of Horatian satire as well. Horace, using to an unknown de-

8. This is Sir Robert Stapylton's translation of J. C. Scaliger's phrase and appears in Stapylton's *Juvenals Sixteen Satyrs* (London, 1647), sig. A6R, the first complete English translation of Juvenal. The preface provides an excellent summary of reasons why the Elizabethans believed that Juvenal exceeded Horace in "heate, in height, and liberty (which is of the essence of Satyr)." Barten Holyday published the second complete English translation of Juvenal and Persius in 1673, and his edition is a monument of humanist scholarship, but Holyday still longs for the "moral Juvenal" of the Middle Ages: "O that we could argue him into a Christian" (sig. A2ᵛ).

9. In recent years critics have been inclined to stress the "Englishness" of the new satires (e.g. Arnold Stein, "Joseph Hall's Imitation of Juvenal," *Modern Language Review, 43* [1948], 315–22), but while it is true that the subject matter is most often native, the formal arrangement of these satires derives from the practice of the Roman satiric authors.

1. *Virgidemiae*, "A Post-script to the Reader," lines 54–6.

gree the earlier satiric writings of Lucilius and Ennius, had
stabilized the form of Roman satire, and both Juvenal and
Persius, though they abandoned the mild Horatian tone,
worked within the Horatian forms.

The reasons for the Elizabethan preference of Juvenal
are fairly clear. Horace, though considered suitably obscure,
maintains an easy distance from the vices he describes,
preferring rather to mock than to rage. Such urbanity did
not fit in with the satyr theory of satire, but Juvenal's saeva
indignatio agreed perfectly, as this typical description of his
style suggests:

> I, Iuvenall: thy ierking hand is good,
> Not gently laying on, but fetching bloud;
> So, surgean-like, thou dost with cutting heale,
> Where nought but lanching can the wound avayle.[2]

Furthermore, Horace's satires do not contain as much of the
sensational as those of Juvenal, and since the satyr was
thought of as a lascivious and scabrous creature, Juvenal's
work was again more congenial. Persius is sufficiently dark
and twisted, but with the exception of his first satire his
writings are more often Stoic homilies than colorful descriptions of a wicked world, and while philosophy has a
place in Elizabethan formal verse satire, it is always sub-
ordinate to the depiction of the actual vices.

But there are stronger ties between this new Elizabethan
satire and Juvenal's than the mere congruence of his work
and Elizabethan critical theory. When seen with the historian's eyes from the vantage point of the twentieth century, the Roman Empire between the death of Augustus in
A.D. 14 and the death of Domitian in A.D. 96 was the usual
mixture of good and bad: palace revolts were balanced by

---

2. *The Second Part of the Return from Parnassus*, I.I.86–9. All citations
of this play in my text are to *The Three Parnassus Plays*, ed. J. B. Leishman, London, Nicholson & Watson, 1949.

the formation of an effective civil service; the extension of
Roman citizenship resulted not only in creating a polyglot
race but in drawing the empire closer together and tighten-
ing the bonds among its diverse peoples; and the bread-and-
circuses policy of the Emperors was no simple attempt to
corrupt but a political necessity forced upon the rulers by
the absolute need for controlling the Roman populace. But
to the writers who lived and wrote in this and the immediately succeeding age—Martial, Seneca, Tacitus, Juvenal,
and Lucan—the Rome of Tiberius, Caligula, and Nero was
a city in which men and their institutions had become
totally depraved: excessive wealth and foreign customs had
sapped the vitality of the Roman stock; government had
been placed in the hands of incompetents, libertines, or
despots; the functions of citizens had been usurped by clever
slaves and freedmen who pursued their own gain rather
than the welfare of the state. In reaction to this situation,
they looked back to a mythical Golden Age when Rome was
still young and its uncorrupted citizens lived the simple life
of the country and emerged, like Cincinnatus, from their
native obscurity only when their country was in danger.

Juvenal's sixteen satires are all built around this contrast of the new luxury and the hardy honesty of Repub-
lican Rome. But while his indignation may flash out against
the depravity of his age, his general tone is one of despair
and dejection, and this same tone dominates most of the
literary works of the period. Seneca's heroes, whose highest
achievement is their Stoic ability to endure inevitable evils,
replaced Aeneas; and the easy, urbane criticism of Horace
gave way to the shrill and elaborately rhetorical voice of
Juvenal. At the same time there was an increasing emphasis
on the macabre, on slaughter and cruelty, and on the sentimental pity evoked by the depiction of innocence and virtue
amidst evil. With certain significant modifications, this age,
in terms of its literature, its outlook on life, and its evalua-

tion of contemporary society, has obvious parallels with the
late Elizabethan and early Jacobean situation, for there too
we find a black despair, a desire for return to primitive
simplicity, an increased interest in a modified Stoicism as
the only possible attitude in a world where as Donne put it,

> New Philosophy calls all in doubt,
> The Element of fire is quite put out;
> The Sun is lost, and th' earth, and no mans wit
> Can well direct him where to looke for it.[3]

Jacobean literature, too, traffics in grotesque sensationalism,
rhetorical effects, and sentimentality. And although to our
eyes Jacobean London, despite certain similarities, was in a
state of pristine vigor compared to first-century Rome, its
inhabitants seem to have felt they were akin to the despairing Stoics of the post-Augustan Empire. As H. B. Lathrop
puts it, "Toward the end of the reign of Elizabeth, the
temper of English literature as of English thought changed
from exuberant enthusiasm to a grave and even bitter tone,
a change evinced in turning from Ovid and Vergil and
frivolous story-tellers to the stern authors of the Silver Age.
Ben Jonson is the leader of the movement; and his works
wide as is their range in ancient literature draw particularly
upon Juvenal and the Senecas, Tacitus and Suetonius." [4]

The Elizabethans are quite explicit about certain stylistic
qualities of Juvenal's satires, qualities which their own intense rhetorical training prepared them to recognize and
discuss. They always call attention to his roughness, his
obscurity, his violence, and his "liberty"—in short, to the
dominant tones of Juvenalian satire which are created by

3. "The First Anniversary," lines 205–18. All citations of Donne are to
The Poems of John Donne, ed. Sir Herbert Grierson, 2 vols., Oxford Univ.
Press, 1912.
4. *Translations from the Classics into English from Caxton to Chapman:
1477–1620,* Univ. of Wisconsin Studies in Language and Literature, 35
(Madison, Univ. of Wisconsin Press, 1933), p. 235.

language and subject matter. But nowhere is there any mention of what we would call, for lack of a better word, his architectonics, the larger elements of style such as the construction of the scene, the management of the themes, and the organization of the whole. This is not surprising, since dazzling rhetoric and sensational subject matter are the most striking elements of Juvenal's satires, and such satiric writers as Marston, Hall, and Guilpin followed Juvenal as ostentatiously as possible in these matters. But they also silently copied his more obvious organizational techniques, and we must examine these briefly.

In all, over a period of thirty years (roughly A.D. 100–30), Juvenal wrote sixteen satires which purport to deal with the events and characters of preceding reigns but are actually attacks on the Rome of his own time. The first satire is a "program" satire in which "Juvenal" first speaks of the inanity of the multitudinous epics he is forced to listen to, and then delivers a long indictment of the Romans by cataloguing their sins. He then tells us that this is the "real" world and that only satire can reveal it, not the lying epic form which makes heroes where there are none. In the course of this catalogue Juvenal manages to construct his satiric personality, a plain, old-fashioned Roman of good family who has fallen on evil days, burning with indignation at the abominations he sees around him and not afraid to speak the truth. The remaining satires, with one exception, deal with various forms of Roman degeneracy: male sexual perversion, the condition of the Roman city, the decay of patronage, the indecent behavior of Roman women, the brutality of the professional army, and the debasement of the great families. One satire only, xv, a description of cannibalism in Egypt, does not seem to bear directly on Rome and its people.

This variety of material constitutes a broad panorama of Roman life about 100 A.D., and it is held together by a

simple theme: money, wealth, luxury, and success have debased Rome and destroyed the ancient virtues which made
her ruler of the world. Juvenal concentrates his attention
on the sensitive areas of cultural life—religion, the law, the
arts, the army, the family, the chastity of women—and using
a multitude of rhetorical devices paints in vivid terms the
corruption of each. By way of contrast we have occasional
glimpses of a plainer and more dignified way of life, the
way of simplicity, hard work, concern for Rome rather than
self, natural sex life, and love of family—the myth of Cicero
and Cato which the satirist embodies. Roman depravity is
given dramatic life in a number of ways. Sometimes it is
presented in the form of a short story as in Satire iv, a mock
epic in which obsequious counsellors are consulted about
how to cook a large turbot; or as a straight sermon, Satire x,
"The Vanity of Human Wishes"; or the satirist will play
the part of a sympathetic listener to an attack delivered by
another figure. His sympathy is ironic in Satire ix where
the professional pathic bewails the "immoral" way in which
his patron has treated him, but the sympathy is genuine in
Satire iii where the satirist listens to an old friend tell why
he is leaving Rome. This latter satire is very close to the
most characteristic Juvenalian form, a dramatic monologue
in which the satirist speaking to an adversarius [5] describes
in vivid terms the corruption of Rome. In Satire iii Juvenal
simply reverses the usual parts and allows the adversarius to
deliver a magnificent attack while the satirist listens, no
doubt in amazement. This satire is typical in all other respects, and a brief résumé of it will make clear certain features of Juvenalian satire which the Elizabethans imitated.

   The satirist begins by saying that an old friend of his is
leaving Rome and settling at Cumae, and though he laments

   5. Persius lays this convention bare in his first satire when he addresses
his adversarius in this manner, "Quisquis es, o modo quem ex adverso
dicere feci" (line 44).

the loss of a friend, he can understand anyone wanting to leave the city where one lives, "in perpetual dread of fires and falling houses, and the thousand perils of this terrible city, and poets spouting in the month of August." Without transition we are swept into a scene in which the goods of the departing friend, Umbricius, are being loaded for the journey. The setting for this incident is a grove once sacred to the gods, but now the native grass has been replaced by a marble fountain in bad taste and the whole area has been given over to indigent Jews. This gives the satirist a chance to expatiate on the contrast between the beauties of un- spoiled nature and the ugly, ostentatious works of men, and allows him to sneer at the Jews who, along with Greeks and other Eastern peoples, are for him symbols of both the adulteration of the Roman stock and the effeminate customs which have debased the citizenry. With the background established and the major themes hinted at, Umbricius delivers his farewell speech, a speech in which he arouses our sympathy for the man who has to leave his native and rightful home and stirs up our indignation at the evils which are driving him thence. He goes, he says, "while my old age is erect and fresh, while Lachesis has something left to spin, and I can support myself on my own feet without slipping a staff beneath my hand." He leaves the city to those "who turn black into white" and to those who were formerly men of the lowest order but have now made for- tunes from contracting city works or running a slave market. He leaves it to them since he no longer has any purpose at Rome: he cannot lie, knows nothing of astrology, cannot act as a messenger between a bride and her paramour, and does not wish to know those dangerous secrets which rob one of sleep but ensure the favor of the man whom the revelation might harm.

At this point old Umbricius abandons his skillfully main- tained attitude of mock humility and launches into direct invective against the sycophantic and parasitical Greeks and Syrians. His anger rises as he recounts how he, a freeborn Roman citizen, must give place to these foreigners. The foreigner, he says, is a natural actor, and even if the true Roman wished to compete with him it would be impossible, for the slave can praise anything, no matter how bad: if one smiles the Greek splits his side with laughter, if one says he is hot the Greek "breaks into a sweat." Besides, this parasite is a lustful creature, and if he fails to debauch the mother of the family, the young daughter, son-in-law, or son, he will attack the grandmother.

Umbricius then commences an attack, still in the vituperative manner, on the prevailing condition where wealth has become the measure of a man in Rome, rather than birth or virtue. You cannot get justice, you cannot even compete for the favors of a courtesan, let alone hope to marry well, unless you have money. And to make these ideas more vivid Umbricius quickly sketches in two brief scenes in which he is forced to give way to slaves while hurrying to see a client, and then because poorly dressed he is forced out of his rightful place at the games by the sons of panders, auctioneers, and gladiators.

Next he turns to a description of rural Italy for contrast. It is here, he says, that the old simplicity is still preserved, and clothes make no difference. We are then shown a sentimental picture of a rustic festival where the "babe on its mother's breast shrinks back affrighted at the gaping of the pallid masks," and where all men are dressed alike. After shifting back briefly to a description of the indignities one must undergo at the hands of a rich man in Rome, Umbricius returns again to the countryside of "cool Praeneste, or at Volsinii," and points out that one can live in these towns in perfect safety, whereas in Rome one is in constant danger of fire and falling buildings.

This is approximately the center of the Satire, and old

Umbricius, still breathing easily, having first decried the moral contamination of Rome and contrasted it with the rural areas where the old virtues are maintained, now begins to dramatize the physical ugliness and dangers of the city. He begins with a scene in which a friend living on the third floor is calling futilely for water to put out a fire. This scene fades into a companion piece, a description of the poor scholar Codrus who loses all his miserable possessions in a fire and is forced to beg—unsuccessfully, of course, for nothing but villainy prospers in Juvenal's satire. But if the house of a wealthy man is destroyed, everyone deplores the fact and hastens to offer valuable gifts. After this the speaker again weaves a description of country life into his tapestry of Rome and then hurries on to descriptions of the noise of the city and the dangers of trying to walk through the Roman crowd. The denunciation of the huge drays passing through the city is made more poignant by drawing a scene in which a load of marble falls from a wagon and crushes, in a most horrible manner, a man so poor that he has not the money to pay his passage over Styx. This scene dissolves into a picture, à la Dickens, in which the dead man's family in their humble (but happy) home are waiting for his arrival. Next Umbricius presents the dangers of the street at night, again in dramatic terms. He describes himself as passing quickly along a street where he is first struck by tiles falling from a badly repaired roof and then by the contents of slop-pails. Having endured these trials, he is robbed and beaten by a bravo, who does not, of course, dare attack the rich. But he ironically consoles himself by saying that even if he should get home safely, the chances are he will be robbed by a burglar and lucky if his throat is not cut in the bargain in a city where there are so many criminals that most of the iron, which should have been used for agricultural tools, goes for making chains. Having completed this magnificent tirade, old Umbricius takes his leave and with mild irony says to the satirist, who has no doubt been listening with mouth agape, "I will come over to your cold country in my thick boots to hear your Satires [i.e. satirists], if they think me worthy of that honour."

Paraphrase is ineffective for rendering the quality of Juvenalian satire for several reasons. First, it misses the lightning speed with which the original moves, an effect achieved by the vigor of the verse and by the rapid shifts from scene to scene and subject to subject without concern for formal transitions. Second, it fails to show the superb manner in which Juvenal manages constantly to keep the ideals of rustic simplicity and antique virtue in contrast with the degenerate city life, not only by alternately presenting scenes of each but by weaving the pastoral world into the texture of the entire satire through the use of imagery and diction which make an invidious comparison with the dirty and wicked town. Finally, it is impossible to suggest the profusion of rhetorical devices used to manipulate the emotions of the reader.[6]

What we have then within the satires is a panoramic view of the dirt and sins of Rome, a camera-eye sweep directed by the satirist over Rome, pausing here and there to focus briefly on a scene or a face, and utilizing every technique known to the rhetorician and the poet to make the pictures vivid and bring into relief their more unsavory aspects. This is one of the primary qualities of formal satire: the display of the world's ills not by concentrating on a single incident, or even a limited number of situations, but rather by presenting a wide variety of brief and carefully constructed pictures and comments, all tending to indict the

6. My discussion of the rhetorical aspects of Juvenal's satires is largely based upon various analyses by W. S. Anderson. His unpublished Yale dissertation, "The Rhetoric of Juvenal" (1954), is a thorough discussion of the skillful manner in which Juvenal used rhetoric. Some of his work has appeared in "Juvenal 6: A Problem in Structure," *Classical Philology*, 2 (1956), 73–94, and "Studies in Book I of Juvenal," *Yale Classical Studies*, *15*.

society in which such things exist. This is the familiar, and difficult, artistic technique of attempting to show the whole through the presentation of as great a number of its parts as possible. The dangers of such a method are characteristic of satire: superficiality and a diversity of events and persons which hinder the emergence of any pattern. But the Juvenalian hodgepodge has a remarkable thematic unity. Each of the innumerable vices and disorders described is traced back to a single source, the possession of excessive wealth which saps Roman vitality and morality.

This horde of hypocrites, foreigners, perverts, whores, sycophants, cowards, murderers, thieves, and sybarites in their dirty, noisy, brawling, and dangerous city is the scene of Juvenalian satire. But strictly speaking this scene, vivid as it is, has no separate existence of its own, for it comes into being entirely through the words of the satirist. He selects the parts, arranges them, and describes them in such a way as to control the reactions of the audience. He stands always in the foreground, pointing out detail after detail, directing our attention from one example of vice to the next, and imparting qualities to each with his language. As a result every detail is reflexive: the words leave the satirist's mouth to describe the scene but they also bounce back to define the satirist who chooses these details and uses this language. This process combined with a variety of direct statements about his feelings and attitudes creates the personality of Juvenal's satirist. He admits to the more attractive characteristics of the satirist—frankness, courage, indignation, and a compulsion to expose vice wherever he finds it. He is a conservative in the best sense, embodying all the primitive virtues Rome now lacks, and as he continues speaking we begin to see the stern old Roman of good family who has fallen on evil days. His money is gone, and since money is the only thing that counts any longer in

Rome, he is shoved about by all, dishonored in being made
to sit below the salt, turned away by patrons, pushed from
his proper seat at the games, and, in general, denied the
dignities to which his name, his profession, and his citizenship should entitle him. To such a man everything about
modern Rome appears debased, and he reacts with violence.
He is the perfect figure to attack Roman depravity, for he
represents an older, healthier society and thus stands always
in contrast to the decadence around him; and he dislikes
everything modern and has the courage to censure it. What
Juvenal has done is to create a character something like
Cato the Censor and place him in the setting of first-century
Rome, and it is as if Cotton Mather were allowed to comment on twentieth-century New York.

But the Juvenalian satirist inevitably has qualities utterly
foreign to Cato the Censor, and these involve him in the
usual paradoxes. For one thing the satirist is a Stoic—at
least from time to time he makes Stoic pronouncements
about denying divinity to Fortune by fortitude, advocates
control of both wrath and desire, and speaks, in Stoic fashion, of the necessity for wisdom and reason. But the pose
of the Stoic conflicts with the furious indignation which is
so omnipresent in Juvenal's satire. The invective is so
powerful, the scorn so biting, the lash so vigorously applied,
the probing so careful and vindictive, the sense of outrage
so apparent, that the satirist is constantly in the position of
denying the same ethic by which he is condemning his
victim. He attacks the wealthy, the hypocritical, the lecherous on the grounds of their being unreasonable, and
simultaneously is outrageously unreasonable, in the Stoic
sense, in his anger which knows no bounds. Juvenal was not
unaware of this predicament and presents the problem in
the line, "si natura negat, facit indignatio versum" (I, 79).
Throughout the satires he argues that the crimes he sees are

so great that no one could resist scourging them, but the fundamental ambivalence in the character of the satirist remains.

Perhaps even more striking is the contrast between the pose of the plain, simple man and the baroque rhetorician who emerges in the satires. By the end of the first century A.D. rhetoric had degenerated from the Aristotelian and Ciceronian ideal of persuasion through reason to a form of public entertainment in which the orator sought to amuse with a display of ornate styles and sensational subject matter. Emphasis was now placed not on *dispositio,* the arrangement of the parts in a logical and orderly fashion, but on *ornatus,* the embellishment of language. The classical ideals of smoothness, concealment, clarity, and organization—*ars est celare artem*—gave way to the baroque rhetoric of the Silver Latin period with its ideals of emotional intensity; elaboration of details; display; and concentration on a single, simple theme. Juvenal was trained in this school of rhetoric, and in his satires the hand of the extravagant rhetorician is apparent in his profuse use of such linguistic devices as synecdoche, metonymy, antonomasia, epithets, allegory, irony, periphrasis. But Juvenal went far beyond the boundaries established by the rhetors for such subjects as he treated. On one hand he made use of elements of the high style: epic catalogues, sonorous meters, archaisms, Hellenisms, weird compounds, and on the other hand he included vulgarisms, obscenities, racy colloquialisms, technical terminology. All this dazzling verbal array is skillfully marshalled to hammer home one single theme, *dépravation du siècle, éloge du temps passé,*[7] one of the standard declamatory topics of the rhetorical schools.

7. Juvenal's use of this theme is treated by Josué de Decker, *Juvenalis Declamans: Étude sur la rhétorique déclamatoire dans les Satires de Juvenal* (Gand, 1913). This work provides a picture of rhetorical practice at the time of Juvenal and investigates the relationship of his satires to the rules of declamation.

The use of this elaborate, showy rhetoric in Juvenal's satires not only endows his stern Roman satirist with contradictory characteristics, a plain man who is at the same time a sophistic rhetorician, but it has led as well to a questioning of Juvenal's motives for writing satire. Once it was shown that his satires conformed to the declamatory exercises of the rhetorical schools, then, given our modern distrust of rhetoric, the truth of Juvenal's charges against the Romans and his indignation became suspect. As H. J. Rose puts it, "Juvenal sometimes leaves a skeptical reader a little in doubt whether he is more angered at the wickedness of the world or obliged to it for giving him such admirable subjects for his great eloquence and extraordinary power of composing vigorous hexameters."[8] There has been no agreement on this point, however, and another scholar can argue that Juvenal's "honesty cannot be questioned. It comes through everything he writes. He is terrifically in earnest, desperately sincere."[1]

The materials of the satires certainly suggest a conscious attempt to capitalize on human delight in the display of depravity. Juvenal's satirist says that he takes for his subject matter "quidquid agunt homines" (I, 85), but since he is always on the attack he seldom, except by way of contrast, introduces any pictures of virtuous Romans, and there must have been many going about their daily business and leading normal lives.[2] Instead we are whisked from scene to

8. *A Handbook of Latin Literature* (London, Methuen, 1936), p. 407.
1. Edith Hamilton, *The Roman Way* (New York, W. W. Norton, 1932), p. 253.
2. The historian's more balanced view of the Rome of the first and second centuries is ably and most interestingly presented by C. N. Cochrane, *Christianity and Classical Culture*, Oxford, 1940. In ch. 4, *Regnum Caesaris Regnum Diaboli*, Cochrane argues that satiric poets such as Juvenal and satiric historians such as Tacitus were fashionable conservatives who completely failed to understand the nature of the crisis through which Rome was necessarily passing on its way to the achievement of stability and order, a crisis made unavoidable by the uncompromising attitude taken in the first

scene of hypocrisy, gluttony, luxury, effeminacy, and in-
gratitude. The whole of this is liberally spiced with explicit
accounts of the sexual perversions of the Romans, and their
moral debilitation is paralleled by descriptions of the ugliness and dangers of their city. There is, of course, always the
possibility that Rome was as thoroughly infected as Juvenal
paints it, but it seems unlikely. What we are facing here is a
problem brought into being by the use of the realistic perspective on satire: i.e. either Rome was completely corrupt
or it wasn't, and if it wasn't then Juvenal's indignation was
sham and he was no more than a Roman muckraker. The
problem is delusive, for we are dealing with art, albeit
highly rhetorical, not history. Rome was somewhat corrupt,
and Juvenal constructed his satires in such a way as to
reveal that corruption in the most striking manner possible.
His satirist, a man who finds everything modern not to his
taste and looks only for evidence of decay, is simply one of
his poetic tools forged to reveal that corruption in a spectacular manner.

I have already suggested the nature of Juvenal's plots in
Chapter 1, but a few words more will be necessary. The
characteristic action of Juvenal's satires, taken singly or as a
group, would seem to be, "to expose the truth," though this
could be stated in a number of other metaphorical ways
such as "to track down the infection." W. S. Anderson has
shown that this action usually takes the form of proving a
startling paradox, as in Satire III "whose theme we may state
as follows: Rome is no longer Rome. . . . Umbricius . . .
takes the Rome of traditional associations—its majesty, justice, wealth, beauty, and honesty—and exposes its self-con-
tradiction. Thus he comments on various conditions, the
lack of opportunity, the aliens, the fires, the thieves, etc., all
of which signify the loss of traditional Roman qualities and

century B.C. by such rugged individualists as Cato and Brutus, who were
regarded by the new conservatives as models of virtue.

cumulate in a totally negative picture of an uninhabitable
city. When he leaves, then, Umbricius symbolizes in his act
what he has been saying, that Roman characteristics no
longer fit the city, for he is the last Roman." ³ While
Juvenal's satirist remains behind to give us thirteen more
satires, his conclusions are always as bleak and unproductive
as those of Umbricius. In each satire he proves his crushing
paradox, which in sum might be stated that men are not
men but beasts, but shows us no possibility of change for the
better. The few instances of good appear in isolated pockets
and seem about to be destroyed. The only "positive" program appears in Satire x where we are advised to cultivate
Stoic fortitude to endure a mad world from which the
satirist has stripped the last shreds of pretense.

All of the various traditions we have examined are to
some degree complementary, and to the Elizabethan writer
they were, of course, not separate traditions but parts of one.
From each the writer of satire could learn that his poetry
should be a frank, outspoken attack on iniquity, with a
heavy emphasis on the sins of the flesh, and filled with
colorful illustrations of these. In addition, Tudor criticism,
native satire, and classical satire all dictated the use of a
base style and scurrilous methods of purging vice. Native
satire provided a precedent for the portrayal of homegrown
villainy and foolishness in a contemporary setting, and pre-
vented the writers of formal verse satire from merely re-
hashing Juvenal's material, though they did not hesitate to
borrow from him in order to enliven their work. Juvenal's
satires provided, most importantly, a model for organization
of the fragmentary materials of the form without resort to
medieval frameworks. The influence of Juvenal is pervasive,
however. There is practically no element of Renaissance
formal satire that does not show traces of borrowing from

3. "Studies in Book I of Juvenal," p. 88.

him. When qualities of the native tradition are present, they have been refined by the practice of Juvenal. The speaker in the satires of Marston and Hall is the satyr of English critical theory, but he speaks in the tones and the curiously mixed style of Juvenal's outraged but always skillful declaimer.

CHAPTER 3

THE ENGLISH SATYR, "THE
TAMBERLAINE OF VICE"[1]

We have seen in the previous chapter that
during the course of the sixteenth century the tone of satire
underwent a gradual change and that by approximately
1590 a new type of satirist had come into being, a satirist
who expressed the values of the Renaissance rather than of
the medieval world. This new satiric personality appears in
a great many different types of satiric writing: in various
literary works of Thomas Nashe, in prose attacks on English
morals by such Puritan reformers as Stubbes and Gosson,
and plays like *A Looking Glasse for London and England*
(1594) by Thomas Lodge and Robert Greene. But in all
these works there are still traces of medieval attitudes and
techniques, and it was not until about 1595 that the satyr
satirist appeared in his characteristic setting of formal verse
satire, the form which displayed him to the best advantage.

Once Joseph Hall in his *Virgidemiae* (1597/8) had employed, apparently with enormous popular success, Juvenalian methods of presenting and organizing his satiric
material, a large number of the new type of satires followed:
John Marston, *Pigmalions Image and Certaine Satyres*
(1598), and *The Scourge of Villanie* (1598, revised and enlarged 1599); Everard Guilpin, *Skialetheia* (1598); T[homas]

---

1. Everard Guilpin, *Skialetheia, or a Shadow of the Truth* (1598), Shakespeare Assoc. Facsimile, 2 (London, 1931), sig. Ci^v.

M[iddleton], *Microcynicon or Sixe Snarling Satyres* (1599);
William Rankins, *Seven Satyres* (1598). To this group we
must add the five satires of John Donne which are impossible to date accurately but clearly belong somewhere in this
period. In June 1599, the Court of High Commission ordered a number of satires burned, and prohibited the further printing of satire without specific license. This action
silenced many of the earlier satiric authors, but a host of
other writers (e.g. Nicholas Breton and Samuel Rowlands)
continued to write and print satires, and the form flourished
for a number of years. The most important works during
this latter period are *The Scourge of Folly* (1611) by John
Davies of Hereford, and *Abuses Stript and Whipt* (1613) by
George Wither—Pope's "Wretched Withers."

These works, which are only a selective sampling of the
large number of satires written in this period, constitute a
new tradition in satire. They are all formal verse satires, and
they all illustrate very clearly a new conception of how
satire should be organized, its proper tone, the correct
persona to be assumed, the fitting style. It is on these satires
that our discussion will be focused, but the material is somewhat unwieldy and it will be useful to have one particular
set of satires as a point of reference. The satiric works of
John Marston are ideal for this purpose: he carried certain
satiric tendencies to the extreme, he was very self-conscious
about his art and frequently explained what he was doing
and why, and since he began writing satiric plays in 1599
his work provides us with a convenient bridge to a discussion of dramatic satire. But I offer Marston's satires as
representative examples of the current understanding and
practice of satiric writing and will substantiate conclusions
drawn from his work with references to other major satires.

In imitation of Juvenal, the new formal satires are composed of a series of short satires which together make up a
book. Each one of the shorter satires is an individual scene

described for us by the satirist. It may be set in the court, the public theater, the streets of the city, or an inn, but ordinarily the Elizabethan satiric writer spends very little time in setting his scene, preferring to concentrate on examples of human wickedness. As each satire opens, we "hear" the voice of the satirist crying out to the world at large or engaged in conversation with an unidentified adversarius, and as he continues speaking a sense of immediacy is gradually created by the use of such rhetorical devices as apostrophe, and we find ourselves on a busy street corner or moving about the city, stopping to notice this incident or that person. The court lady, face covered with cosmetics, rattles by in her coach on her way to an assignation; her husband steals down an alley to the side door of the citizen's house; the citizen lends money to the young gentleman fresh up from the country who has diced his own money away and forces him to take part of the loan in brown paper or worthless cloth; the gentleman hurries to the tailor for the latest in fantastic fashions and then goes to the tavern where he drinks and gambles again—to lose once more—with idle fustian poets, cony-catchers, bragging soldiers who have never been beyond Dover, panders, and young men from the Inns of Court. The satirist cries out with surprise at the ostentatious size of Luxurio's town house; repeats the shouts of the gambler, "Come on five, S. George, by heaven at all"; gasps with horror at the sight of a son tearing the lead from his father's tomb; describes a man taking the sweating cure for venereal disease; shows us the secret practices of a lady of pleasure; points out a usurer committing himself to the Fleet in order to live more cheaply; and stops to advise a father who has vainly locked up a son to curb his monstrous sexual appetites. Frequently the satirist pauses to deliver a brief sermon on the wickedness of London, to discuss the ancient hardihood of the English yeomanry, or to prophesy the impending doom and

destruction of this "sin-drowned world." There is always
in these satires a pronounced declamatory tendency which
constantly threatens to overwhelm the dramatic elements.
Hall's satires are often no more than discussions of a particular theme, and even Donne and Marston, the most vivid
of the new satiric writers, frequently fall back into the ora-
torical mode.[2] But whenever the satires are noticeably dramatic, we find the usual satiric scene: the insolent, proud,
luxurious, and stupid are present everywhere, and this
"inundation of luxuriousness / Fatts all the world with . . .
grosse beastlines." [3]

Within this satiric scene we find what at first appears to
be a vast and infinitely varied collection of individual fools
and villains, and specific forms of vice and folly. But after
reading a number of these works one begins to find familiar
faces appearing with the monotonous regularity of the
cuckold in Restoration drama. Not only do these standard
figures appear in the works of different authors, but the
same figure, only slightly modified, will reappear frequently
within the satires of the same writer. The immediate impression of variety is achieved by the use of three elements
in the formation of each character to be held up for scorn.

2. The similarity of these satires to rhetorical themes and declamations
is probably no accident. Juvenal's satires were themselves declamatory in
origin (see Decker, *Juvenalis Declamans*) and after the humanist reform
of education in the early 16th century the English schoolboy's training was
almost identical to that of the 1st- and 2nd-century Roman. One of the
standard exercises in the English grammar school was the writing of
themes on set topics. One judicial class of theme, *Laus et Vituperatio*,
praise and blame, has marked resemblances to the new formal satires. For
examples see George Gascoigne's *A Hundreth Sundrie Flowers* which includes five poems that are extemporary developments of such topics as
durum aeneum & miserabile aevum. A number of Hall's and Marston's
satires also begin with the statement of topics which would have fallen
within the *Vituperatio* class of theme, and in Marston's play *What You
Will* the satirist Lampatho Doria is asked to deliver one of these themes
on the topic, "In Heaven's Handiwork There's Naught" (II.2.128).

3. *The Scourge*, II, p. 25.

By shuffling these elements the author is able to avoid repeating exactly the same pattern. The system works in this way. You begin with a number of basic characters: the fop, the courtier, the country boy come to the city, the Catholic or Puritan, the soldier, the graybeard, the traveler, the lover, the amorous poet, the frugal yeoman, the bawd, the merchant or his wife, the lawyer, the doctor, the highborn lord, the *arrivé*. To these characters it is then possible to attribute any one of a number of general sins. Vanity, greed, lust, hypocrisy, and ambition are the most popular, but any one of the Seven Deadly Sins, as well as a number of minor ones, serves. Once the type character has been assigned a species of sin, then the failing is dramatized in a number of stock situations: fantastic dress, mistreatment of wards, whoring, pretensions to learning, usury, miserliness, extravagance, love of luxury, lying about travels, cowardice, bragging, sycophancy. The following typical cases will serve for examples. The noble motivated by greed and lust forgets his moral responsibilities, begs monopolies, dresses fantastically, leaves his lands to ruin, forgets his tenants, pursues common wenches, mistreats wards, and gets the pox. The squire puts all his lands on his back, goes to London, brags of amours with every lady in court, flatters the great outrageously, uses fantastic language, allows his estate to go to ruin, gets the pox. The soldier returns from the wars, brags, lies about travels, pretends to a fashionable melancholy, dices, wenches, is continually drunk, bullies the weak, gets the pox. The merchant puts money out at exorbitant rates, is cuckolded by a fop, starves his servants, cheats his friends, is miserly, while his son at one of the Inns of Court spends his income riotously and gets the pox.[4]

4. Various critics have made widely differing estimates of the degree to which the scene of Elizabethan satire squares with the reality of Tudor England. Ben Jonson (*Poetaster*, "To the Reader," pp. 54 ff.) accuses the satiric writers of gross distortion, and John Davies of Hereford in *The Scourge of Folly* (London, 1611) admits that he writes for two purposes,

This is the standard side show of the Elizabethan satirist, and he is often quite skillful at presenting his individual characters and creating the effect of a world given over to vice, but he never quite manages to bind his diverse materials together. One of the major problems of the satiric author has always been to create an ordered disorder. He must present us with a rabble to suggest the multiplicity of vice and its chaotic nature, but he must also find at the same time some way of preventing his own composition from being ultimately as fragmentary as the world it mirrors. In great satire the binding element is always some relatively simple concept of the nature of the disease—e.g. wealth, dullness, fear—which is destroying civilization, society, and the decent life. In works where an organizing concept of this kind is present it will find expression, either directly or by contrast, in each of the diverse parts of satire: the incidents and characters created to hold vice up to scorn, the plot, the satirist, and the elements of the ideal which still exist in the midst of depravity.

Unfortunately, no author of Elizabethan formal satire had a clear idea of what was basically wrong with his society, but the traditional fools and villains he displays in his satire do have an innate similarity. Where the standard targets of medieval satire had been the clergy and professional men who were more concerned for their individual welfare than the good of the Christian commonwealth, the common butts of the new satire are the members of the

---

"Lechers *paine,* and Printers gaine." ("Of the Printer," sig. A3R). In our own time both J. B. Leishman (*The Three Parnassus Plays,* p. 49) and C. R. Baskerville (*English Elements in Jonson's Early Comedy,* Chicago, 1911) have argued that the standard targets of satire are conventional and derivative. But Hallett Smith (*Elizabethan Poetry,* ch. 4) and L. C. Knights (*Drama and Society in the Age of Jonson,* London, 1937) have stated, very persuasively, a number of reasons for believing that there is a close connection between the types of fools and practices scourged by the satirists and actual contemporary men and their activities.

rising middle class, the new-made knights, the yeomen's sons come to London to the Inns of Court, the merchant adventurer who buys a great estate and a coat-of-arms. During the course of the sixteenth century in response to actual social conditions these figures, as well as many others, gradually hardened into type characters, caricatures of more complex living men. And if the creation of this rogues' gallery was a somewhat sporadic and not entirely conscious process, it was not haphazard, for each of the type characters described earlier in this chapter is a mocking portrait of some particular form of what L. C. Knights, discussing Ben Jonson, has suggested as the basic subject of Renaissance satire, "inordinate desire—for power, for money, or for the enjoyment of the senses," [5] the sinister side of Renaissance individualism, energy, and daring. But no satiric author before Ben Jonson perceived and took advantage of the fact that the stock targets which he worked and reworked— the fop, the usurer, the projector, the bombastic poet, the *miles gloriosus,* the sycophant, and the insatiable lecher— were but various manifestations of a boundless desire for self-gratification that escaped the restraints hitherto placed on it by tradition and common sense.

The failure of the satiric poets to grasp the innate unity of their raw materials is manifest in the organizational weaknesses of both the individual satires and the collected books.[6] George Wither was at least aware of the tendency of his chosen form to heterogeneity and offered a lame ex-

5. "Ben Jonson, Dramatist," in *The Age of Shakespeare,* ed. Boris Ford (London, Pelican Books, 1955), p. 369.

6. Dryden in his "Discourse on Satire" is doubtless glancing at the excesses and peculiarities of the type of satire we have been discussing when he tells us that Persius was the first author to discover "this important secret, in the designing of a perfect satire—that it ought only to treat of one subject; to be confined to one particular theme; or at least, to one principally. If other vices occur in the management of the chief, they should only be transiently lashed, and not be insisted on, so as to make the design double." In *Works, 2,* 102.

cuse for his own inability to bring order out of chaos: "Although some may thinke I have not so well ioyned things together as I might have done, I know when you have considered the nature of the *Subiect,* & the diversity of things therein handled, you wil accept my good-wil, and let my yeeres be an excuse for that & all other ignorant over-sights whatsoever." [7] But other satiric authors, unwilling or unable to plead their youth, either paid not the slightest attention to unity, contented themselves with loose collections of examples of the same type of vice, or introduced some elaborate and ingenious principle of organization which is more decorative than functional. In *Pigmalion,* for example, Marston, who seems to have understood that Juvenal's satires were basically variations on declamatory themes, introduces his first satire with a theme: *Quaedam videntur, et non sunt.* The next two satires are then given related themes as titles: *Quaedam sunt, et non videntur,* and *Quaedam et sunt, et videntur.* After this the cumbersome scheme breaks down, and while the themes continue to be supplied both in *Pigmalion* and *The Scourge,* they have no relationship to one another and, often enough, no real bearing on the kinds of villainy dealt with in the satires. William Rankins' *Seven Satyres*—actually there are eight —is, however, the extreme instance of the failure of the satiric poet to see that in satire true unification of the material can only be brought about by a firm, definite understanding of the moral issues involved. Rankins' satires "are constructed on the ingenious idea of exploiting the connection between the days of the week, the corresponding astrological planets, the influence of those planets on temperaments, and the contemporary manifestations of such temperaments." [8]

7. "To the Reader," *Abuses Stript and Whipt* in *Workes of George Wither,* sig. B1R.
8. Davenport, *Seven Satires,* pp. vii–viii.

The structural weakness of Elizabethan formal verse satire is ultimately traceable to the almost exclusive interest
of the satiric poets in the figure of their satyr satirist. Each
component part of these satires, e.g. language and subject
matter, is chosen not for its contribution to the total unity
of the poem but for its appropriateness to the accepted character of the satirist. His dominance is suggested by his place-
ment in the scene. Where the medieval plowman-satirist
was partially absorbed by his scene, blending into the pilgrimage or humbly surrendering the foreground to some
other more colorful speaker, the swaggering satyr is always
at the front of the stage. His victims, and even his adversarius, remain nearly always mute, while his voice roars
on without pause. He stands solid and isolated before the
restless world of giddy change and the crowds of fools who
pass behind him. As they move by he hurriedly directs our
attention to this one or that one, and his eye pierces through
the masks of gravity, the fine clothes, the cosmetics, to the
physical and moral ugliness which lie beneath the various
human pretenses of decency and beauty.

This *mise en scène* is taken directly from Juvenal, and
if the Elizabethan satirist's moral point of view had been
as clear and consistent as that of Juvenal's satirist, Elizabethan satire would have been far more consistent. But the
Elizabethan satirist was a strange, twisted character, and
the poets seem to have delighted in multiplying his peculiarities—so much so that it often appears that they were
more interested in creating a sensational satirist than in
writing satire. But, for all the bizarre touches added by the
Elizabethans, the satiric character defined by the critics
and elaborated by the authors of satire is simply an extension—perhaps an extrapolation—of the basic satiric character defined in Chapter I. What the Elizabethans did was
to intensify certain standard satiric traits and repress others.

The association of satire and satyr is the fundamental

assumption made by nearly all Elizabethan satiric authors, and for them a poem in which the writer wore the mask of the satyr and displayed the appropriate savage characteristics was by definition a satire. Forty-five years after Joseph Hall, who claimed priority in the new satire, wrote his first three books of satires and called them "Tooth-lesse Satyrs," his learning and logic could be attacked as deficient by another classicist who knew that satire and biting harshness were synonymous. "But that such a Poem should be toothlesse I still affirme it to be a bull, taking away the essence of that which it calls it selfe. For if it bite neither the persons nor the vices, how is it a Satyr, and if it bite either, how is it toothlesse, so that toothlesse Satyrs are as much as if he had said toothlesse teeth." [9]

This flat definition was the fundamental tenet of the new satire, and, from approximately 1590 on, every author of satire labored to create the biting satyr. Some writers took the idea quite literally, and the satiric persona became in their hands an actual mythological satyr, half man, half goat. William Rankins, for example, in the "Induction" to his *Seven Satyres* depicts his speakers in such a fashion:

> My shaggy Satyres doe forsake the woods,
> Theyr beds of mosse, their unfrequented floodes.
> Their Marble cels, their quiet forrest life,
> To view the manner of this humane strife.
>
> (lines 3–6)

And throughout Rankins' satires occasional references to fauns, silvanes, and rough woods suggest that the voice we hear is that of an actual satyr with hoofs and tail. But this interpretation of the convention is relatively rare. For most Elizabethan satiric writers playing the part of the satyr appears to have meant the display of certain personality

9. John Milton, "An Apology for Smectymnuus" ed. H. M. Ayres in *The Works of John Milton*, ed. F. A. Patterson et al. (Columbia Univ. Press, 1931), *3*, Pt. I, 329.

traits—roughness, crudity, lasciviousness, and frankness—
although a number of the title pages of satiric works carry
the picture of a satyr. This understanding of the convention is suggested by Wither's lines,

> Though in shape I seeme a Man,
> Yet a Satyr wilde I am.[1]

By far the greatest number of references to the physical
characteristics of the satyr occur in metaphor and in such
a way as to suggest a satyr-personality rather than the genuine creature. Marston's satirist speaks of the speech proper
for "a Satyres lips," of "sharpe-fang'd poesie," and references to snarling and biting are frequent. Later on he discusses his "respectlesse rude Satyrick hand," and adds,

> Unlesse the Destin's adamantine band
> Should tye my teeth, I cannot chuse but bite.
> *(The Scourge,* VIII, p. 82)

And in a fit of rage he asks if the world shall continue in
its iniquity,

> Whilst my satyrick vaine
> Shall muzled be, not daring out to straine
> His tearing paw?   *(The Scourge,* III, p. 36)

The choice of the satyr as a model for the satiric character had a number of far-reaching consequences. The
various critical passages quoted earlier make it clear that
the Elizabethans considered the satyr to be lustful, rough,
cruel, and railing, and the descriptions of satyrs in *The
Faerie Queene* confirm this as the established image of
the satyr personality. In Book I, Canto 6, the best picture
of "the salvage nation," we learn that these creatures troop
wildly about, "a rude, misshapen, monstrous rablement." [2]

1. "The Satyrs Selfe-description of himselfe," in *Workes,* sig. X8R.
2. Stanza 8. Citations of *The Faerie Queene* are to *The Works of Edmund
Spenser, A Variorum Edition,* ed. Greenlaw, Osgood, and Padelford, Baltimore, Johns Hopkins Press, 1932.

They are capable of sympathy for the unfortunate Una, but we are told that their pity for her is "unwonted ruth." The story of the birth and training of Sir Satyrane, half satyr and half man, further illustrates certain conventional views of the satyr. Sir Satyrane is the product of an adulterous union of the lustful Thyamis who, searching for pleasure, wandered into the woods where,

> A Satyre chaunst her wandring for to find,
> And kindling coles of lust in brutish eye,
> The loyall links of wedlocke did unbind,
> And made her person thrall unto his beastly kind.
>
> (I, 6, 22)

He holds her captive to his "sensuall desyre" until she presents him with a boy whom he trains up to be a true satyr:

> For all he taught the tender ymp, was but
> To banish cowardize and bastard fear;
> His trembling hand he would him force to put
> Upon the Lyon and the rugged Bear,
> And from the she Beares teats her whelps to teare.
>
> (I, 6, 24)

Such is the success of this educational process that Satyrane grows "so fearlesse and so fell" that he frightens his sire and becomes a tyrant over all the beasts, whose "sturdie courage" and "stubborne harts" he delights to "tame with dreadfull aw."

The virtues and failings of uncivilized man, reckless courage, cruelty, delight in combat, lustfulness, lack of discipline, strength, hardihood, are the attributes of the Elizabethan satyr. None of these qualities squares very well with the traditional public personality of the satirist, the character he assumes to persuade us that he is the plain, straightforward, modest chider of vice; but the satyr as the Elizabethans conceived him is in many ways similar to what I have called the private personality of the satirist. Ferocity, sadism, concupiscence, and an inability to control the passions by reason are prominent features of both personalities. Thus, the Elizabethan authors were committed from the beginning to developing the darker and less pleasant aspects of the satirist and to playing down the sunnier side of his nature. There are, of course, in these satires the usual protestations of truthfulness, honesty, decency, and interest in justice. But, in contrast to medieval satire, there is no mock humility, no pretension of being simply a plain, pious man walking the well-worn ways of the past. Instead, every satirist is, or tries to be, a raging satyr, a Tamburlaine of vice, an insolent swaggerer, the utter foe of vice, just Rhammusia's whip, the scourge of villainy, the only champion of truth. He pictures himself as a healer of a sick society, but he is no tender ministrant. He is the barber-surgeon who burns, probes, cuts, and purges. His medicines are no soothing ointments but verjuice, gall, vinegar, salt, wormwood and *aqua fortis*. On occasion he employs instruments of torture—the scourge, the rack, the strappado, the bastinado —to shock the mad world back into sanity. He admits that his style is rough and plain as befits an honest man who intends to speak the truth, but rather than make mock apologies for his "carelesse rymes" he scorns other kinds of poetry and boasts,

> Nor Ladies wanton love, nor wandring knight,
> Legend I out in rymes all richly dight.
> Nor fright the Reader with the Pagan vaunt
> Of mightie Mahound, or great Termagaunt.
> Nor list I sonnet of my Mistresse face,
> To paint some Blowesse with a borrowed grace.
>
> .   .   .   .   .
>
> Nor under every banke, and every tree,
> Speake rymes unto my oten Minstralsie.
>
> (*Virgidemiae*, I, 1, 1–16)

Having rejected the lying ways and specious styles of the more conventional kinds of poets, it was necessary for the satirist to create a new style which would express his own rugged honesty, his savage hatred of all false-seeming, and his determination to cleanse the world of its impurities. The result was the most fantastic and mannered style ever written. Since the satyr was rough, crude, and frank, decorum required that his style should be harsh and plain; and without exception every author of the new satire calls attention to these qualities in his verse. Sometimes he complains of the difficulty of writing in this manner. George Wither, whose verse is actually monotonously regular, anticipates criticism of his style by pointing out, "I could with ease have amended it, for it cost mee (I protest) more labour to observe this plainenesse, than if I had more Poetically trimd it." [3] Usually, however, the authors self-consciously exult in their use of the rough style and boldly call attention to it as does Everard Guilpin in his address to his satiric Muse:

> Thou must have words compact of fire & rage:
> Tearms of quick Camphire & Salt-peeter phrases,
> As in a myne to blow up the worlds graces,
> And blast her anticke apish complements.
>   (*Skialetheia*, I, C3R–C3V)

Every formal satire of the period is filled with terms for this rough style: "cancered," "rough-hewed," "stuttering," "invective," "ragged," "tart."

To understand just what kind of style is referred to it is necessary to turn to examples, and the works of Hall and Marston provide instances of both the normal manner and the extreme. Hall defends the style of *Virgidemiae* by saying, "It is not for every one to rellish a true and naturall Satyre, being of it selfe besides the native and in-bred bitter-

3. "To the Reader," *Workes*, sig. B2R.

nes and tartnes of particulers, both hard of conceipt, and
harsh of stile, and therefore cannot but be unpleasing both
to the unskilfull, and over Musicall eare." [4] But he then
goes on to apologize for both the clarity of his work and
the relative ease of the style which he has adopted, he says,
despite the practice of Juvenal and Persius because "English is not altogether so naturall to a Satyre as the Latin."
Elsewhere he also recognizes the softness and easiness of
his satire, but he hopes that

> from the ashes of my quiet stile
> Hence forth may rise some raging rough *Lucile.*
>
> (v, 3, 13–14)

Comparatively speaking Hall is correct in his estimate of
his own style, for his meter is far less rugged, his meaning
less obscure, his diction and imagery less harsh and cryptic,
and his tone in general less frantic than is usual in the new
satires:

> Would now that *Matho* were the *Satyrist,*
> That some fat bribe might greaze him in the fist,
> For which he need not braule at any barre
> Nor kisse the booke to be a perjurer;
> Who else would scorne his silence to have sold,
> And have his tongue tyed with strings of Gold?
>
> (IV, 5, 1–6)

The lines stumble here and there, but on the whole they
proceed fairly easily with the noticeable aid of frequent
alliteration; and the diction is fairly respectable despite
the use of such words as "fat bribe," "greaze," and "braule."
For the modern reader accustomed to the practice of the
Metaphysical poets the passage seems quite tame, but we
must remember that to the ear adjusted to the lyric ease
and the seemly idiom of Surrey, Spenser, Sidney, and Daniel,

4. "A Post-script to the Reader," lines 1–4.

Joseph Hall's lines must have sounded grating and crude.

John Marston was the "raging rough *Lucile*" whom Hall had hoped for, not anticipating that the style would be employed against him.[5] Marston opens his first satiric work, *The Metamorphosis of Pigmalions Image and Certaine Satyres* with an insolent dedication, "To the Worlds Mighty Monarch, Good Opinion" which he signs with the initials "W. K." These stand for the name "W. Kinsayder," we learn in Marston's subsequent volume of satires, *The Scourge of Villanie*. Kinsayder is apparently a pun on Marston (Mar-stone) since "*kinsing* seems to have been an operation which castrated unruly dogs and docked their tails."[6] The coinage suggests the violent qualities Marston believed fitting for the satyr satirist, and the language with which Kinsayder attacks the world is appropriately violent. He specifically disavows the lyric tradition:

> I invoke no *Delian* Deitie,
> Nor sacred of-spring of *Mnemosyne:*
> I pray in ayde of no *Castalian* Muse,
> No Nimph, no femall Angell to infuse
> A sprightly wit to raise my flagging wings,
> And teach me tune these harsh discordant strings;
> I crave no Syrens of our Halcion times,
> To grace the accents of my rough-hew'd rimes;
> But grim *Reproofe*, a stearne Hate of villany,
> Inspire and guide a Satyres poesie.
>
> (*The Scourge*, III, Prologue, p. 78)

The most exaggerated instance of Kinsayder's "stuttering style" (*Pigmalion*, IV, 157) occurs in the first satire of *The Scourge*, which Marston admits he wrote "in some places too obscure, in all places mislyking me"[7] to show that he

5. The full details of the literary quarrel between Hall and Marston are recounted by Arnold Davenport, "The Quarrel of the Satirists," *MLR*, 37 (1942), 123–30.

6. Theodore Spencer, "John Marston," *The Criterion*, 13 (1934), 581.

7. "To those that seeme iudiciall perusers," p. 9.

could write in the approved obscure manner. An example drawn from this satire will be useful, however, for here we find the boldest employment of the standard techniques used to create the required harshness and obscurity. Kinsayder begins by addressing an unidentified person with whom he is debating:

> Fond Physiognomer, *Complexion*
> *Guides not the inward disposition,*
> *Inclines I yeeld.* Thou sayst Law *Iulia,*
> Or *Catoes* often curst *Scatinia*
> Can take no hold on simpring *Lesbia,*
> True, not on her eye, yet Allom oft doth blast,
> The sprouting bud that faine would longer last.
> Chary *Casca,* right pure or *Rhodanus,*
> Yet each night drinks in glassie Priapus.
>   Yon Pine is faire, yet fouly doth it ill
> To his owne sprouts, marke, his rank drops distill
> Foule Naples canker in their tender rinde!
> Woe worth when trees drop in their proper kinde!
> *Mystagogus,* what meanes this prodigy?
> When *Hiadolgo* speakes gainst usury.
> When *Verres* railes gainst thieves. *Mylo* doth hate
> Murder, *Clodius* cuckolds.

(pp. 13–14)

The most obvious quality of these lines is their rugged, uneven progression which is achieved by use of a number of devices: short phrases or words which break up the flow, e.g. "True," or "marke"; difficult and harsh words, "Physiognomer," "Hiadolgo," "Mystagogus"; prosaic phrases, "Inclines I yeeld," "not on her eye"; and a high proportion of monosyllabic words. With one exception each line contains ten syllables, but the accents do not, of course, fall with steady regularity.

A reader is impeded here not only by the sound of the verse, but by awkward syntax, by elisions, and by the rapid

transitions from one subject to another. For example, in
the third line the satirist says, "Inclines I yeeld," which
means, I take it, that complexion, or humor, inclines (in-
fluences) the nature of a man but does not determine his
character. The effort required to discern that "inclines"
is a verb rather than a noun retards understanding, and the
analysis is made even more difficult by the absence of any
grammatical link between the first clause and the second.
While one does not expect any poetry to be written in strict
grammatical form, extreme ellipsis and cryptic references
in the same clause make for considerable difficulties. Immediately after this the satirist jumps without transition
to a discussion of obscure Roman laws dealing with marriage and adultery, the "law *Iulia*" and "*Scatinia*" and their
effect on "simpring Lesbia." After considerable effort a
logical connection is discernible: the physiognomer, who
does not speak, has argued that character is determined by
the governing humor and that law has little effect in controlling a human being in the grips of his particular humor.
Apparently he has offered a libertine as an example. Kinsayder counters with a denial of the dominance of humor in
formation of character and the assertion that while Lesbia
may not heed the law, she may be cured by it. Immediately
after this Kinsayder hops to a description of the obscene
private practices of Casca and Rhodanus who take care to
appear virtuous. Some thought reveals that Kinsayder is
offering these two as support for his thesis that the harshness of the law is effective in curbing those evil instincts
which the Physiognomer believes cannot be resisted. Casca
and Rhodanus are naturally inclined to filthy ways, but
they have also realized that they must control their vices
until they are out of the sight of men. Therefore, complexion can be controlled by threat of punishment.

Next we get an extended metaphor of a tree which infects
its own sprouts, but obscurity is achieved by leaving the

reader to guess just what it is that the tree is being compared to. The key lies in the words "Foule Naples canker," a term for venereal disease, which suggests that the satirist is attacking the roués who pass on the effects of their loose living to their children. Next, the satirist swivels his gaze to a murderer, a thief, a usurer, and a cuckold, whom he flays by ironically describing the miraculous nature of their rejection of their former habitual sins. Thus in the short space of seventeen lines, five descriptions or ideas related in only the most tenuous fashion are presented, and each idea is purposely made difficult. Marston probably derived this technique of rapidly moving by association from one subject to another from Juvenalian satire and from the style of Seneca, but in the works of both of these writers there is a firm logic underlying a fragmentary surface, whereas in the case of Marston the bits and pieces never quite form a definite pattern. The passage just discussed and the remainder of Satire I are more inchoate than the rest of Marstonian satire or the satires of his contemporaries, but the elements of style which have been isolated in these lines are present in varying amounts in all Elizabethan formal verse satire.

In the dramatic monologue of formal satire this "stuttering style" creates for us a character who is rough, powerful, and earnest. The twisted verse suggests the explosive force of his indignation. His sense of the omnipresence of vice and the need for haste in describing it is revealed in the plenitude of examples offered and the speed with which he moves from one manifestation of evil to the next without concern for transitions or full explanations of his meaning. His rugged honesty is reflected in his drive straight to the mark without concern for lyric grace or poetic ornamentation. These traits of character are reinforced by Kinsayder's choice of language. Decorum required, as we have seen, that in satire the diction be base to agree with the matter, and accordingly the lines of *The Scourge* and *Pigmalion,* and other satires as well, contain a great many low words drawn from the language of the streets. The reader will be aware of this aspect of the satiric style from the quotations already given, but a random sampling from Marston's satire will be helpful. We find such words as "chuffe," "shaking-fittes," "drab," "cleane forsake," "candid potatoes," "greasie," "salt-proud bitch," "fat-paunch'd," "cogs," "packstaffe," "garboiles," "jade," "brat," "lousie," "muzled," "currish," "puling." [8] Kinsayder, however, goes beyond mere plainness and employs a great number of unusual and coined words like "jobernole," "barmy froth," "glibbery," "bitcherie," "ierk," "wambling," and "guzzel dogs." [9] The vulgarity of this vocabulary is further intensified by constant references to decay, disease, and dirtiness of the human body: "halfe-rot finger," "infectious blood," "gouty humor," "tender breech," "maggot-tainted,"

8. While it is fairly certain that none of these words would have been used in an epic or sonnet, it is difficult to determine whether they would have been considered entirely appropriate in the low style. No Elizabethan is very explicit about the exact nature of any of the three recognized styles. But in Spenser's *Mother Hubberd's Tale,* a good example of the use of the base style in satire, the language is more "seemly" and generally on a higher level than is ordinarily the case in Elizabethan formal satire. If Spenser be taken as a guide, it is clear that Marston's diction lies for the most part entirely outside the area recognized as suitable for poety of any kind. This would seem to be borne out by the objections raised to Marston's language in the *Poetaster* by the classically correct Jonson, and by Puttenham's dictum that base matters should be conveyed in a "low, myld, and simple maner of utterance, creeping rather than clyming" (*The Arte of English Poesie,* in *Elizabethan Critical Essays,* 2, 158).

9. Ben Jonson attacks such innovations in *Poetaster,* v.3.275–92, 465–527, where the satirist Crispinus, probably a caricature of Marston, is made to vomit up his fantastic vocabulary. Arthur H. King. *The Language of the Satirized Characters in Poetaster,* Lund Studies in English, Vol. *10* (Lund, 1941) provides an excellent analysis of the kinds of linguistic practices which Jonson is attacking and shows that the vocabulary which Jonson gives Crispinus is typical not only of Marston's work but of all the new formal satires.

"pox," "itch-allaying," "big paunch'd wife," etc. It is impossible to convey through quotation the remarkable effect
achieved by the continual focus on physical nastiness which
Kinsayder maintains, but perhaps a few of the more sensational passages will show the lengths to which he goes. A
pompous critic examining a piece of poetry is described in
this manner:

> And all as thanklesse as ungratefull Thames
> He slinks away, leaving but reeching steames
> Of dungy slime behind, all as ingrate
> He useth it as when I satiate
> My spaniells paunch, who straight perfumes the roome,
> With his tailes filth: so this uncivill groome,
> Ill-tutor'd pedant, *Mortimers* numbers
> With muck-pit esculine filth bescumbers.
>
> (*The Scourge*, IX, p. 93)

The necessity for the writing of satire is thus described:

> O what dry braine melts not sharp mustard rime
> To purge the snottery of our slimie time?
>
> (*The Sourge*, II, p. 21)

The critics of *Pigmalion* are attacked in this way:

> O these same buzzing Gnats
> That sting my sleeping browes, these Nilus Rats,
> Halfe dung, that have theyr life from putrid slime,
> These that doe prayse my loose lascivious rime;
> For these same shades, I seriously protest
> I slubber'd up that Chaos indigest.
>
> (*The Sourge*, VI, p. 62)

The use of this remarkable vocabulary does suggest a
character who is not only rough and honest, but sickened
at the spectacles of vice he sees around him and determined
to open up the rotteness and bestiality of the world. But,
as is always the case in Juvenalian satire, the satirist goes

too far. His language begins very shortly to seem excessive,
a mere tour de force rather than an attempt to describe the
world accurately. And as the satirist continues to look into
one sewer after another, turning always to the nasty, the
rotten, and the obscene for his imagery; finding dropsy,
pox, madness, itch, tetters, and maggots everywhere, it begins to appear that he has a fixation or obsession of some
unhealthy variety. He seems to delight in seeking out and
describing in loving detail the most unpleasant functions
of the human animal. This impression is further strengthened by the frequency with which he describes the more
sensational varieties of lust, zoöphilia, incest, homosexual-
ity. Ben Jonson, identifying author and satirist, provides
us with a classic description of this part of the Elizabethan
satirists' character.

> Good troth, if I knew any man so vile,
> To act the crimes, these whippers reprehend,
> Or what their servile apes gesticulate,
> I should not then much muse, their shreds were lik'd;
> Since ill men have a lust t'heare others sinnes,
> And good men have a zeale to heare sinne sham'd.
> But when it is all excrement, they vent,
> Base filth, and offal: or thefts, notable
> As *Ocean* pyracies, or high-way stands:
> And not a crime there tax'd, but is their owne,
> Or what their owne foul thoughts suggested to them.
> And, that in all their heat of taxing others,
> Not one of them, but lives himselfe (if knowne)
> *Improbior satyram scribente cinaedo.*[1]

The elements of style which we have isolated satisfy the
Elizabethan critical requirements that satire should be

1. *Poetaster,* "To the Reader," lines 54–67. All citations of Jonson's works
are to *Ben Jonson,* ed. C. H. Herford and Percy Simpson, 11 vols. Oxford
Univ. Press, 1925–52.

rough in verse, harsh and low in language, and dark in sense. But from Juvenal the authors learned that the satirist was no mere crude, straightforward satyr or unlearned Piers, but the heroic scourge of vice as well, the very Nemesis of evil, inspired with moral if not poetic frenzy; and the style of Elizabethan satire reflects this understanding. Kinsayder and other Elizabethan satyrs frequently shift from their broken verse and low language to lofty epic tones and "the soaring style of oratory." [2] Kinsayder, for example, directs attention to his employment of the high style and justifies it, though he recognizes that satiric decorum is being violated:

> Grim-fac'd *Reproofe,* sparkle with threatning eye
> Bend thy sower browes in my tart poesie.
> Avaunt yee curres, houle in some cloudy mist,
> Quake to behold a sharp-fang'd Satyrist.
> O how on tiptoes proudly mounts my Muse,
> Stalking a loftier gate than Satyres use.
> Me thinks some sacred rage warmes all my vaines,
> Making my spright mount up to higher straines
> Then wel beseems a rough-tongu'd Satyres part,
> *But Art curbs Nature, Nature guildeth Art.*
>
> (*The Scourge,* IX, p. 92)

And so, his nature curbed by Art, Kinsayder turns to his rough style again and shouts at his victims, "Come down yee Apes, or I will strip you quite." Joseph Hall also calls attention to the heroic qualities of his satirist's verse and gives his reason for the use of a more elevated style than was strictly proper:

2. Eugene Waith, *The Pattern of Tragicomedy in Beaumont and Fletcher,* Yale Studies in English, *120* (New Haven, Yale Univ. Press, 1952). Ch. 2, "Satyr and Shepherd," is an extremely interesting discussion of the Elizabethan and Jacobean employment of the satirist, a discussion to which my own work is heavily indebted.

Goe daring Muse on with thy thanklesse taske,
And do the ugly face of vice unmaske:
And if thou canst not thine high flight remit,
So as it mought a lowly Satyre fit,
Let lowly Satyres rise aloft to thee:
Truth be thy speed, and Truth thy patron bee.

(Virgidemiae, I, Prologue, 19–24)

In keeping with their heroic view of the satiric function, Kinsayder and his fellows display a marked taste for both the language and constructions of the high style. To his realistic expressions and vulgarisms, Kinsayder juxtaposes such elevated words and phrases as "catastrophe," "impious," "callenture," "Hymen's sacred bands," "loftie cedars," "exequies," "elegies," "obloquie," "dalliance," "lave," "magnificate," "authenticall." His lines contain a great many classical references: "Areopagites," "Hermes," "Theban," "Mirmidon," "Dolopian," "Cyclopian," "Heccatombe," "Thracian," "Paphian." Various tropes strictly considered proper only to the high style are used profusely: metaphor, epic similes, catalogues, invocations. According to Renaissance theory metaphor was a type of ornamentation not allowed in the *genus humile.* Thomas Wilson, for example, advocates that in writing in "the lowe kinde . . . we use no *Metaphores* nor translated words, nor yet use any amplifications, but goe plainly to worke, and speake altogether in common wordes." [3] Yet the pages of the new satires, and particularly those of Marston, abound with metaphors, and these, typically, are the usual mad mixture of high and low materials. In the following examples the "high" construction, the metaphor, draws on the basest aspects of life for its comparisons: "Let custards quake, my rage must freely runne"; "He'le cleanse himself to Shoreditch purity"; "So like a crabfish Sporo still doth move";

3. *The Arte of Rhetorique* (1560), ed. G. H. Mair (Oxford Univ. Press, 1909), p. 169.

"the Orbes celestiall / Will daunce Kemps Iigge." On occasion Kinsayder unlooses a flood of invective in which vulgar and elevated images are indiscriminately mixed together within a purely epic construction, the catalogue:

> These are no men, but *Apparitions,*
> *Ignes fatui, Glowormes, Fictions,*
> *Meteors, Ratts of Nilus, Fantasies,*
> *Colosses, Pictures, Shades, Resemblances.*
>
> (*The Scourge,* vii, p. 66)

This peculiar mixture of gutter language, stuttering style, epic constructions, and ornate bombast did not pass unnoticed by Marston's contemporaries, and in *The Second Return from Parnassus* this style is characterized in the following fashion:

Judicio: What, Monsier Kinsayder, lifting up your legge and pissing against the world? Put up man, put up for shame.

Ingenioso: Me thinks he is a Ruffian in his stile,
Withouten bands or garters ornament.
He quaffes a cup of Frenchmans Helicon,
Then royster doyster in his oylie tearmes,
Cutts, thrusts, and foines at whomsoever
    he meets,
And strewes about Ram-ally meditations.
Tut, what cares he for modest close coucht
    termes,
Cleanly to gird our looser libertines?
Give him plaine naked words stript from
    their shirts
That might beseeme plaine dealing *Aretine.*

Judicio: I, there is one that backs a paper steed
And manageth a pen-knife gallantly,
Strikes his poinado at a buttons breadth,

> Brings the great battering ram of tearms
>   to towne,
> And at first volly of his Cannon shot
> Batters the walles of the old fustie world.
>
> (1.2.267–84)

All the qualities of Marston's satiric style are noted here, particularly the mingling of high and low elements: "Royster doyster in his oylie tearmes" captures the quality precisely. This use of the soaring style to deliver base matter is parodied hilariously in the speeches of *Furor Poeticus,* a character in *The Second Return* who is probably a caricature of Marston's satiric personality:

> The Gods above that know great *Furors* fame,
> And do adore grand poet *Furors* name,
> Granted long since at heavens high parliament
> That who so *Furor* shal immortalize,
> No yawning goblins shall frequent his grave,
> Nor any bold presumptuous curr shall dare
> To lifte his legge against his sacred dust.
> Where ere I leave my rymes, thence vermin fly,
> All save that foule fac'd vermin poverty:
> This sucks the eggs of my invention,
> Evacuates my witts full pigeon house.
>
> (IV.2.611–22)

After which Sir Raderick exclaims, "He is ether a madde man or a conjurer: it were well if his words were examined, to see if they be the Queenes [frends] or no." Marston himself was not unaware of the peculiarities of Kinsayder's style, and in Satire v of *Pigmalion* after a particularly elevated passage there is the ironic marginal note (line 15), "*Huc Usque Xylinum,*" i.e. "thus far bombast." Even in the minor satires one finds an amused awareness of the ridiculousness of this feature of the satiric style. In Satire vi of *Microcynicon,* for example, there is a somewhat cryptic conversation between a fool and the satirist, where, in a manner reminiscent of *Lear*, they debate the question of who is the true fool. The satirist to establish his primacy delivers a lengthy, bombastic explanation of why he must rail:

> Streams that are barr'd their course
> Swell with more rage and far greater force,
> Until their full-stuft gorge a passage makes
> Into the wide maws of more scopious lakes,
> Spite me! not spite itself can discontent
> My steeled thoughts, or breed disparagement.[4]

The Fool's comment is pointed and direct: "A resolute Ass."

John Milton describes this peculiar mixed quality of the satiric style accurately and with considerable distaste. He speaks of the sixth satire of Hall's second book in *Virgidemiae* "where having begun loftily *in heavens universall Alphabet,* he fals downe to that wretched poorenesse and frigidity as to talke of *Bridge street in heav'n, and the Ostler of heav'n,* and there wanting other matter to catch him a heat . . . with thoughts lower than any Beadle betakes him to whip the signe posts of *Cambridge* Alehouses, the ordinary subject of freshmens tales, and in a straine as pitifull." [5] But the practicing satiric writer found the mixture of styles congenial, and it became one of the trademarks of the new satire.

It is by now evident that the character created by the style thought appropriate for satire is a strange and somewhat unstable one compounded of many elements. The satirist is the savage satyr, rough in speech, harsh and direct in attack. He is also the heroic scourge of vice inspired

4. Pp. 134–5. All citations of *Microcynicon* are to *The Works of Thomas Middleton,* ed. A. H. Bullen (Boston, 1876), Vol. *8*. Bullen provides no line numbers for the formal satires attributed to Middleton.

5. "An Apology for Smectymnuus," pp. 328–9.

by indignation, who expresses his dedication to truth in an elaborate epic style. Furthermore, he is the surgeon seeking out the moral diseases of the city and curing them by cruel methods. These various characteristics are created largely by the indirect method of style, but there are further complexities of the satiric character which though suggested by his style are developed more fully by direct statement.

Thomas Lodge in his description of the satyrs of the ancient satiric drama tells us that "these monsters were then as our parasites are nowadays: such as with pleasure reprehended abuses." [6] Moral correction is then not the satyr's only reason for engaging in satire; he finds swinging the lash a congenial occupation. Lodge, who is a most uninventive critic and author, appears to be deriving the satyr's pleasure in giving pain from his traditional character, but he is also expressing the common feeling that writing satire is a most unnatural business and that some extraordinary explanation is required to account for the cruelty and gusto with which the satirist attacks his victims. Simple and uncomplicated sadism is Lodge's answer, and there is a distinct strain of cruelty in all the satyr satirists. It appears in their harsh and unnecessarily obscene language, in their brutal invective, and in the waspish speed and range of their attacks. The authors of satire were fully conscious of this aspect of the satyr and advertised it openly. Hall's satirist admits that he relishes his cruel trade:

> Now laugh I loud, and breake my spleene to see
> This pleasing pastime of my poesie,
> Much better than a Paris-garden Beare,
> Or *Mimoes* whistling to his tabouret
> Selling a laughter for a cold meales meate.
>
> (*Virgidemiae*, IV, 1, 74–9)

6. *Defence of Poetry*, in *Elizabethan Critical Essays, I*, 80.

George Wither is explicit about the satyr's joy derived from giving pain and further tells us that the satyr lures men into foolishness so that he can then lash them:

> Ape-like-fac't, Spaniell tayl'd,
> Fawning till I have prevayl'd;
>   My pleasing left hand hath a pipe,
>   On which I play till Folly's ripe;
> To carelesse Fooles in a Trance,
> I doe pipe and they doe Dance;
>   Like mirth-full Syrens that doe charme,
>   Delighting those they meane to harme;
> Teaching men to hold their way,
> Not from their right course to stray:
>   The other hand a whip doth beare,
>   With which (provok't) I surely teare
> Skin from flesh, and flesh from bone
> Of such as I hap upon:
>   I'me sent abroad the World, to purge
>   Mans vile Abuses with my scourge;
> Oft I make my Master sport,
> When men sinne to lash them for't.[7]

In *The Scourge* Kinsayder derides other kinds of poetry and then adds,

> But as for me, my vexed thoughtfull soule,
> Takes pleasure, in displeasing sharp controule.
> (Proemium, p. 11)

Again, speaking of the pleasure he derives from writing satire, he says,

> My pate was great with child, & here tis eas'd,
> Vexe all the world, so that thy selfe be pleas'd.
> (VI, p. 65)

7. "The Satyrs Self-description," *Workes*, pp. 307–8.

And in words which suggest willful cruelty, he boasts, "I will plague and torture whom I list" (II, p. 18).

While sadism is a prominent part of the satyr character, the Elizabethans were not content with this explanation alone, and they gave the figure other equally dark, unpleasant motivations. Envy is chief among these. Nashe's Pierce Penilesse, who is a satyr in everything but name, is a disappointed scholar who not having received what he believes to be his due from the world vents his spite in satire. Hall says of his satirist,

> Envie belike incites his pining heart,
> And bids it sate itself with others smart.
> (II, Prologue, 7–8)

And elsewhere he describes his satiric efforts in this way:

> Envie waits on my backe, Truth on my side:
> Envie will be my page, and Truth my Guide.
> Envie the margent holds, and Truth the line;
> Truth doth approve, but Envy doth repine.
> (I, Prologue, 5–8)

And Kinsayder characterizes his satires in this fashion,

> From a sickly bed,
> And from a moodie minde distempered,
> I vomit foorth my love, now turn'd to hate.
> (*Satyra Nova*, pp. 103–4)

Marston is here suggesting a state of mind rather more complicated than simple envy. Kinsayder, Timon-like, appears to hate the world now and scourge it because he once loved it and was disappointed by it. This theory is not developed in any of the poetic satires but is picked up and exploited, as we shall see in the next chapter, in the stage satire.

The satyr is then both sadistic and envious, and it was inevitable that the standard Elizabethan medical explanations for such characteristics should be applied to him. In

the Prologue to Book I of *The Scourge* Kinsayder invokes
Melancholy as his muse:

> *Thou nursing Mother of faire wisedoms lore,*
> *Ingenuous Melancholly,* I implore
> Thy grave assistance, take thy gloomy seate,
> Inthrone thee in my blood; Let me intreate
> Stay his quicke iocond skips, and force him runne
> A sadde pac'd course, untill my whips be done.
> *Daphne,* unclip thine armes from my sad brow,
> Blacke Cypresse crowne me whilst I up doe plow
> The hidden entrailes of ranke villanie.
> Tearing the vaile from damn'd impietie.
>
> (pp. 11–12)

And in the opening lines of *Satyra Nova* he says that his
satires spring,

> From out the sadnes of my discontent,
> Hating my wonted iocund merriment.
>
> (p. 99)

When in Satire x he turns to lighter subjects he commands
"Dull sprighted *Melancholy,* leave my braine" (p. 105).
Elsewhere he speaks of the "cold black frost" that "con-
geales" his "nūmed brain" (p. 58).

The same use of melancholy as a motivation for writing
satire is found in William Rankins' *Seven Satyres* where the
satirist leaves his natural habitat for a time to visit the world
of men:

> Farewell awhile chill and unhallowed caves,
> Where *Saturne* with devouring mischiefe frets,
> Where Melancholy chafes, and madnes raves,
> Where pain dead torments torments death begets,
> Where discontent in ragged habit sits.
>
> (VI, 1–5)

Nashe in *The Anatomie of Absurditie* also traces his satires
to a melancholic condition, though he does not identify the
disease by name. "What I have written, proceeded not from
the penne of vain-glory but from the processe of that pen-
siveness, which two Summers since overtooke mee: whose
obscured cause, best known to everie name of curse hath
compelled my wit to wander abroad unregarded in this
Satyricall disguise, & counsaild my content to dislodge his
delight from traytors eyes." [8] While Hall does not refer to
melancholy in his satires, he does make an association in his
later writings between satire and the "malcontent," a word
which to the Elizabethans "implied melancholy—denoted,
like 'cynicism' with us today, an exacerbated form of it." [9]
"Nothing but feare," says Hall, speaking of the malcontent,
"keeps him from conspiracies, and no man is more cruell
when he is not manicled with danger. He speakes nothing
but *Satyrs* and Libels, and lodgeth no guest in his heart but
Rebels." [1]

Melancholy as an explanation for the character of the
satiric speaker is hinted at as early as 1566 by Drant in the
preface to his edition of Horace where he suggests, among
other possibilities, that,

> Satyre of writhled waspyshe Saturne may be namde,
> The Satyrist must be a waspe in moode.[2]

8. *Works*, p. 5.

9. E. E. Stoll, "Shakespere, Marston and the Malcontent Type," *MP*, *3*
(1906), 284. This point of view is confirmed by the research of Laurence
Babb, *The Elizabethan Malady, A Study of Melancholia from 1580 to 1642*
(East Lansing, 1951), p. 75. O. J. Campbell, "Jaques," *Huntington Library
Bulletin*, 8 (1935), 71–102, however, expresses some dissatisfaction with the
linking of malcontent and melancholic and argues that "the Elizabethans
recognized no 'malcontent' type" (p. 79). Stoll successfully defends his view
in "Jaques and the Antiquarians," *Modern Language Notes*, 54 (1939), 79–85.

1. *Heaven upon Earth and Characters of Vertues & Vices* (1608), ed.
Rudolph Kirk, Rutgers Studies in English, *6* (New Brunswick, Rutgers
Univ. Press, 1948), p. 179.

2. Thomas Drant, *Horace His Arte of Poetrie, Pistles, and Satyrs Eng-*

Since melancholy had not by Drant's time become the popular disease that it was to become later in the century, he was not thinking of the satirist as the familiar melancholic, but merely as an icy, sinister figure whose character, formed under the influence of the planet Saturn, would make the "waspish" business of writing satire congenial to him. It may well be that this suggested etymology was the basis for the later use of melancholia as a motivation for the satirist since melancholy was considered by the Elizabethans to be a cold, dry humor and had, therefore, obvious affinities with Saturn, the cold, dry planet.

It would appear from these connections of melancholy and satire that from the time that Elizabethan writers began to think seriously about the nature of the satiric form, there was a vague but tenacious link between the writing of satire and an abnormal mental state variously identified as saturnine, malcontent, pensive, and finally as melancholic. Such an association no doubt resulted from the slashing brutality which was judged the distinguishing mark of satire and the necessity for accounting for it in some way. Normal, healthy individuals simply could not write in this fashion. When in 1608 Gervase Markham translated the mild satires of Ariosto into English he felt it necessary in his preface to list a long series of lamentable events which had brought Ariosto to the state of mind in which he could write even such gentle satire: unhappy love, difficulties in ruling a tributary state, disappointment in the new Pope, the death of a father, and the brutal blinding of his employer's brother, Julio.[3]

Before attempting to bring the character of the satyr

---

lished (London, 1567), sig. H8ᵛ. Drant's discussion of satire appeared first in the 1566 edition, but his complete translations of Horace were not printed until 1567.

3. Gervase Markham trans., *Ariostos Satyres in Seven Famous Discourses* (London, 1608), sigs. A3ᴿ–A4ᵛ.

satirist together, one further quality which contributes to his contradictory nature must be examined. The Elizabethan critics are agreed that the satyr—both the beast and the writer—is by nature "lascivious" and "wanton." In other words, he is himself guilty of at least one of the sins for which he attacks his victims. The authors of satire expand this idea considerably. Envy, sadism, and discontentedness subtract from the satyr's moral stature; a constant interest in sins of the flesh and near obsession with disease and bodily functions suggest his prurience; and the stuttering style manifests an unhealthy state of frenzy. But some of the authors frequently go beyond mere suggestion and allow their satyrs to admit openly that they are themselves tainted by the very crimes which they so roundly condemn. Wither's satyr admits his own culpability in this startling manner:

> An Execut'oner am I,
> Of Lust, and wanton Venery.
> Thus are vices scourg'd by mee,
> Yet my selfe from vice not free;
> Like to Sumners that cite others,
> When themselves defile their mothers.
>
> ("Satyrs Selfe-description," p. 308)

And Kinsayder bares his own sinful nature in a moment of ironic honesty:

> But since myself am not immaculate
> But many spots my mind doth vitiate,
> I'll leave the white robe and the biting rhymes
> Unto our modern Satire's sharpest lines.
>
> (*Pigmalion*, II, 11–14)

He then, of course, goes on to the most vicious kind of attack on Hall and other satiric writers. T. M.'s satyr in *Microcynicon* freely admits that in his time he has frequently visited the very bawdy house he is preparing to attack and practised the same sins which he is about to

castigate (V, p. 131). In the same satire he describes how he
lusts for a "maiden" he encounters in the street, but unfortunately for him it develops that "she" is an "ingle."
The satyr's anger derives not from moral indignation but
from outrage at having been gulled:

> Fair words I had, for store of coin I gave,
> But not enjoy'd the fruit I thought to have.
>   (p. 133)

The ultimate and perfectly logical extension of the satyr's
moral hypocrisy is found in *The Blacke Booke* (1604),
probably written by Thomas Middleton. Here the satirist is
the Devil himself, who has come to earth in reply to the
letter sent by Nashe's Pierce Penilesse. The Devil, of course,
is a past master of all the forms of human sinfulness which
he discovers in his London wanderings, and like his more
commonplace satyr cousins encourages vice and feels a
twisted delight in the depravity of mankind:

> Hence springs my damned joy; my tortured spleen
> Melts into mirthful humor at this fate,
> That heaven is hung so high, drawn up so far,
> And made so fast, nail'd up with many a star;
> And hell the very shop-board of the earth.
>   *(Lucifer's Prologue, p. 7)* [4]

The absolute separation of heaven and earth is, of course,
occasion for rejoicing on the Devil's part. And where the
ordinary satirist only relieves his compulsive hatred of
mankind by luring the fools of the world into a position
where they can be scourged, the Devil obtains the practical
result of enlarging his kingdom.

Examples of the contradictory and twisted nature of the
satyr can be endlessly multiplied by a close critical reading of any of the satires of the period. Kinsayder particularly
involves himself in a morass of contradictions and am-

---

4. *The Black Booke* is reprinted in *Works of Middleton,* Vol. *8.*

biguous moral situations. One recent critic, John Peter, who identifies Marston with Kinsayder, tells us that he came to Marston's satires "with the expectation of coherence and consistency," but found himself "flabbergasted by the wildness and uncertainty of his [Marston's] contradictions." [5] Peter then proceeds to pile up nearly two pages of examples of inconsistencies in *Pigmalion* and *The Scourge* and deduces from these a description of Marston which is an excellent description of the satyr: "a personality the native instability of which has been exaggerated to the point of incoherence" (p. 174). Instability, incoherence, wildness, uncertainty, contradiction, these are the very essentials of the satyr character and are part, as Peter admits,[6] of all the satirists of Elizabethan formal satire.

The main features of the satirist's character are now clear, and we can attempt to construct a composite picture without taking note of every minor "confusion." The satirist is above all harsh, honest, frank, and filled with indignation at the sight of the evil world where the fools and villains prosper by masquerading as virtuous men. This same honest man happens also to be the heroic scourge of vice capable of rising to the heights of the elevated style. Furthermore, although he is the inveterate foe of vice, he himself has dark twists in his character: he is sadistic and enjoys his rough work; he is filled with envy of those same fools he despises and castigates; he has a taste for the sensational and delights in exposing those sins of which he is himself guilty; he is a sick man, his nature unbalanced by melancholy, whose

5. *Complaint and Satire in Early English Poetry*, p. 174.

6. "As we close *The Scourge of Villanie* it is difficult to resist the conclusion that we have been witnessing an utterly insincere and possibly pathological performance. But the disease is wider than Marston's case as the works of other satirists like Guilpin and Richard Middleton suffice to prove" (p. 176). Peter goes on to argue that the satires reflect a character-split typical of the age, but he does not explain why it appears only in satire.

perspective of the world is distorted by his malady. The
satyr personality is complex, but it is by no means un-
believable. In fact, with all its tensions and confusions it is
far more lifelike, more vital, than a completely logical and
balanced character would be in the context of satire. The
full exercise of the satiric function is not, as the Elizabethans knew, a logical, balanced activity.

The picture I have drawn in the preceding pages of the
satyr personality is admittedly a composite one, and no
single satyr except Kinsayder has all of the characteristics
I have isolated. Or, to put it more accurately, the various
tendencies present in the satiric character are not always
fully developed or overtly stated. Thus the relatively quiet
style of Hall's *Virgidemiae* detracts from the harshness and
crudity of his satirist, although he lays claim to these
qualities. Guilpin's satirist, while sufficiently rough, makes
no boasts about his own culpability, nor does he openly
reveal any envy, melancholy, or sadism, even though all of
these qualities are suggested by his vicious treatment of his
victims and his obvious hatred of them. Rankins' shaggy
satyrs may be subject to melancholy, but they express themselves in relatively gentle terms which greatly lessen the
characteristic violence. The satires of John Donne, however,
constitute the most notable modification of the tradition.
Donne imitates both Juvenal and Horace, particularly in
the arrangement and dramatic handling of his satiric material, and he is sufficiently insolent in manner and coarse and
rough in speech to make it clear that he is writing in the
satyr tradition. But he does not elaborate on the satiric
character. He employs no satyr imagery to suggest that his
satirist is allied to the woodland creatures of antiquity;
there are no open revelations of a twisted, complex character venting its own disappointment and mental sickness
in satire; and the linguistic extremes of billingsgate and the
soaring style are absent. Donne concentrates on cudgeling

the fools for their ostentation, their pursuit of meaningless goals, their bad manners, and their persistent, boring
attempts to talk to that humble and retiring scholar, John
Donne. As a result he creates the most consistent and
ordered formal satires of the period; but our interest here
is not so much in the artistic excellence of Elizabethan formal satire as in its conventions and, in turn, their relationship to the basic principles of the satiric genre.

We come now to the philosophy of the satirist, that
ethical system which he employs to measure the deficiencies
of his contemporaries. In actual practice the satirist may
lack any coherent philosophy and his individual judgments
may seem most often to be the result of random maliciousness, hatred, or an innate conservatism which characterizes
as evil any conduct incompatible with the way things were
done in the "good old days." But in order to strengthen
the impression of his probity and dispassion the satirist will
usually make certain formal statements about his adherence
to some philosophical system of his time. Juvenal had made
use of some loose variety of Stoicism as his formal philosophy, and probably in an attempt to imitate him as closely
as was possible in a Christian era the majority of the Elizabethan authors of formal satire present their satirists as neo-
Stoics. It is, of course, extremely difficult to distinguish
neo-Stoicism absolutely from Christian stoicism, but when
a writer insists on the dominance of reason in man and his
ability to use it to shape his own life and to endure the evils
of the world; when he emphasizes control of the passions,
contentment with station, the simple life uncomplicated by
luxury and wealth; and when he spends little time discussing humility and God's ultimate justice and mercy, then it
seems fairly certain that he has been influenced more immediately by Seneca, Marcus Aurelius, and Epictetus than
by St. Paul or St. Augustine.

Hall's satirist sums up his outlook on life in this manner:

To know much, and to thinke we nothing know;
Nothing to have, yet think we have enough,
In skill to want, and wanting seeke for more,
In weale nor want, nor wish for greater store;
Envye ye Monarchs with your proud excesse
At our low Sayle, and our Hye Happinesse.

(IV, 4, 84–9)

Most of the philosophy of Hall's satires is concentrated in
the first satire of Book III where the Golden Age is pictured in Stoic fashion as an age of simplicity when men ate
acorns, drank water, dressed in hides, and respected au-
thority; trouble came with the accretion of wealth:

But when by *Ceres* huswifrie and paine,
Men learn'd to bury the reviving graine:
And father *Ianus* taught the new found vine,
Rise on the *Elme,* with many a friendly twine:
And base desire bad men to delven low,
For needlesse mettals: then gan mischiefe grow,
Then farewell fayrest age, the worlds best daies,
Thriving in ill, as it in age decaies.
Then crept in *Pride,* and peevish Covetise:
And men grew greedy, discordous and nice.

(lines 34–43)

Nowadays, the satirist goes on to say, men seek the rarest
foods, drink wine, dress fantastically, seek to be king, and
"one confusion another brings." While Hall did not intro-
duce a large amount of philosophical discussion into his
satires, the ideals set forth in these passages are implicit
throughout *Virgidemiae* where evils are regularly con-
demned because they represent needless ostentation or
luxury and are therefore contrary to right reason and the
dictates of Nature. These same classical ideals are invoked
to condemn the popular poetry of the day which lacks

decorum, balance, and control, and fails to adhere to the
rules laid down by ancient writers.

The early Elizabethan formal satires are filled with re-
sounding Stoic statements in which the satirist assures us
that "in dying well is onely happines," that Reason is "the
soules bright genius / Sent downe from *Joves* throne," that
the good man is "no slave to censures" but negligent of the
world's opinion. Epictetus, Socrates, and Seneca are put
forward as models of virtue whose lives manifested that
"resolve" and "perfect temperature" required for the good
life. Bishop Hall is fairly successful in keying his satirist to
his philosophy of measure, restraint, and control, but in the
satiric works of Rankins, T. M., and particularly Guilpin,
these Stoic pronouncements sound very strange coming
from their biting, slangy, frenzied, sadistic satyrs. The dramatists, once they began to deal with the satirist in the
theater, exploited this conflict, but before that strangest of
creatures, the Stoic satyr, became a theatrical convention
John Marston attempted to provide his satirist with a more
suitable philosophy.

Marston's first satiric effort, *Pigmalion,* is signed, "Epictetus," the paragon of the Stoics, and while the volume contains little overt philosophizing, the general basis for criticism is vaguely Stoic. But in *The Scourge* Epictetus gives
way completely to the coarse and savage W. Kinsayder who
shows a more pained awareness of man's depravity than
do the other Elizabethan satirists. Speaking of mankind in
general, he can say:

> each Ape,
> Than can but spy the shadow of his shape,
> That can no sooner ken what's vertuous,
> But will avoyd it, and be vicious.
>
> (IV, p. 43)

Or, after describing the world in bitter terms, he laments,

> *Would truth did know I lyed, but truth, and I,*
> *Doe know that sence is borne to misery.*
>
> (II, p. 21)

He rejects optimism with crushing definiteness, "Some
Sophy say, *The Gods sell all for paine.* / Not so." (v, p. 52);
and bitter disillusionment appears in his words, "I dare
sweare, the soules of swine / Doe live in men" (vII, p. 66).
But the most direct insight into the soul of Kinsayder is
provided by his endless references to the functions and
diseases of the human body. Thus in a few pages of *The
Scourge* the following words are introduced: "dung,"
"putrid slime," "slubber," "undigested," "blood," "maggots," "corruption," "itching," "bodies scum," "blemish,"
"deformity," "scabs," and "muddy dirt." The sense of the
innate foulness of man which results from the consistent use
of this kind of language is further reinforced by the frequent associations made between man and animals, the
goat, ass, pig, and monkey. Kinsayder is obsessed with a
sense of man's decay and beastliness.

Although Stoicism was a pessimistic philosophy formed
to deal with a world in which righteousness seemed to have
been lost, it was supposed to lead its practitioners to a state
of controlled endurance of the human condition. But the
attitude that emerges from *The Scourge* passes the bounds
of reason and borders on the psychotic. At times, like Gulliver's feelings about the Yahoos, the pessimism is so
extreme that it becomes merely ludicrous. To account for
such a violent detestation of man, which far surpasses that
found in other satire of the period, some darker view of
humanity than Stoicism was required, and Kinsayder specifically denies the traditional philosophy:

> Preach not the Stoickes patience to me,
> I hate no man, but mens impietie.
>
> (II, p. 18)

Stoicism as an explanation and salve for the beastliness of
humanity is rejected at greater length in Satire IV (the rejection is somewhat complicated by the fact that Kinsayder
seems to regard Zeno and Seneca as Cynics rather than
Stoics, although the philosophy he describes is Stoic):

> *I will,* cries *Zeno,* ô presumption!
> *I can,* thou maist, dogged oppinion
> Of thwarting Cynicks. To day vicious,
> List to their precepts, next day vertuous.
> Peace *Seneca,* thou belchest blasphemy.
> *To live from God, but to live happily*
> (I heare thee boast,) *from thy Philosophy,*
> *And from thy selfe,* ô ravening lunacy!
> Cynicks, yee wound your selves, for Desteny
> Inevitable Fate, Necessity,
> You hold doth sway the acts spirituall,
> As well as parts of that we mortall call,
> Wher's then (*I will?*) wher's that strong Deity,
> You doe ascribe to your Philosophy?
> Confounded Nature's brats, can *will* and *Fate,*
> Have both their seate, & office in your pate?
>
> (p. 45)

The denial of the validity of human will in these lines
suggests Kinsayder's philosophic orientation, and he spells
it out for us in Satire VII where, after reviling the world, he
explains its evils in this fashion:

> Sure I nere think those axioms to be true,
> That soules of men, from that great soule ensue,
> And of his essence doe participate
> As't were by pipes, when so degenerate,
> So adverse is our natures motion,
> To his immaculate condition:
> That such foule filth, from such fair purity,
> Such sensuall acts from such a Deity,

Can nere proceed. But if that dreame were so,
Then sure the slime that from our soules doe flow,
Have stopt those pipes by which it was convai'd,
And now no humane creatures, once disrai'd
Of that faire iem.
Beast's *sence,* plants *growth,* like being as a stone,
But out alas our *Cognisance* is gone.

                                                                (p. 76)

The satire in which these lines appear is labeled "A Cynicke
Satyre," and while the view of human depravity presented
here fits well enough with the philosophy of Diogenes, the
Renaissance Englishman would have been far more aware
of the Calvinism of the lines than their Cynic qualities. The
emphasis here on man's "foul filth," the innate human
nastiness and slime which choke off the flow of grace from
God to man, and the denial of the validity of the human
will in Satire IV suggest a much closer connection with
Geneva than with Athens and Rome. This impression is
further strengthened by the fact that Kinsayder, after re-
jecting the explanations of good and evil given by Ovid
(based on Aristotle), Duns Scotus, Zeno, and Seneca, expresses the doctrine of justification by faith through a denial
of the efficacy of good works and the power of the human
will:

In earnest thus, *it is a sacred cure*
To salve the soules dread wounds; Omnipotent
That Nature is, that cures the impotent,
Even in a moment; Sure Grace is infus'd
By divine favour, not by actions us'd.
Which is as perminent as heavens blisse
To them that have it, then no habite is.
To morrow, nay, to day, it may be got;
So please that gracious Power clense thy spot.[7]

7. IV, p. 43. In the third line the word "Nature" appears, but Nature

And a few lines later he advises, "To day, to day, implore obsequiously," for grace. There are also occasional attacks in *The Scourge* on those beliefs and groups which the Tudor Puritans railed against so determinedly: the doctrine of literal transubstantiation (II, p. 22); the Papists and their immorality (III, p. 29; VIII, pp. 84–5); and idle, inept absentee clerics holding several cures (III, p. 35; V, p. 55).

But Kinsayder shares more than a Calvinistic philosophy with English reformers such as Stubbes and Gosson. One historian of English Puritanism talks of the "white-hot morality" which "made the Puritan a prophet in his generation, one who freely rebuked both high and low alike," [8] and, drawing from various Puritan writings, he presents a composite picture of the Puritan zealot outraged by the evils of the time who, reckless of his own safety, described things as they were without mincing words. Thomas Drant, the translator of Horace, appears to have been in life something very like the fearless satirist in Juvenal and in the new English satire. On January 8, 1569/70, he preached before the Court at Windsor on the vanity of dress and took for his text, "They were both naked, Adam and Eve, and blushed not"—this before Elizabeth who reputedly had over three thousand dresses! On Easter Tuesday, 1570, he preached to a congregation that filled the largest hall in England, St. Mary's Spital. His subject was sensational enough for any satire, the carnality of London.[9]

---

here is emphasized by the word "that" and by capitalization to distinguish it from the *natura* of the Stoics.

8. M. M. Knappen, *Tudor Puritanism* (Univ. of Chicago Press, 1939), pp. 334–5.

9. This sermon is reprinted in C. H. and Thompson Cooper, *Athenae Cantabrigienses* (Cambridge, 1858), *1*, 384; It shows clearly the similarity between Elizabethan formal satires and sermons. It is interesting to note that in these sermons, though the preacher quite obviously did everything possible to prevent it, the face of the satyr is gradually shaped by the language of denunciation. Such an event is predictable, of course, since sermons of this type are fierce attacks on vice, and we have seen that

I have called Marston's Kinsayder a Puritan reformer, and he certainly shares a number of qualities with this type, but on a number of occasions in *The Scourge* this same satirist castigates the nonconformist excesses of precisians and sectarians (II, pp. 22–3; IX, p. 98). Furthermore, there is nothing in his theological pronouncements that cannot be found in Hooker's classical definition of Anglicanism. Yet Kinsayder's intemperate denunciation of vice and his nearly psychotic awareness of the depraved nature of man distinguish him from the unimpassioned and measured Hooker. A Calvinist Kinsayder certainly is, but beyond that we can merely say that he shows the burning zeal usually identified with the left wing of the English Church.[1] Without raising the question of why Marston substituted Calvinism in his satires for the traditional Stoicism, it may be said that this change has an important effect on his poetry. It imparts to the satires a vividness and quality of reality which is ordinarily lacking in the other contemporary examples of this genre with their evocation of a dim Golden Age and the sages of classical antiquity. One has the feeling

---

whenever an attack of this kind is made the satiric tensions will inevitably be generated. The difference between the writer of literary satire and the sermonist is, very simply, that the former is free to employ the character thus created in a dramatic fashion, while the latter must make every effort to prevent the identification of himself with the sadistic, hypocritical. scandal-mongering satirist.

1. The full extent of Kinsayder's resemblance to the Puritan reformer is more a matter of curiosity than critical interest, but I cannot resist pointing out that the two figures share an ideal of style. The satirist espouses the plain style and attacks other forms of poetry than satire because their ornate language and verbal ornaments are no more than plausible ways of telling lies about the state of man and the world. The Puritan was also a linguistic reformer who distrusted "eloquentia," and defended the vulgar language as an instrument for speaking bare truth and translating the simple words of God in the Scriptures. See Richard Foster Jones, "The Moral Sense of Simplicity," in *Studies in Honor of Frederick W. Shipley*, Washington Univ. Studies, New Series, Lang. and Lit., *14* (St. Louis, 1942), 265–88.

that *The Scourge* is no mere classical exercise but rather a
street corner in Elizabethan London where the raging
evangelist bitterly denounces the sinful nature of mankind
and the wickedness of the new Sodom. Marston's use of
Calvinism as a satiric philosophy appears to have been no
more than a temporary interest, however, for when he began writing satiric plays in 1599 his dramatic satirists again
declare themselves Stoics. However, in the printed formal
satire written after *The Scourge* some stern variety of Prot-
estantism or fundamentalism became fairly standard for
the satirists.

No more fantastic literary figure has ever been created
than the satyr satirist just described. Kinsayder is certainly
the extreme example, but each of the other satirists is very
nearly as bewildering a creature. Since my argument that
this personality is an artistic construction rather than a
direct reflection of the authors' psychic make-up runs
counter to the usual understanding of the situation, it seems
necessary to offer further confirmation at this point. Because of the nature of the material being dealt with, elaborate documentation is not feasible, for it would be un-
bearably tedious to list every satiric pronouncement on
style or every line where the author makes it plain that he is
using an assumed character for his satiric purposes. Two
other ways of verifying the conventional character of the
satyr present themselves: a brief examination of the work
of inferior satiric authors, and a look at a caricature of the
satyr satirist as he appears in a work not primarily satiric.

Nowhere does convention appear more openly than in
second-rate poems where the author trying to work in a
well-defined poetic tradition fails to blend his matter and
his style, for the contrast between the various components
brings the conventions into relief immediately. This is
exactly the situation in a vast number of formal satires

written during the first twenty or thirty years of the seventeenth century. After Hall and Marston had made the new satire popular and then abandoned it, a great many imitators began to turn out crude satires in the new form, and the authors discussed in the following pages are only a small fraction of this large and undistinguished group.

Richard Braithwaite wrote in 1621 *Natures Embassie or The Wilde-Mans Measures: Danced Naked by Twelve Satyrs*,[2] and his title undoubtedly reflects his belief that if one satyr was popular, twelve naked ones would be at least twelve times as attractive. The title page carries a woodcut of a number of dancing satyrs, and under the picture are the lines,

Wilde men may dance wise measures; Come then ho,
Though I be wilde, my measures are not so.

This suggests a modification of the rough satiric style, but later on Braithwaite's satyr speaks of his "ragged lines," his "cancred style," and compares his satires to rough bear cubs which have to be licked into shape. But satyrs and roughness are mere trappings here, not an integral part of the poetry, for the body of the work is composed of flat, generalized discussions of Nature and how it flows from God and directs us to him. Endless exempla are drawn from classical history, and these together with the droning quality of the verse and the moral earnestness everywhere apparent create an effect very much at odds with the savagery and roughness the author has been at pains to advertise. Braithwaite does no better in *A Strappado for the Divell* (1615), but takes more care to establish the satyr persona. He begins by invoking Bacchus as his muse, and crowns himself not with laurel but with nettle. Juvenal is frequently mentioned and quoted, and there are constant references to "sharp-tooth'd Satire," and "unripping" the crimes of the

2. Ed. J. W. Ebsworth, Boston, Lincolnshire, 1877.

city. At the end of the introduction we get a description of
what Braithwaite considered "true" satire.

> But now (my nimble Satyre) for to thee
> Tends this impolisht piece of poesie:
> How wilt thou taxe, or where wilt thou begin
> With thy tart phrase, to stinge and nettle him?
> Thou must be bitter (for in greatest grieves)
> And festered wounds we use no lenitives
> To mollifie, but corrasives to gall.[3]

But again the substance of the work falls far short of the
promises of the title and such lines as those above. The most
constant element in the *Strappado* is a fanatical religious
strain expressed in such pious exclamations as "Oh *London*
how thy vanity abounds" (p. 32), and in frequent identifications of God and the satirist as allies in unmasking sin.

Perhaps the most humorous of these formal satires is
*Times Whistle, or a New Dance of Seven Satires and Other
Poems* (c. 1615) written by "R. C." R. C. borrows heavily
from Marston's *The Scourge* and attempts to imitate the
coarseness and insolence of that work, but only succeeds
when he paraphrases Marston. In the introduction R. C.
paints himself as the usual biting satyr, but in fact he is
very much the country bumpkin amazed by lewd talk, rich
feasts, and dancing, which is, he adds righteously, "a cause /
That many unto fornication drawes." [4] The incongruity of
the satyr persona and the actual character becomes com-
ically apparent when he records a visit to Islington in the
company of a number of young ladies and gentlemen to
eat cream. After some dalliance the young gentlemen and
ladies steal away to indulge their pleasures, and R. C., left
alone, finally perceives with horror just what kind of trip
this is. He leaves, but not without

3. Ed. J. W. Ebsworth (Boston, Lincolnshire, 1878), p. 35.
4. Ed. J. M. Cowper, Early English Text Society (London, 1871), Satire
VI, lines 2677–8.

having defraide
A great part of the reckning; *which* I paide
Whilst they were all full busie in the darke,
Because they should not thinke I came to sharke
Only for vittailes.

(vi, 2691–5)

At least *he* did not forget his moral duty. All of this would be not only amusing but effective if the part of the simpleton did not conflict with the satyr characteristics which are constantly introduced by direct statement.

Richard Johnson gives his satires the long and ferocious title, *Look on Me, London. I Am an Honest Englishman, Ripping up the Bowels of Mischiefe, Lurking in Thy Suburbs and Precincts* (1613), but the satire itself turns out to be a Polonius-like warning to a son, "thou unhappy young gentleman," who is about to go to London to make his way in the world. This middle-class satyr points with indignation to the foulness of the town, but more often than not he is more worried about his son squandering money than any moral or physical dangers he may encounter. "But yet take this admonition from me, thy father. In this good city are many alectives to unthriftinesse; by which meanes, where the father hath beene at charge to make his sonne a lawyer, to doe his country service . . . his aforesaid sonne (for want of government) many times spends his whole substance." [5] The book was probably written for the country trade, nervously curious about the terrors of London, and Johnson lures his readers on shamelessly by promising after a number of pages filled with abominations, "I have but yet begun to anatomize the head of these sanctuaries of iniquity; there are heapes and whole bodies of evils to follow."

Our old friend Piers Plowman turns up in John Taylor's *Superbiae Flagellum* (1621) where the author identifies him-

5. In *Illustrations of Early English Popular Literature,* ed. John Payne Collier (London, 1864), p. 5.

self as a humble and unlearned Waterman who can praise
Piers for his traditional characteristics:

> The painfull Plowmans paines doe never cease
> For he must pay his Rent, or lose his lease.
>
> (sig. Ci^v)

The Waterman then goes on to attack pride, particularly
as it is manifested in dress, by tracing it in the best homiletic
fashion from Adam to the present. But this kind of approach and the humble Waterman's character are at odds
with the title, which suggests the whip of the satyr, and with
the various references to "satyre-like" verse and "invective
style." Taylor does provide an interesting comment on the
enormous number of new satires being written. He despairs,
he says, of writing anything new about pride and dress because,

> these things have so well bin bang'd and firk'd,
> And Epigram'd and Satyr'd whip'd and Ierk'd,
> Cudgeld and bastinadoed at the Court,
> And Comically stag'de to make men sport.
>
> (sig. C8^v)

The implication here is that the writing of satire was rather
a thriving trade than any attempt at moral correction, but
whatever the motive behind the works we have been looking at, the point is clear, I believe, that in the early seventeenth century anyone who wrote satire felt that he must
assume the mask of the satyr and use the prescribed rough
style. In the majority of cases—and, like Johnson's abominations, the examples I have given can be endlessly extended
—this satyr personality is a mere trapping which rather than
corresponding with the actual spirit of the satire stands in
direct contrast to the drab style, plodding earnestness, and
naïveté which dominate the works.

Abraham Holland characterizes this stumbling kind of

satire perfectly in his continuation of John Davies' "Papers Complaint." [6] He is speaking of various "Paper-Persecutors" and turns to the writers of satire:

> Others that ne're search'd new borne Vice at all,
> But the seven deadly Sinnes in generall,
> Drawne from the tractate of some cloyster'd Frier,
> Will need write Satyrs, and in raging fire
> Exasperate their sharpe Poeticke straine,
> And thinke they have toucht it, if they raile at Spaine,
> The Pope and Devill; and while thus they urge
> Their stingless gall, there's none deserve the Scourge
> More than themselves, whose weaknesse might suffice
> To furnish Satyrs and poore Elegies.
>
> (p. 80)

The same weaknesses we have already noted constitute the grounds for this attack. The general ineptitude of these authors in playing the part of the satyr is the fundamental complaint: their gall is "stingless," i.e. their style lacks sharpness and bite; and they merely rehearse the traditional and by now old-fashioned evils—the Seven Deadly Sins, the various corrupt practices dealt with by the church fathers, and the Elizabethan *bêtes noires*, Spain, the Pope, and the Devil. But such was the strength of the tradition that the would-be authors of satire, no matter how inept, had to "exasperate their sharp Poeticke straine," and the results were often ludicrous. The sight of these poets trying desperately to play the prescribed satyr's part provides further proof that many of the traits heretofore confidently ascribed to Hall, Marston, and the authors of satire were in fact no

---

6. "Papers Complaint," which is an imitation of Juvenal's 1st satire, is appended to the 1st edition of Davies' *Scourge of Folly*. It was reprinted in 1625 as *A Scourge For Paper-Persecutors* with additions by Abraham Holland. The lines given here are part of Holland's work and are quoted from Davies' *Complete Works*, ed. A. B. Grosart, Chertsey Worthies' Library (Edinburgh, 1878), Vol. 2.

more than qualities attaching to the fictitious character of the satyr satirist.

The inferior writers of satire in the earlier seventeenth century provide evidence for the existence of a tradition of roughness and biting harshness, but their works do not show many traces of the more twisted and diabolic features of the satyr. That these darker characteristics were also conventions can fortunately be verified by an examination of the character of Jaques in *As You Like It*. Written in 1600 when satire had just been banned and was at the peak of its notoriety, *As You Like It* satirizes in a gentle fashion a number of the popular attitudes or poses which were celebrated in the romances, a form which included elements of the heroic, the pastoral, and the amorous. Perfectly appropriately, mythologically speaking, Shakespeare set a satyr in the midst of the idyllic forest of the romance, but this satyr acts and thinks in a manner proper to his sixteenth-century representative, the melancholy satirist developed by the satiric writers of the preceding decade. Jaques,[7] though he is used as a device for deflating the poses of the other characters, is satirized in turn, and the principal method by which he is attacked is caricature, the process of seizing on his more ridiculous attitudes and magnifying them to the point where they are patently laughable. This is fortunate: it allows us to see which features of the satirist were considered traditional, for burlesque of this type must be built on the familiar. If it were to rely on the unique, the audience would miss the point.

Jaques possesses practically every characteristic of the satirist as we have seen him. His pessimism grows out of a melancholic condition so exaggerated that he "can suck

7. It seems likely that the name "Jaques," pronounced Já-kes, or Jakes, i.e. a "privy," is a reference to the quality of the satirist's thoughts and language. The evidence for this pronunciation is summed up by G. B. Harrison in the note added to his edition of *The Scourge*, pp. 124–6.

melancholy out of a song as a weasel sucks eggs." [8] He views man's life as a meaningless progress from one state of nastiness to another, from "the infant, / mewling and puking," to old age, "sans teeth, sans eyes, sans taste, sans everything" (II.7.139–66). This extravagant pessimism is most effectively ridiculed in Touchstone's clever parody, which Jaques foolishly admires and repeats:

> 'It is ten o'clock.
> Thus we may see,' quoth he, 'how the world wags.
> 'Tis but an hour ago since it was nine,
> And after one hour more 'twill be eleven;
> And so, from hour to hour, we ripe and ripe,
> And then, from hour to hour, we rot and rot;
> And thereby hangs a tale.'
>
> (II.7.22–8)

The satirist's insatiable and sadistic craving for targets, his delight in attack, is made ridiculous in Jaques' statement, "I'll go sleep, if I can; if I cannot, I'll rail against all the first-born of Egypt" (II.5.62–3). His hypocrisy is mentioned by the Duke:

> Most mischievous foul sin, in chiding sin.
> For thou thyself hast been a libertine,
> As sensual as the brutish sting itself;
> And all th'embossed sores and headed evils
> That thou with license of free foot hast caught,
> Wouldst thou disgorge into the general world.
>
> (II.7.64–9)

Jaques' defense of his railing is the typical satiric one that he attacks no particular person but the general vice, and that by registering indignation at his attack an individual convicts himself.

In style, too, Jaques fits the pattern. He admires Touch-

8. II.5.12–14. All citations of Shakespeare are to *The Complete Works,* ed. G. L. Kittredge, Boston. Ginn, 1936.

stone's speech because he "rail'd on Lady Fortune in good terms, / In good set terms" (II.7.15–16). And in his "All the world's a stage," speech Jaques reveals his own skill at "set terms" and the lofty style of oratory, but characteristically mixes in such vulgar words and phrases, as "mewling," "whining," "fair round belly with good capon lin'd," and "shrunk shank." Elsewhere he uses the typical medical imagery of satire:

> Give me leave
> To speak my mind, and I will through and through
> Cleanse the foul body of th' infected world,
> If they will patiently receive my medicine.
>
> (II.7.58–61)

Jaques has only a small part in the play and therefore very little opportunity for launching attacks, but the sallies he does make are all directed against the types who provided grist for the mill of the verse satirist: the lover, the quarrelsome soldier, the lawyer, the woman who dresses extravagantly. He does not display much interest in sexual abnormalities, though it is clear from the Duke's speech quoted above that he is, or once was, concerned with such matters. To have emphasized this part of his character or even to have given him much space for ranting would have seriously upset the balance of the play, for it is light and gentle comedy at its best, and even a ridiculous satirist tends always to the dark and vicious. Perhaps the only really somber moment in the play occurs when Jaques delivers his famous speech beginning "All the world's a stage." By the end of the play, however, he is enough softened toward men to wish his companions well, but hugging his melancholy to him, he declines to share in their good fortunes and prefers to go with Duke Frederick who has entered a religious order. Jaques and the satirist he mirrors were truly, as he says, "For other than dancing measures."

We are now in a position to deal with the question of why the Elizabethans created this strange, contradictory satirist, and why they elaborated rather than concealed his peculiarities. The traditional answer has been the biographical one that the personalities of the authors and their satirists were identical, but such a view is no longer tenable once it becomes clear that the various characteristics attributed to the authors are parts of a convention and that the authors were clearly aware of these characteristics and stressed them. It would be strange indeed if every author of formal satire from Nashe to George Wither was sadistic, rough, frank, lascivious, fired by envy, subject to melancholy, guilty of the same sins he castigated, and so stupid that he was unable to conceal any of these weaknesses.

In part, no doubt, the satirist came into being as a result of the authors' desire to be classically correct, to recreate the woodland satyr who was supposed to have been the original satirist and whose voice and mannerisms were, the Elizabethans believed, still to be heard and seen in the works of Juvenal, Horace, and Persius. But no Elizabethan satirist was created simply to resemble the satyr. That is, the authors and critics did not imagine that the purpose of satire was to present satyrs, though in fact such writers as Marston and Guilpin may have done little more than this in their satiric poems. Instead, the Elizabethan belief that satire had originally been spoken by satyrs is but one manifestation of a much more dynamic and artistically sophisticated theory of art applied particularly to the satiric genre. The reason consistently given in Elizabethan criticism and satire for playing the part of the satyr is that wearing this specialized mask is necessary for the achievement of the satiric end, the successful attack on foolishness and vice. Thomas Lodge puts it very straightforwardly: the satyr play came into being, he tells us, so that men "might wiselye, under the abuse of . . . [the satyr's] name, discover the

follies of many of theyr folish fellow citisens." John Marston
makes the same point somewhat more cleverly in a passage
in which his satirist simultaneously recognizes his own peculiarities and offers an explanation for them:

> Who would imagine that such squint-eyed sight
> Could strike the world's deformities so right.
>
> (Pigmalion, II, 37–8)

This justification of the "squint-eyed sight" of the satyr,
i.e. that it is necessary to employ a distorted lens to bring
man's moral ugliness into true focus, is not only stated in
every satire of the period, but is latent in every aspect of
the satyr's character. Hall's satirist, motivated by both envy
and truth, also has the biased viewpoint. The truth about
the world's deformities is his aim, but envy, the "squint-
eyed sight," is the bias which forces him to describe the
world in the most vicious and intemperate terms, terms
which a normal man would shrink from using, but which
catch the world aright. Each of the satirist's many moral
weaknesses, his melancholy, his sadism, his prurience, his
intemperance, are, paradoxically, the sources of his satiric
strength. Everard Guilpin provides us with a comprehensive
statement of this theory of satire and makes it perfectly
clear that he is fully conscious of using the satirist to en-
compass his satiric goal:

> Viewing this sin-drownd world, I purposely,
> Phisick'd my *Muse*, that thus unmannerly,
> She might beray our folly-soyled age,
> And keepe *Decorum* on a comick stage,
> Bringing a foule-mouth Iester who might sing
> To rogues, the story of the lousie King.[9]

9. *Skialetheia*, Epigram 70. Although the lines refer immediately to the
preceding epigrams they describe the satires as well, for the only difference
between satires and epigrams which the Elizabethans recognized was that
of length. An epigram was for them simply a short satire.

The "foule-mouth Iester" is the satirist, and the "lousie King" is depraved mankind. Guilpin offers two reasons for the creation of his "Iester": to reveal the world for what it truly is, "beray our folly-soyled age," and to "keepe *Decorum,*" i.e. to write in the manner considered proper for this poetic kind.

In 1599 when Ben Jonson attempted "to make *Every Man Out of His Humor* a recognizable equivalent of formal verse satire," [1] he went to some trouble to make clear that the character of the satirist is a mask which an author assumes for the purpose of making some lasting impression on the world he is attacking. The play begins with the appearance on stage of the angry Asper who expresses feelingly the Juvenalian sentiment copied by all the Elizabethan authors of satire, *Difficile est saturam non scribere:*

> Who is so patient of this impious world,
> That he can checke his spirit, or reine his tongue?
> Or who hath such a dead unfeeling sense,
> That heavens horrid thunders cannot wake?
> To see the earth, crackt with the weight of sinne,
> Hell gaping under us, and o're our heads
> Blacke rav'nous ruine, with her sail-stretcht wings,
> Ready to sinke us downe, and cover us.
> Who can behold such prodigies as these,
> And have his lips seal'd up? not I: my language
> Was never ground into such oyly colours,
> To flatter vice and daub iniquitie:
> But (with an armed, and resolved hand)
> Ile strip the ragged follies of the time,
> Naked as at their birth. . . .
> . . . and with a whip of steele,
> Print wounding lashes in their yron ribs.
>
> (Induction, lines 4–20)

1. Campbell, *Comicall Satyre,* p. 56. The satiric aspects of *Every Man Out* are discussed in detail by Campbell in ch. 3.

But while Asper resembles the satirist in his outraged indignation at the evils of the time, he is not morally culpable
like the satyr. Rather, he is "an ingenious and free spirit,
eager and constant in reproofe, without feare controuling
the worlds abuses. One whom no servile hope of gaine, or
frosty apprehension of danger, can make to be a parasite,
either to time, place, or opinion." But such honesty prevents
him from attacking vice effectively, and in order to scourge
the fools he assumes the character of Macilente: "A man
well parted, a sufficient Scholler, and travail'd; who (wanting that place in the worlds account, which he thinks his
merit capable of) falls into such an envious apoplexie, with
which his judgement is so dazeled, and distasted, that he
growes violently impatient of any opposite happinesse in
another." Motivated by envy, like Nashe's and Hall's satirists,
Macilente proceeds in the play to despise everyone and plan
the downfalls of the fools with sadistic joy. So depraved is
his own nature that he can stoop to poisoning Puntarvolo's
dog and calling it "the onely true jest in the world" (v.1.69).
By the end of the play Macilente has managed to reveal each
fool for what he is and laugh him from the stage. He then
turns to the audiences and says:

> Nowe is my soule at peace.
> I am as emptie of all envie, now,
> As they [the fools] of merit to be envied at.
> My humor (like a flame) no longer lasts
> Than it hath stuffe to feed it.
>
> (v.11.54–8)

And he reveals himself as Asper. The more unsalutary aspects of the character of the satirist are thus treated as
merely the tools which the writer of satire uses to accom-
plish his end. What Jonson did in *Every Man Out* was to
develop in dramatic terms the relationship between author
and satirist which is axiomatic in both Elizabethan formal
verse satire and critical discussions of the genre.

What the Elizabethans perceived with remarkable clarity was the primary relation of satire to its goal, not its author, and the necessity for constructing the character who delivers the satiric attack in terms of his function. With this in mind, we can go a step farther than they explicitly did. We have seen in the first chapter that whenever satire is written a certain unwholesome personality is created by the very act of attack, and that the primary problem of the author is how to handle this personality. At the expense of power and vividness, the authors of medieval satire either obliterated or subdued the more unsalutary tendencies of the satirist. But the Elizabethans chose rather to make their attacks on vice and foolishness as powerful and harsh as possible, and they thus allowed the satirist his full organic development. All the ugliness of character and peculiar instabilities congenital to the expression of the satiric sense of life are given expression in Elizabethan satire; indeed, they are openly stated, elaborated, cultivated. The result was the creation of the satyr personality, which was ultimately formed not by the personalities of the authors nor by a false etymology but by the very nature of satiric expression.

The interrelated tensions which are present in varying degrees in all satire are the very essence of the satyr. He is at once the simple, plain man who speaks plain truth, and the heroic Nemesis of vice who uses all the elaborate tools of the baroque rhetorician. He is the savage enemy of all evil, who is himself tainted with the same failings with which he charges others. He argues that he alone of the poets tells the truth about the world, and yet his obviously melodramatic tone, his mental sickness, and his sadism suggest that his is a totally perverted and twisted view of humanity. He attacks others for their lack of reason or Christianity, and no one could be more unreasonable or unchristian than he in his viciousness, scurrility, and pessimism. He belabors others for pride and yet is proud as

Satan and eaten up by envy. He attacks others for sins of the flesh, yet he is himself lascivious and wanton. In no other period have the innate tensions of satire been allowed such free play in the formation of the satirist.

The history of Elizabethan formal satire is the story of the gradual growth and development of this satyr personality, but after 1599 when the further printing of satire was prohibited, the most interesting developments took place in the theater. The number of printed satires increased after this date, but without exception the later productions were uninspired imitations of the earlier satires, particularly of Marston's, and the satyr we encounter in printed formal satire after 1600 is simply a standardized version of the figure defined by Nashe, Hall, and Marston.

CHAPTER 4

THE SATIRIST IN
THE THEATER

For Elizabethan critics and authors the art of satire was largely a matter of creating the correct personality to deliver the attack. Both the theoretical discussions of the genre and the actual satires center on the satirist, often to the detriment of the attack on folly and vice; and it is no exaggeration to say that for most Elizabethans, satire and the satyr satirist were synonymous. For this reason we can, to a large extent, follow the development of the satiric drama during the late Elizabethan and early Jacobean period by tracing the fortunes of the satirist —by now as much a type character as the *miles gloriosus* or the Machiavel—and noting the modifications he underwent at the hands of the dramatists. One exception to this procedure is, however, necessary. The satiric plays of Ben Jonson written after 1604, and after a number of unsuccessful efforts on Jonson's part to include the figure of the satirist in his drama, constitute a movement away from the use of the satirist. Since *Volpone* and *The Alchemist* are both the finest examples of Renaissance satire and extremely interesting instances of the satiric form in general, it will be necessary to discuss these and other later Jonson plays in some detail.

Considering the pronounced dramatic features of formal verse satire as the Elizabethans wrote it, it should have been a simple matter for the playwrights to adapt it for the stage. The satirist need only be given a name, the fools allowed to speak for themselves, and some rudimentary plot devised to hold the scenes together, and the satiric poem would become a satiric play. But the theater, it developed, was not such a congenial environment for the satirist as formal verse satire had been. The different literary modes are not, finally, interchangeable ways of making the same statement, but distinct perspectives that reveal the world on which they open from different angles. The dramatic monologue, the mode of formal satire, has a rather narrow focal point—the mind of the single character from whom the voice emanates; but in drama the single, narrow focus is lost and we have instead a wider and much more complex scene. The difference between the two modes can best be understood by imagining the satirist first in the setting of formal satire and then on the stage. In formal satire he always remains half-hidden. We seem to stand behind him and follow his finger as it singles out fool after fool from the endless crowd passing before him. We hear only his voice as he strips from his mute victims their various pretenses and calls attention to their concealed deformities. His insistent rhetoric and violent indignation divert attention from himself to his satiric objects, who, always silent, have only those qualities he assigns them. Since the face of the satirist is turned away from us, we must infer his true character from his language and from the tantalizingly brief glimpses he gives of himself in passages of self-revelation. But the stage shifts our perspective. The shadowy face is now turned toward us and we see its full ugliness, the features twisting with hate and envy at the sight of the prosperous fools, the tongue nervously moving around the lips in the presence of the folly and villainy which is found simultaneously loathsome and attractive. The mask is transformed into a character—Jaques, Timon, Thersites, Macilente, Malevole, Bosola. The satirist's various contradictions, confusions, and tensions are realized dramatically, and the dramatic perspective reveals them unambiguously. Not only are the outlines of the figure clarified, but we escape the control of his headlong rhetoric, for the scene comes to life, the characters speak for themselves; and while they may damn themselves from their own mouths, they nevertheless make some claim on our sympathies, for they are now human beings, not mere collections of loathsomeness. Most importantly, in drama the satirist must take his place in some type of plot. His speeches, attitudes, and gestures now have consequences, and he can be measured by the effects of which he is the cause. No longer can he merely rail and commend himself as the only absolute foe of vice because he does so. His railing becomes action which can be judged by its issue.

The tendency of the drama to intensify and make explicit the traditional tensions of the satirist can easily be illustrated. In 1599 three plays which feature the new satirist appeared: *As You Like It, Every Man Out of His Humor,* and Marston's *Histriomastix*.[1] The obvious imperfections of Jaques and Macilente have already been discussed, so despite the slight merits of *Histriomastix* as a play, we shall begin with an anatomy of its satirist, Chrisoganus. *Histriomastix* is essentially a morality play tracing in six acts the decay of a society from peace and plenty to war and poverty. The body of the play consists of a series of thematically related scenes in which representatives of the various social classes demonstrate the human propensity for pride and quarreling. The inevitable result is a disordered society in which no one is willing to work, prices rise, and civil war

1. The date, authorship, and origin of *Histriomastix* are all in doubt. In an article, "John Marston's Play, *Histriomastix*," *Modern Language Quarterly, 19* (June, 1958), 134–40, I have discussed the various reasons for assigning the play to Marston and have tried to demonstrate that the play is not a hasty and uneven revision of an older play, but a unified whole.

breaks out. In the midst of this process of social degeneration we find the satirist Chrisoganus [2] who, like Kinsayder,
thinks he carries "just *Ramnusia's* whippe," [3] makes "stab-
bing Satirs," and uses the stuttering style to describe the
iniquities of the world. Here he is attacking the players and
the vulgar plays they produce:

> VVrite on, crie on, yawle to the common sort
> Of thickskin'd auditours: such rotten stuffs,
> More fit to fill the paunch of Esquiline,
> Then feed the hearings of judiciall eares,
> Yee shades tryumphe, while foggy Ignorance
> Clouds bright *Apollos* beauty.
>
> ⟨II, pp. 273–4⟩

As the social situation deteriorates from a state of pride
and idleness to civil war and famine, Chrisoganus, like an
Old Testament prophet, cries woe upon the "grosse and
impious times," and warns the people that the "vulture, vile
Ambition," is destroying religion, law, pity, and piety. But
these denunciations are unavailing, and the commonwealth
passes on to disaster. From the ruins Chrisoganus emerges
to recommend Stoic fortitude and to point the lesson of the
play, while proudly exempting himself from any responsibility:

> When thou wast rich and Peerelesse in thy pride,
> Content did never harbour in thy brest,
> Nor ere had love, her residence in thee,

2. The unusual name "Chrisoganus," i.e. "golden-born," was probably
borrowed from Cicero's oration *Pro Sexto Roscio Amerino*, where "Crysogo-
nous," a sinister and greedy freedman of Sulla, is attacked. The choice of
this name for the satirist suggests that Marston was fully aware of creating
a repulsive character.

3. *Histriomastix*, Act II, in H. H. Wood's edition of *The Plays of John
Marston* (Edinburgh, Oliver & Boyd, 1934–9), 3, 258. Wood does not give
line numbers or scene divisions, so all references are to act and page numbers.

(I meane the love of perfect happinesse)
But skillesse grudging from a haughty spirit
Did blind thy sences with a slender merit.
Whil'st I (poore man) not subject to such thought
Gave entertaine to those sweet blessed babes,
Which Sapience brought from Wisedomes holy brest,
And thought me rich to have their company.
By nursing them in Peace I shun'd all Sloth,
Nor yet did *Plenty* make me prodigall:
Pride I abhor'd and term'd the Beggers shield:
Nor ever did base *Envie* touch my heart.
Yet alwayes loov'd to beare (as *Solon* sed,)
A Turtles eye within an Aspicks head.

(VI, p. 296)

The "turtles eye within an Aspicks head" is, of course, the
exact equivalent of Kinsayder's "squint-eye'd sight," the
assumption of a fierce mask for a sanative purpose.

Chrisoganus, in the common manner of all satirists, is
placing himself in the best possible moral light. He maintains after disaster that he has nourished wisdom while
shunning sloth, envy, pride, prodigality, and that his "stab-
bing satirs" had their source in a love for mankind, the
"turtles eye," not in hatred. But his past actions do not bear
him out, for he has been as proud and as envious as the
other characters in the play. He begins the play not as a
satirist but as a scholar to whom Reason entrusts the moral
education of the nobility. Specifically, Reason enjoins him
to train men to use their minds to control their brutish
appetites. Instead Chrisoganus leads them into the bogs of
scholastic epistemology and so loads his discussions with
the technical language of philosophy and Latin tags that
he merely bewilders his pupils:

If this bee certaine then which comes from sence,
The knowledg proper to the soule is truer;

For that pure knowledg by the which wee know
A thing to bee, with true cause how it is,
Is more exact then that which knowes it is,
And reacheth not to knowledge of the cause.
Besides; that knowledge (that considers things
Abjunct from sencive matter) is exacter
Then that which joynes it selfe with elements;
Arithmetick ever considers numbers
Abstract from sencive matter: *Musick* still
Considers it with sence, as mixt with sound:
Therefore *Arithmeticque* is more exact,
And more exact then is *Geometrie:*
Since *unitas* is still *simplicior puncto,*
And number simpler then is magnitude.
For *Unitas* may still be *sine puncto,*
But *Punctus* never without Unitie,
Nor; *Magnitudo sine Numero,*
Dum (enim) punctus ponitur, ponitur (ex necessitate) unitas.

(I, p. 249)

Mavortius, one of the nobles, replies to this schoolman's speech with exasperating and delightful common sense, "But all this prooves not wee may know a truth."

There is nothing wrong philosophically with Chrisoganus' argument, and it can be followed fairly easily on the printed page, but in the mouth of an actor it would, like speeches in *The Alchemist* composed of alchemical terms, sound like so much pedantic gibberish. Shortly after this lecture, Chrisoganus, still avoiding his duty to discuss moral problems, soars into a description of celestial mechanics, and here the jargon, the ostentatious display of recondite learning, and the drift away from the point confirm Chrisoganus as a vain pedant devoid of common sense:

Why you shall meet with projects so remov'd
From vulgar apprehension, (as for instance,)

The Sunne heere riseth in the East with us,
But not of his owne proper motion,
As beeing turn'd by *primum mobile,*
(The heaven above *Cœlum stellatum*)
Whereas his true asscent is in the West,
And so hee consummates his circled course
In the Ecliptick line, which partes the Zodiack,
Being borne from Tropick to Tropick: this time
Wee call a yeere; whose *Hierocliphick* was
(Amongst the *Egyptians*) figured in a Snake
Wreath'd circular, the tayle within his mouth:
As (happily) the Latines (since) did call,
A Ring, (of the word *Annus*) *Annulus.*

(I, p. 253)

But Chrisoganus fails again to interest the nobles, and in the next act he tries to persuade them to investigate theological matters, arguing that there are no "better recreations" than "sacred knowledge in divinest thinges" (II, p. 257). He has thus tried to lead his charges into three areas, epistemology, cosmology, and theology, where reason can only produce endless speculation, and men, like Milton's fallen angels who puzzle over the same questions, can only find themselves in "wandr'ing mazes lost."

It is only after Chrisoganus has been rebuffed by the nobles and dismissed from his post as their tutor that he becomes a railing satirist. He turns at first to playwriting, but his play is rejected by a company of strolling players because of the high price of ten pounds which the proud Chrisoganus places on it. Then, and only then, does he begin to rage and roar in the familiar style of the satyr. He now becomes "halfe starv'd in Envie" of "Fat Ignorance and rammish Barbarisme," and begins to "eate his marrow, and him-selfe devoure" (III, p. 277). Chrisoganus has thus degenerated from scholar to hack playwright to satirist, and his downward course parallels that of the other characters.

The nobles, the professional men, and the artisans all misuse peace and plenty. They become rich and proud, vie with one another, abandon their proper places in society, and engage finally in civil war. The play is a study of social collapse, and the satirist is presented as one form of social abnormality.

Histriomastix is not a distinguished play by any standard, but it is an interesting one, for it makes clear the major Elizabethan assumptions about the nature of the satirist and the satiric impulse. Satire is an abnormal and fallen activity which has no place in a well-ordered society. The satirist himself is a scholar who has misused his gifts.[4] His reaction to his sufferings is not self-examination but hatred and envy of the more prosperous. He is, as he stands among the ruins of the society he has helped to destroy, reading hard lessons to the ragged survivors, a most unsavory creature who completely lacks humility and understanding. But his own moral stains do not impair the ultimate correctness of his judgment, and his exemption of himself from responsibility is necessary if he is to criticize the world with

4. It was fairly standard for Elizabethan and Jacobean authors to present their satirists as men who in their younger days had been overly curious scholars and who on entering the world discovered that their bookish wisdom was of no value. They react by becoming parasites, flatterers, and satirists. This is the development of Nashe's Pierce Penilesse, of Lampatho Doria in Marston's *What You Will*, of Ingenioso in *The Second Return from Parnassus*, and of Bosola in *The Duchess of Malfi*. Robert Burton, digressing on "The Miseries of Scholars," in *The Anatomy of Melancholy* traces this pattern with his usual clinical exactitude. After pointing out that the "irksome hours, laborous tasks, wearisome days" of scholars make them susceptible to melancholy, he then goes on to show us that the disease becomes inevitable because of the poverty and contempt with which the world rewards scholars after their Herculean feats of learning. Since this is the case, Burton says, *"their Rhetorick only serves them to curse their bad fortunes,* and many of them for want of means are driven to hard shifts; from Grasshoppers they turn Humble-Bees and Wasps, plain Parasites, and make the *Muses,* Mules, to satisfy their hunger-starved paunches, and get a meals meat." ed. F. Dell and P. Jordan-Smith (New York, Farrar & Rinehart, 1927), p. 265.

sufficient harshness to effect its cure. Chrisoganus, of course, is not aware of playing a part. His personality and the mask of the satyr are identical, but Marston the author stands apart from his creation and treats him as but one more example of thwarted pride and ambition.

In a number of ways the dramatic form sharpens our critical faculties and forces us to scrutinize Chrisoganus with a more curious eye than we usually turn on the satirist of formal verse satire. The dramatic contexts of scene and plot provide reference points from which his measure can be taken, and thus we can judge him by the effect his railing has upon events, by comparison with other characters, by their comments on him, by his various actions, and ultimately by his contribution to the catastrophe and his reaction to it. In other words, that perennial contrast between the public and private personalities of the satirist which is partially concealed in formal satire becomes glaringly apparent in the drama. Since the Elizabethan satiric authors had always understood their satirists as fallible dramatic characters, this situation created little difficulty, and the playwrights simply carried to the extreme the practice of the satiric poets of elaborating on the peculiarities of the satiric personality. Very roughly, the satiric drama in which the satyr satirist is developed in this way falls into two categories: "Comicall Satyre," i.e. the Horatian variety; [5] and Tragical, or Juvenalian, satire. The two kinds are not mutually exclusive, but for the sake of clarity it will be useful to treat them separately.

5. The term "Comicall Satyre" is used by Ben Jonson to describe three of his satiric plays, *Every Man Out of His Humor, Cynthias Revels,* and *Poetaster.* In each of these he draws heavily on Horace, who is actually the nominal satirist in *Poetaster,* for definitions of satire and comedy. For a description of Jonson's theories about the nature of comedy and satire see Campbell, *Comicall Satyre,* ch. 1.

Comicall Satyre

"Good Thersites, come in and rail," [6] says Shakespeare's Patroclus when he discovers the satirist skulking outside his tent; and Achilles when he returns is delighted to find the railer there, "Art thou come? Why, my cheese, my digestion, why hast thou not serv'd thyself in to my table so many meals?" (11.3.40–3), and he teases him into performing, "Come, what's Agamemnon?" Thersites responds with vigor and unanticipated thoroughness, "Agamemnon is a fool; Achilles is a fool; Thersites is a fool; and, as aforesaid, Patroclus is a fool." The satirist Thersites is, as Achilles points out, "a privileg'd man," a licensed jester to the Greek camp, taken seriously by none and vastly enjoyed by all. In a majority of the other plays in which a satirist appears he is also treated as a buffoon by the other characters, who are quite proud to have such a distinguished performer in their midst, although they pay no attention to the meaning of his words. He storms and raves while they smile approvingly and comment enthusiastically that "he beats the ayre the best that ere I heard," [7] or remark admiringly that he is "more discontent than Lucifer when he was thrust out of the presence." [8]

Apparently the theater audiences of the early seventeenth century shared this admiration for the satirist and his sensational rhetoric, as the following lines from Marston's *What You Will* (1601) suggest:

> This is the strain that chokes the theatres;
> That makes them crack with full-stuff'd audience;
> This is your humour only in request,
> Forsooth to rail; this brings your ears to bed;

6. 11.3.25–6.
7. *Histriomastix,* Act 111, p. 274.
8. *The Malcontent,* 1.1.28–9.

> This people gape for; for this some do stare.
> This some would hear, to crack the author's neck;
> This admiration and applause pursues.
>
> (III.2.165–71)

Alfred Harbage classifies as satirical comedies all but a dozen of the fifty-five extant plays produced in the private theaters between 1599 and 1613,[9] and a large number of these plays contain ranting satirists. Even the public theaters, where railing and satire were never as popular as in the private houses, were forced for a time to meet the new demand and present satirical plays. Tucca, in Jonson's *Poetaster*, attacks a player from one of the popular companies for putting on the new satires: "They say, you ha' nothing but *humors, revells*, and *satyres*, that girde, and fart at the time, you slave."[1] But the common player, Histrio, denies this humbly and points out that the lack of satiric plays has nearly ruined the popular companies. To remedy the situation his group has hired Demetrius (Dekker?) to write a satire for them and he hopes that "it will get us a huge deale of money . . . and we have need on't; for this winter ha's made us all poorer, then so many starv'd snakes; No bodie comes at us" (lines 327–30).

The flamboyant character of the satirist, his colorful railing, and his parade of fools were, it appears, simply theatrical sensations which were added to the set rhetorical speeches, swordplay, gorgeous costumes, dancing, songs, exchanges of wit, *sententiae,* and low comedy devices which were jumbled together in most Elizabethan drama. The better dramatists, of course, managed in time to make of the satirist something more than a mere "getpenny," just as they had already made serious use of other sensational theatrical material; but throughout his stage career the satirist was first of all a spectacular figure designed to attract

9. *Shakespeare and the Rival Tradition* (New York, 1952), p. 71.
1. III.2.165 ff.

and delight the audience. For such a task the satirist developed by the authors of the new formal satire was ready-made, and although the dramatists served him up in a variety of sensational combinations, he remained essentially the same exaggerated railer created by Nashe, Hall, and Marston.

Marston's *What You Will* shows very clearly the manner in which the satirist could be exploited for his comic possibilities. The play is a collection of spectacular scenes which are only loosely held together by a rambling Plautine plot. Among the songs, the dances, the exquisite rhetoric, and the pages' bawdy jokes, we find Lampatho Doria, a satirist directly descended from W. Kinsayder, to whom he is specifically compared (ii.1.134–5). Like his forebears he delights in railing on any subject, and his foolish friend Simplicius becomes incoherent with joy in his praise of this faculty, "He'll rail against the court till the gallants—O God! he is very nectar" (ii.1.32–3). Lampatho is prepared at any moment to denounce the general wickedness of man, and when Quadratus, another satiric figure in the play, gives him a rhetorical topic, "In Heaven's handiwork there's naught," to develop, Lampatho replies splendidly, like a well-prepared schoolboy, with a set speech on the wretchedness of humankind:

> In Heaven's handiwork there's naught,
> None more vile, accursed, reprobate to bliss,
> Than man; and 'mong men a scholar most.
> Things only fleshly sensitive, an ox or horse,
> They live and eat, and sleep, and drink, and die,
> And are not touched with recollections
> Of things o'er-past, or stagger'd infant doubts
> Of things succeeding; but leave the manly beasts,
> And give but pence apiece to have a sight
> Of beastly man now—
>
> (ii.2.128–37)

As Lampatho continues to dilate on the vanity of human wishes his lines are punctuated by the shouts of Simplicius who calls from off stage intermittently to remind him that if he doesn't come at once his meal will not be paid for.

Lampatho's other satiric traits are made equally ridiculous. His language is the usual mixture of Ciceronian phrases and billingsgate:

> Dirt upon dirt, fear is beneath my shoe.
> Dreadless of racks, strappadoes, or the sword—
> Maugre informer and sly intelligence,—
> I'll stand as confident as Hercules,
> And, with a frightless resolution,
> Rip up and lance our time's impieties.
>
>   .   .   .   .   .
>
> Now is my fury mounted. Fix your eyes;
> Intend your senses; bend your list'ning up;
> For I'll make greatness quake; I'll taw the hide
> Of thick-skinn'd Hugeness.
>
>   (III.2.144–61)

The style here is obviously overdone, but the joke is made even more pointed. After nearly twenty lines of build-up to a heroic denunciation of "hugeness," Lampatho balks. His auditors wait anxiously for the magnificent tirade which should follow, but it never comes. This deflationary technique is used throughout the play. While Lampatho threatens again and again to rhyme his enemies dead or "pickle" them in "the sour juice of a tart brain" (II.1.122–3), he is always either bought off with money or a free meal, or frightened from delivering any specific attack on vice. Elsewhere, he proposes to deliver a satire on that ever popular subject, the ladies of the court, but decides instead, when encouraged, to make love to one of them. He professes to hate his benefactors, but is careful never to attack them openly. Instead he lives on the scraps they fling him, fawns over them, and praises them in ridiculously inflated language.

Lampatho is, quite clearly, a caricature of the conventional satirist developed in formal satire. He is also the satiric character as the harshest critic would describe him: a *poseur,* a coward, a mere rhetorician, a hypocrite, a lecher, and an opportunist. The ironic treatment of Lampatho is too consistent and too pronounced to be an accident, and this fact makes it impossible that he was either Marston's spokesman or his image. No author would discredit his own spokesman in this way or burlesque himself and his views in such a carefully planned manner.

The anonymous author of *The Second Return from Parnassus,* also written in 1601,[2] plays the same game with the satirist. After following in the first two Parnassus plays the misfortunes of two Cambridge scholars, Philomusus and Studioso, for whom the world has no suitable place, he brings them to London in *The Second Return* where they encounter two other disappointed scholars from Cambridge, Ingenioso and Furor Poeticus, the latter almost certainly a caricature of the literary personality of John Marston. Ingenioso—perhaps Thomas Nashe—opens the play reading Juvenal and vowing to model himself on that Roman worthy and whip the world which has treated him so badly. Neither Furor nor Ingenioso has any moral scruples about wringing a living from the world. Ingenioso tries to keep alive by writing sensational pamphlets—his latest is *A Catalogue of Cambridge Cuckolds.* But such a living is hazardous, so he and Furor, who is no more than a mad, fantastic cadger of drinks, plan to flatter a wealthy noble, Sir Raderick. The scheme fails, and when we last see the two, Furor is picking lice from himself while Ingenioso describes their future:

2. The date of this play is discussed by Leishman, *Three Parnassus Plays,* pp. 24–6. All citations of *The Second Return* are to this edition.

> Faith we are fully bent to be Lords of misrule in the
> worlds wide hall; our voyage is to the Ile of Dogges,
> There where the blattant beast doth rule and raigne,
> Rendinge the credditt of whome ere hee please;
> Where serpents tongs the pen men are to write,
> Where cats do waule by day, dogges [barke] by night:
> There shall engoared venom be my inke,
> My pen a sharper quill of porcupine,
> My stayned paper, this sin loaden earth:
> There will I write, in lines shall never die,
> Our feared Lordings crying villany.   (lines 2108–18)

The author of *The Second Return* does not attempt to
avoid any of the unpleasant characteristics which were traditional in the satirist. Instead he capitalizes on them and
makes Ingenioso and Furor, particularly the latter, as foolish and as base as possible. They rant, they preen themselves, they scheme, they flatter, they will stop at nothing
to get money, and when they fail to improve their fortunes
they go to the "Ile of Dogges," that mythical "liberty" of
satirists created by Thomas Nashe,[3] where they may give
vent to their spite in suitable surroundings and without
interference. But the blame for their baneful natures is
placed on the world which has not found a suitable place
for such learned scholars:

> A gentle wit thou hadst, nor is it blame
> To turne so tart, for time hath wronged the same.
>   (lines 2119–20)

No doubt the plays in which the satirist's bizarre style,
melancholy, railing, venality, and interest in those same
vices which he finds loathsome in others were held up for

---

3. Nashe's play *The Ile of Dogs* (c. 1597) is lost, but from the frequent
references to it in other works of the time it was clearly one of the most
successful satiric plays of its day. For a description of the play see E. K.
Chambers, *The Elizabethan Stage* (Oxford, 1923), *3*, 453–5.

laughter were popular successes, but the dangers of this approach are apparent. By discrediting their satirists so thoroughly, the authors ran the risk of discrediting satire itself, for if the satiric spokesman becomes too ridiculous or too depraved, then his criticisms are apt to seem merely laughable (the case of Furor Poeticus and Lampatho) or the poisonous mouthings of an envious failure (the case of Chrisoganus). But many Eliabethan dramatists seem only to have been interested in providing sensational theatrical fare, and they continued to elaborate on the satirist's character and present him in a ridiculous light without regard for his function in the satiric design. But Ben Jonson, perhaps the only thoroughly serious satiric author in this period, was concerned with the moral and sanative purpose of satire, not just with exciting theater, and in his three plays which he called "Comicall Satyres," *Every Man Out of His Humor* (1599), *Cynthia's Revels* (1600), and *Poetaster* (1601) he attempted to limit the satirist to his proper place in satiric drama. Or, put in another way, he tried in these plays to solve the recurrent problem of formal satire, a problem intensified by the shift to the theater: how to manage the unruly satirist needed for the castigation of the fools. Each of these plays has elaborate prologues, inductions, epilogues, and scenes where Jonson or one of his characters discusses with a great deal of care the problems of satire. He accuses the other authors of dramatic satire of being no more than,

> Fellowes of practis'd and most laxative tongues,
> Whose empty and eager bellies, i' the yeere,
> Compell their braynes to many desp'rate shifts.[4]

4. *Poetaster,* "To the Reader," lines 89–91. This brings us to the famous "War of the Theaters" in which Jonson is supposed to have quarreled with Marston and Dekker and satirized them in his plays after Marston first caricatured Jonson as Chrisoganus in *Histriomastix.* There was undoubtedly a quarrel of some sort here, but of late there has been a tendency among

That is, these authors write satire not to correct the manners of the times, but merely for profit. Furthermore, Jonson charges earlier in this same passage that these scribblers write out of personal malice; that they feed the baser appetites of their vulgar audience with the foulest kinds of material, much of which is stolen from other authors; that they themselves have dirty minds; and that their language is wild and outlandish.[5]

These charges certainly have some foundation, as any reader of the satires Jonson is attacking can testify, but it is interesting to note that the specific counts in Jonson's indictment are identical with those of the traditional attacks on authors of satire. He is fastening on the inherent tensions of satire, which are given open expression in the new Elizabethan satire, and using them to discredit this particular kind of satire and the authors of it. Having associated other authors of satire with their satirists, Jonson then sought to disengage his own personality from his satirists' and present his own satiric motives and methods in the best light. His arguments are stated well, but they are not particularly novel, being no more than the conventional explanations offered by all satirists in the moments when they stop belaboring their victims long enough to tell us that while it might appear that they are sadists, lechers, hypocrites, and just plain liars, in actuality they are honest, moral, forthright, judicious citizens of the commonwealth. Jonson admits that his satiric plays have some salt and gall, but he argues that he is free from any personal malice. It has always been his aim, he says piously, "To spare the person and speak the vices" (*Poetaster*, "To the Reader," line

---

critics to avoid specific identifications of various characters in these plays. See R. W. Berringer, "Jonson's *Cynthia's Revels* and the Wars of The Theaters," *PQ*, 22 (1943), 1–22; William Talbert, "The Purpose and Technique of Jonson's *Poetaster*," *SP*, 42 (1945), 225–52; Herford and Simpson, *Ben Jonson, 1*, 24–31.

5. *Poetaster*, "To the Reader," lines 54–68.

85). Elsewhere, drawing on Cicero, he presents his ideal of Comicall Satyre, *"Imitatio vitae, Speculum consuetudinis, Imago veritatis;* a thing throughout pleasant, and ridiculous, and accommodated to the correction of manners" (*Every Man Out,* iii.6.206–9). In short, Jonson presents himself as free from the sensationalism and personal malice which mar other satires. Rather, he gives us "deedes, and language, such as men do use," for the purpose of "the correction of manners."

In these plays Jonson attempts to cultivate an attitude as balanced and detached as that of Horace, to whom he compares himself and on whose writings he draws heavily. But the frequency with which Jonson returns to discussions of satire throughout these three plays suggests that putting the Horatian attitude into practice was considerably more difficult than might have been anticipated. There were a number of reasons for this, some of them peculiarly contemporary and bound up with personal quarrels and the economic problems of the theater, but the principal cause was the ancient dilemma that no matter how wise and just and restrained the original impulse to satire may be, an effective attack on vice inevitably creates a character who is unpleasant and inconsistent. Jonson was fully aware of his problem, and where the earlier satirists had simply plunged ahead and encouraged the satyr to evolve, Jonson attempted to control his development. In each of his three Comicall Satyres he made a distinct effort to find some satisfactory way of handling the conflict between the sane, reasonable author interested in correction of vice, and the unbalanced, intemperate railer who inevitably becomes his theatrical persona.

In his first attempt, *Every Man Out of His Humor,* Jonson created as unprepossessing a satirist as appeared in the Elizabethan theater. Macilente has every twisted impulse, every dark and unpleasant characteristic of the satirist. He

is a disappointed scholar, "a lanke raw-bon'd anatomie,"
who "walkes up and downe like a charg'd musket." During
most of the play he lurks on the edge of the scenes, eaten
up with envy and hatred—envy of those who have the
wealth and position he desires, and hatred for those who
have nothing he wants. So powerful is his anger at the world
which has disappointed him that he would like not to mend
it, but to destroy it utterly in order to blot it from his sight:

> I wish the organs of my sight were crackt;
> And that the engine of my griefe could cast
> Mine eye-balls, like two globes of wild-fire, forth,
> To melt this unproportion'd frame of nature.
>
> (1.1.25–8)

His monstrous pride and tormented hatred are constantly
revealed in his imagery. The fools are "clods," "bull-rushes,"
"mushrompe gentlemen," "slaves," "scorpions." He compares them to animals: whales, snakes, lice, hogs, horses,
dogs; and makes all human activity no more than animal
functions, swilling, gorging, digesting, and discharging offal
and venom. He curses the fools and hopes they will be
infected with the "plague," "leprosie," or the "hecticke."
His fury also finds expression in the headlong rhythms,
jagged phrasing, and profusion of epithets which constitute
his harsh satiric style. This intense anger burns inwardly
as well, for he exclaims, "I could eate my entrailes, / And
sinke my soule into the earth with sorrow."

Ben Jonson was, however, a greater poet than the majority of the Elizabethan satiric authors, and occasionally he
gives Macilente lines which sound new depths in the satiric
character. "Would to heaven," says Macilente,

> I were turn'd
> To some faire water-*Nymph,* that (set upon
> The deepest whirle-pit of the rav'nous seas,)

My adamantine eyes might head-long hale
This iron world to me, and drowne it all.

(II.4.161–6)

The sheer ferocity of the desire to be the agent of a universal cataclysm, a return to primal chaos, expressed here
interacts strangely with the optative tone of the passage.
"Would," "were," "might" are key terms embodying a longing for an event which is known to be an impossibility,
and the heavy accents of the last three lines rather than
suggesting determination express a feeling of blocked desire for action. Frustration is implicit everywhere in the
speech. Macilente's desire to be a "faire water-*Nymph*" is
most immediately a reference to the mermaids' practice of
luring sailors to their wrecks, but the word "faire"—it has
an extrametrical stress—suggests by contrast that Macilente
knows his own ugliness and longs to be free of it.

Despite Macilente's frequent attempts to proclaim himself the heroic champion of virtue and foe of vice, he is
no protagonist in a great action. He is, as a stage performance of *Every Man Out* shows more clearly than a reading,
a mere railer. Although he engages in some petty actions
such as poisoning a dog, betraying a woman and her lover,
and revealing a female courtier for a fool, for the greater
part of the play Macilente is merely an observer of the action. He stands on the edge of the scene, gritting his teeth
with anger, until he explodes with rage and delivers a bitter
speech anatomizing the particular brand of idiocy he has
been watching. Usually these speeches are in the form of
asides directed at the audience alone, and Macilente is far
less open and intemperate in his denunciations when they
are addressed to the other characters. In so placing Macilente, Jonson is making fully visible the implicit scenic
arrangement of nondramatic satire where the satirist appears to stand on the edge of a turbulent and silent mass
of humanity and characterize the fools as they pass. In the

nondramatic satire this positioning is advantageous to the satirist, for his physical steadfastness images his rocklike moral stance before a world of giddy change. But his immobility has quite a different effect on the stage, for the essence of drama is movement, and the audience no longer stands still with the satirist but sits outside observing both him and the moving crowd of fools. In this new context the satirist like Macilente who merely stands and rails at the world without attempting to move in it, appears futile, sterile, and cowardly.

Macilente is thoroughly detestable, and all of his detestable qualities are those necessary to the satirist to achieve his satiric ends. But Jonson took considerable pains in *Every Man Out* to make it clear that Macilente is his satiric instrument, not his spokesman. A character called Asper is introduced in the Induction who has all of the virtues of the satirist with none of his defects. He is indignant at the time's iniquities; outraged by the impudence of folly; frank; unafraid; and free from any personal malice, envy, or profit motive. Like Juvenal and the Elizabethan satyr he is determined "with a whip of steele" to "print wounding lashes" in the "yron ribs" of the foolish and vicious who "grow ranke in sinne." But his two questioners, Mitis and Cordatus, point out to Asper the various dangers incumbent on the actual work of printing wounding lashes. He will be thought "too peremptorie," he is a "madman" in this mood, and he is "transported with violence." To these objections they add the practical arguments that it is dangerous to attack evil in these days, and that such an attack will effect no changes. Asper, however, avoids these difficulties by assuming the character of Macilente, and under the cover of this persona he accomplishes his satiric work. When the play is finished and the end of satire achieved, at least theoretically, with each fool having been driven out of his humor, Asper drops the disguise of Macilente. Asper corresponds to the public personality of the satirist and Macilente to the private personality, and by splitting the satiric character in this Jekyll-and-Hyde fashion Jonson attempted to make certain that his attack on vice would not be invalidated by the methods his satirist used to attack folly.

In his next two Comicall Satyres, *Cynthia's Revels* and *Poetaster,* Jonson abandoned the somewhat cumbersome method devised in *Every Man Out,* and created satirists who have only admirable qualities. Crites in *Cynthia's Revels* is "a creature of a most perfect and divine temper. . . . His discourse is like his behaviour, uncommon, but not unpleasing. . . . Hee will thinke, and speake his thought, both freely: but as distant from depraving another mans merit, as proclaiming his owne" (II.3.123–36). Horace, the satirist of *Poetaster,* is equally judicious, well balanced, and free from unpleasant psychic twists. Like the Horace of the *Sermones* who is the model for Jonson's satirist, the Horace of *Poetaster* writes "sharp, yet modest rimes / That spare mens persons, and but taxe their crimes" (III.5.133–4). Their moral characters may be thoroughly admirable, but Crites and Horace are ineffective as satirists, for their probity and stern sense of decorum prevents them from making any very cutting attack on foolishness. Crites wanders loosely about in his play and has to be forced by Mercury and Cupid, who actually provide the satiric commentary, to engage in a plot to reveal the fools. Once his reluctance has been overcome, his dignity and sense of justice do not allow him to give the fools the thorough scourging they require, and his assaults on them are chaste and vapid. Horace does no better. He does bring the false satirists Demetrius and Crispinus to the bar of justice and forces them to recant, but he does so without any savage intensity, and throughout most of the play he is so busy explaining the beauties of his own character that he has no time to engage in satiric activities. In worrying too much about placing his satirists in the best possible light Jonson robbed them of their raison d'être, effective attack. If he allowed them to rail they would inevitably acquire the more detestable satiric qualities, but if they were not allowed to rail then they had no function except to serve as an apology for Jonson's own satiric activities.

It was in this latter fashion that Jonson's contemporaries chose to understand the characters of Asper, Crites, and Horace. In *Satiromastix or The Untrussing of the Humorous Poet* (1601) Thomas Dekker, perhaps with some help from Marston, delivered the counterblast to Jonson's argument. Horace, the satirist of the play, is a caricature of Jonson. He is presented as a cringing, cowardly, basely descended, ex-bricklayer and ex-player who has ranted in Hieronimo's part. Horace, like Jonson, argues that he turned his *"Muse into a Timonist"* only because he loathed "the general Leprozie of Sinne" (v.2.195–6).[6] But this motive is not allowed to stand, and we are shown a Horace who spits in the face of his enemies because they have attacked him, who hunts not "for mens loves but for their feare," [7] who writes a satire on baldness for a fee, and who becomes a biting satirist only after the players banish him to the Ile of Dogs. In the end Horace, costumed like a satyr, is arraigned, tried, and forced to renounce his excessive pride, his literary borrowings, and his personal appearances at the theater when his plays are being performed. The specific touches of the satire doubtless refer to actual details in the life of Jonson, but it is necessary to note, again, that these details are manifestations of general failings which are traditional parts of the satirist's character—disappointment, pride, personal animus, and a desire for power. Dekker

6. *The Dramatic Works of Thomas Dekker*, ed. Fredson Bowers (Cambridge Univ. Press, 1953), Vol. *1*.

7. II.2.62.

simply presents Jonson under the figure of Horace as a living example of the standard satiric character.

Jonson's various attempts to produce a "clean" satirist ran contrary to the tendency of Elizabethan and Jacobean drama, and he himself abandoned the effort after *Poetaster*. He continued to write both tragical and comicall satyres after 1603, and *Sejanus, Volpone, The Alchemist, Bartholomew Fair*, and *The Devil is an Ass* are without question the most impressive English satires of the Renaissance, but in these plays Jonson no longer tried to imitate the practices and organizational techniques of formal satire. The satirist is gone, though there are characters, such as Mosca, Truewit, and Humphrey, in whom residual traces of the old satyr are evident; and the scenes, which in the early plays are arranged in the loose, episodic manner of formal verse satire, are now held together by a more complicated plot and by a much more rigorous conception of the basic causes of the diverse instances of depravity and foolishness which are dramatized. In short, Jonson turned to writing Menippean satire, stressing the scene rather than the satirist. But while the method may have changed, the world which Jonson creates in his later plays is the same world found in Elizabethan formal satire and the earlier satiric plays; and it is at the same time a magnificent instance of the typical satiric scene. Outwardly we are shown Elizabethan London and Renaissance Venice, but the bits and pieces of contemporary life which are the playwright's raw material are arranged in the unchanging configurations of the standard satiric scene, and their thrust and pressure are along the usual satiric lines of force.

In Act II, Scene 2 of *Volpone*, Volpone, in order to gain a sight of the pure Celia, whom he desires, assumes the mask of a mountebank, Scoto of Mantua, and delivers a long harangue on the virtues of his medicinal oil. Aside from its slight function in the plot, the speech serves to characterize Volpone and suggest his unlimited confidence in himself, his joy in skilfully playing a part, his delight in words, and his pleasure in bilking the ignorant clods of the world. But in Jonson's satiric plays the assumption of a mask usually has an ironic function: it serves to reveal the character for what he truly is. Thus in this play Volpone's assumed physical diseases,

> Those filthy eyes . . . that flow with slime,
> Like two frog-pits . . . those same hanging cheeks,
> Cover'd with hide, in stead of skin. . . .
>
> (1.5.57-9)

reveal his true spiritual state, his moral ugliness, his animal nature. Similarly at the conclusion of the play when the advocate Voltore escapes from a difficult situation by pretending to have been possessed by the devil "in shape of a blew toad, with a battes wings" (v.12.31), the pretense reveals the truth about him, that he has in spirit been owned by the evil one in a bestial and unnatural shape. Volpone's mask of the mountebank, the charlatan, thus permits us to look at him clearly for a moment, for he is, in actuality, a great quack who while seeming to offer well-being to the men who flock around him hoping to become his heir, is in actuality offering only a worthless pseudomedicine, gold, and endangering the moral health of himself and of his society.

But there appears to be still another level of meaning in the mountebank's long spiel. At one point in his diversified entertainment, Volpone has his attendants sing the following song:

> You that would last long, list to my song,
> Make no more coyle, but buy of this oyle.
> Would you be ever faire? and yong?
> Stout of teeth? and strong of tongue?
> Tart of palat? quick of eare?

Sharpe of sight? of nostrill cleare?
Moist of hand? and light of foot?
(Or I will come neerer to't)
Would you live free from all diseases?
Doe the act, your mistris pleases;
Yet fright all aches from your bones?
Here's a med'cine, for the nones.

(II.2.192–203)

Most immediately the song is, of course, typical of the attitudes Volpone represents in his own person, for we are offered here only physical well-being, and this freedom from the pains that flesh is heir to is offered on the impossible terms of perpetuity. But read in a metaphorical rather than a literal fashion, the song suggests the sanative goal of the satirist, the return to health of the individual and society through the curative properties of satire itself. Quickness of ear, sharpness of sight, clearness of nostril would correspond on this level to moral rather than sensual alertness, an ability to see, hear, and smell the moral foulness of the greedy, self-centered, and unnatural men and women presented in *Volpone*. Finally, and most importantly, the "oil" would restore man to his procreative functions and allow him to reproduce his kind, to give life and beauty to the world, rather than the misshapen creatures, the dwarf, hermaphrodite, and eunuch, produced by Volpone. In terms of this metaphorical interpretation of the song—and the scene of which it is a part—the mountebank's nostrum or oil would be Jonson's satiric plays, and the mountebank would become Jonson the satiric poet.

Certain details of the speech suggest this interpretation, for at times the language of the mountebank gives way entirely to the language of a poet defending the peculiar value of his own satiric plays. For example, the mountebank attacks "these ground *Ciarlitani*, that spread their clokes on the pavement, as if they meant to do feates of activitie, and then come in, lamely, with their mouldy tales out of *Boccacio*" (II.2.49–51). And he goes on to inveigh against these same rogues who "with one poore groats-worth of un-prepar'd *antimony,* finely wrapt up in severall *'scartoccios* [papers], are able, very well, to kill their twentie a weeke, and *play.*" But, the mountebank goes on, "these meagre starv'd spirits . . . want not their favourers among your shrivel'd sallad-eating *artizans.*" This poet-mountebank sounds very like the Ben Jonson who under many guises in the various prologues and epilogues of his plays praised the soundness of his own inventions, their decorousness and moral purpose, and berated the sensational, imitative, formless, and stale, but unfortunately popular and profit-able plays of his contemporaries. Certain other details of the mountebank speech seem also to bear on Jonson's per-sonal situation: Scoto speaks of his recent imprisonment (line 45), suggesting Jonson's own recent imprisonment in 1605 (shortly before *Volpone* was written) for his hand in the satiric play *Eastward Ho;* the reference to the extensive studies that have gone into the preparation of the nostrum, "whil'st others have beene at the *balloo,* I have beene at my booke: and am now . . . come to the flowrie plaines of honour, and reputation" (lines 167–70), sounds much like Jonson's usual boast of intensive scholarship and studies in preparation for writing plays. The description of a new playing place, "I . . . who was ever wont to fixe my banke in face of the publike *piazza,* . . . now (after eight months absence, from this illustrous city of *Venice*) humbly retire my selfe, into an obscure nooke of the *piazza*" (lines 34–8), perhaps refers to the presentation of the play at the two universities rather than in the public theater.[8]

8. *Volpone* was first played, according to the title page of the first quarto, in 1605/6 by the King's Men at the Globe and then at Oxford and Cam-bridge in 1606 or 1607. For details see Herford and Simpson, *9,* 196. If the "obscure nooke of the *piazza*" refers to the two universities, then the passage was interpolated for the later performances; there is, of course, no way of

The mountebank's speech makes it clear, if my reading is correct, that while Jonson's methods of constructing satiric drama have changed, his aims have not. Under cover of the medical metaphor, so typical in satire, the satiric author now offers his play as a purge for the ills of the time. The medicinal properties of his product are no longer concentrated in the railing speeches of a satyr satirist but are present in the entire spectacle he places before us. The materials out of which the mountebank compounds his medicinal oil and the materials out of which Jonson the satiric poet constructs *Volpone* are one and the same:

> All his ingredients
> Are a sheepes gall, a rosted bitches marrow,
> Some few sod earewigs, pounded caterpillers,
> A little capons grease, and fasting spittle.
>
> (ii.6.17–20)

These chunks of matter constitute the underlay, the basic substance of all of Jonson's satiric plays. These are the basic elements, the primal stuff, on which all the swirling life of the plays rests, and the base material which Jonson's alchemists—and all of his characters are in their many vanities alchemists—attempt to transmute into gold.

> . . . materialls
> Of pisse, and egge-shells, womens termes, mans bloud,
> Haire o' the head, burnt clouts, chalke, merds, and clay,
> Poulder of bones, scalings of iron, glasse,

---

determining this. Another possible interpretation of the lines presents itself, however. Since 1599, the year in which *Every Man Out of His Humor* was presented by the Chamberlain's Men, Jonson's plays had been acted with one exception—the unfortunate *Sejanus* which was hissed from the stage—in a "private" theater, Blackfriars, by one of the boy companies. Blackfriars was in the center of the city, "in the face of the publike *piazza*," while the Globe, being on the Bankside, might well be described as an "obscure nooke." Such speculation would, of course, be idle if the other details of the Mountebank's speech did not clearly suggest a biographical element in the lines.

> And worlds of other strange *ingredients,*
> Would burst a man to name.
>
> (The Alchemist II.3.193–8)

This dense substratum is created in the plays not only by
catalogues such as these but by an enormous amount of
incidental reference to a world of unregenerate, roiling
biological substance and mere chemical process. Never in
Jonson's plays are we very far above this world of sodden
ale, pellitory of the wall, fat ram-mutton lying heavy on
the stomach, torsion of the small gut, the scotomy, golden
lard, cramps, convulsions, paralyses, the stranguary, hernia
ventosa, a spoonful of dead wine with flies in it, hot blood,
scalded gums, gobs of phlegm, the swelling unctuous paps
of a fat pregnant sow. This world of chemical process and
layers of organisms exists along side another equally dense
stratum of inanimate things: plate, gold, carbuncles, dia-
monds, gingerbread, tobacco, feathers, wax, and clay.

No amount of quotation can convey the incredible
density of *things* which Jonson rams into his plays, but perhaps a few examples of concentrated references will suggest
the quality he achieves. Here is Captain Otter, in *The
Silent Woman,* describing his wife: "A most vile face! and
yet shee spends me fortie pound a yeere in *mercury,* and
hogs-bones. All her teeth were made i'the Blacke-*Friers:*
both her eye-browes i'the *Strand,* and her haire in *Silver-
street.* . . . She takes her selfe asunder still when she goes
to bed, into some twentie boxes; and about next day noone
is put together againe, like a great *Germane* clocke"
(IV.2.91–9). Or here is another instance of density but in
this case on a more "heroic" level:

> We will be brave, *Puffe,* now we ha' the *med'cine.*
> My meat, shall all come in, in *Indian* shells,
> Dishes of agate, set in gold, and studded,
> With emeralds, saphyres, hiacynths, and rubies.

The tongues of carpes, dormise, and camels heeles,
Boil'd i' the spirit of *Sol,* and dissolv'd pearle,
(*Apicius* diet, 'gainst the *epilepsie*)
And I will eate these broaths, with spoones of amber,
Headed with diamant, and carbuncle.
My foot-boy shall eate phesants, calverd salmons,
Knots, godwits, lamprey's: I my selfe will have
The beards of barbels, serv'd, in stead of sallades;
Oild mushromes; and the swelling unctuous paps
Of a fat pregnant sow, newly cut off,
Drest with an exquisite, and poynant sauce;
For which, Ile say unto my cooke, there's gold,
Goe forth, and be a knight.

                .   .   .   .   .

My shirts
I'll have of taffeta-sarsnet, soft, and light
As cob-webs; and for all my other rayment
It shall be such, as might provoke the *Persian;*
Were he to teach the world riot, a new.
My gloves of fishes, and birds-skins, perfum'd
With gummes of *paradise,* and easterne aire—
                        (*The Alchemist,* II.2.71–94)

Out of materials such as these, organic and inorganic,
Jonson creates in his satiric plays a dense layer of primal
stuff, what Subtle calls "remote matter," or *"materia
liquida,"* existing anterior to any human meaning or purpose. It is important to note, however, that this remote
matter is not treated as inherently hideous and repulsive. It
is raw life full of potential, and as such is exciting. The
phrases and passages in which Jonson describes it, even
when it is being misused by a Volpone or Sir Epicure, are
never merely grotesque, but pulsing, vital, and thoroughly
exciting.

Just above this layer in Jonson's plays, but still existing
only in the form of metaphor and incidental reference, ap-

pear the first forms of complex life, the animal world. On this level the vulture, the raven, the crow, and the flesh-fly hover over the body of the dying, decaying fox, while to one side the parrot (Sir Pol) chatters away, miming those whom he takes for his betters and his models. Here the parrot and monkey parade "with all the little long-coats about him, male and female" (*Bartholomew Fair* 1.4.115–16). The "wel-educated Ape" jumps "over the chaine, for the *King of England* and backe againe for the *Prince,*" but sits "still on his arse for the *Pope,* and the *King* of *Spaine!*" (*Bartholomew Fair,* Induction, lines 17–20). The sub-devil Pug lames a cow, or enters into a sow "to make her cast her farrow" (*The Devil is an Ass,* 1.1.9). This is the world of the pig led forth squealing to slaughter, the flea and the dog-leech sucking blood, the bear or horse at the stake striking out frantically at the savage, snarling dogs, the rat daintily picking its way into the garbage. References to animals are everywhere, the calf, the brach, the horse leech, the boar, the stallion, the cat, the turtle, the mouse, the monkey, the swallow. Only slightly above these animals appear such malformations of humanity as Volpone's dwarf, eunuch, and hermaphrodite. Paralleling the crude arrangements of organic matter into animal forms, we have the equally crude arrangement by man of inorganic matter into compounds, forms, and machines: drums, hobbyhorses, cosmetics, alembics, perpetual motion devices, windmills, elaborate foods, rich clothes, coaches, puppets, weapons, stills, clocks, palaces, money. Human artifacts in these plays are as numerous and most often as devoid of practical purpose or expression of ethical values as the raw materials out of which mankind has ingeniously constructed them to satisfy his animal desires for material display and for conquest of his fellows.

At this point we emerge from the subhuman into the human world, but we are still not at the level of plot and dramatis personae, for at this level we encounter, by means again of indirect reference and metaphor, the vast, busy, noisy world of humankind. The sprawling metropolis of London with its countless numbers of men going about their varied activities is ever present in Jonson's plays. The cooks sweating over their ovens, the glass blowers at their smoky trade, the bell founders casting metal; fishwives, orange-women, broom-men, costard-mongers crying out their wares in the streets; the braziers, armorers, pewterers and other "hammer men" pounding metal on the anvil; Here are the sword-and-buckler man, the tooth-drawer, the juggler, the hobbyhorseman, the horse-courser, the tapster. At one place the Puritan drones a grace "as long as thy tablecloth," while elsewhere the parasite, he who has "your bare town-arte," fawns, fleers, and licks "away a moath" in his nervous efforts to please; the "sonnes of sword and haz-zard," longing for satin cloaks lined with velvet, swagger into Madam Augusta's in their rude homespun and "fall before / The golden calfe, and on their knees, whole nights, / Commit idolatrie with wine, and trumpets!" While the young dandy gathers his "learned counsell" "your *french* taylor, barber, linener" about him in the morning and the lady of fashion excitedly plans to take coach for "Bedlam . . . the China-houses and . . . the Ex-change," the young punk at the fair is being stood on her head "with her Sterne upward" to be "sous'd by my wity young masters o' the *Innes o' Court.*"

The various details on the preceding pages have been drawn from all of Jonson's later satiric plays, but the quality of scenic density which they illustrate is present to an al-most incredible extent in each individual play. This dense mass of life, composed of successive layers of being rising gradually from primal matter into the animal kingdom and then into the town, is the basic scene of Jonson's plays and the background for the plot. It is also, of course, an excellent example of the typical satiric scene, for here is raw life and being, surging, noisy, dense, gross, weighty, and chaotic— the great fair of the world, the field full of folk. Jonson's unparalleled ability to manufacture this hubbub of creation accounts for half of the greatness of his plays; the other half results from his rock-hard, unrelenting moral grasp of this material, his ability to marshal it into significant forms and subject it constantly to the play of ironic wit.

The chemical life, the inert matter, the animals, the men have, in my illustrations, been arranged into a hierarchy of being extending from the lowest and simplest forms of matter and process to the highest and most complex. What I have done, in short, is to take the "stuff" of Jonson's plays and fit it very roughly into its proper place in that all-inclusive and familiar scheme, the great chain of being. But in the actual plays these things and processes are jumbled together in a fantastic mixture, and no one layer ever stands out distinctly from those above and below it. Life in Jonson's plays is not still and at rest at any one point on the great chain, but moves ceaselessly up and down it in an unending cycle of aspiration and fall. We can perhaps best see this by employing one of Jonson's own central metaphors, that of alchemy, as an organizing principle of discussion. In dealing with this movement up and down the ladder of existence we shall necessarily come forward from the scene, which is built up primarily by incidental reference and metaphor, into the world of dramatis personae and plot, the more obvious elements used by the playwright in constructing his dramatic image of the world.

In a very real sense, life in all of Jonson's plays is viewed as a process of alchemy, the transmutation of base matter into gold; and each of the characters is an alchemist attempting to transform himself by means of his particular "philosopher's stone" into some form higher up on the scale of being than the point at which he began. The lady who paints, the young man who dresses himself in silks and feathers, the pedant who pretends to vast amounts of learning, the fool who seems to know all the great men of the world, the amorous fop who sighs after his lady and writes her sugared sonnets, all these are alchemists trying by various means to transmute their base metal into the gold of beauty, learning, sophistication, love. And while their particular "stones" or "elixirs"—cosmetics, books, a grave demeanor—may vary, in the final analysis the ultimate "stone" of all the fools is language. Jonson must have had the most sensitive ear in the kingdom for colloquial speech rhythms, tricks of phrasing, misuse of metaphor, and other verbal peculiarities. His plays are one vast din, a true Babel, where the magniloquent, Messianic tones of a Sir Epicure Mammon and a Volpone, announcing the dawn of a world of unlimited sensuality and joy, mingle with the pious apocalyptic mouthings of Zeal-of-the-Land Busy, the chatter of the Collegiate Ladies discussing books, fashions, and lovers, Subtle's mishmash of alchemical terms, the soaring phrases of business and finance rolled out endlessly by the projector Meerecraft, the lists of Latin authors proudly recited by Sir John Daw. Every character seems to be talking endlessly, seeking—as is actually the case in *The Silent Woman*—to empty the world of all sounds but that of his own voice and create a silence of sameness. This vast flow of language, for all the different tones employed, has, however, a common denominator, for in every case—from the chattering sound of Sir Politic Would-Be's discussion of political plots to the soothing, oily tones of Mosca duping some fool with praises —the intent of the language is an alchemical transformation of the foolish and vicious into something "rich and strange," or of a vulgar, unlawful act into decent and honorable conduct.

A particularly striking instance of this kind of transformation occurs in *The Alchemist* where Subtle finds it

necessary to encourage the Puritans, Tribulation Whole-
some and Ananias, who are waiting impatiently for "projection" to occur. He offers to counterfeit some Dutch
"dollers" for them which will "bide the third examination."
Greedy but cautious, Tribulation asks, "This act of coyning,
is it lawfull?" (III.2.149). Subtle replies, "It is no coyning,
sir. It is but casting." Miraculously, language has transformed an unlawful act into honest labor! and Tribulation
can now exclaim joyfully, "You distinguish well. Casting of
money may be lawfull." Ananias and Tribulation—and all
of Jonson's Puritans—are particularly skilled in this kind
of linguistic alchemy, and their stone is always a greasy piety
expressed in Old Testament language. These two brethren
are in actuality "fences" dealing in stolen goods, and they
are particularly anxious to acquire a basement full of metal
which Face and Subtle have persuaded Sir Epicure Mammon to send them to be turned into gold. This shady deal
is neatly turned into a beneficent and worthy act by verbally
transforming the stolen articles into "widows and orphans
goods," and so careful is Ananias that before he will pay
for the goods he insists on knowing that the orphan's parents
were "sincere professors." In the course of *The Alchemist*
Jonson carries us beyond these particular bits of Puritan
alchemy and depicts the entire Puritan movement as an attempt to transform the base human motives of greed and
desire for political power into piety and religious zeal. The
stones used to create the transmutation are a "holy vizard"
and such

> scrupulous bones,
> As whether a *Christian* may hawke, or hunt;
> Or whether, *Matrons, of the holy assembly,*
> May lay their haire out, or weare doublets:
> Or have that idoll *Starch,* about their linnen.
>
> (III.2.78–82)

Libelling prelates, long graces, railing against plays, lying with "zealous rage," and the use of such names as "Tribulation, Persecution, Restraint, Long-patience" round out the list of stones used by those "as are not graced in a state" to gather a flock and gain power. For the Puritan, of course, these are all but "wayes . . . invented for propagation of the *glorious cause.*"

What the Puritans achieve in their own way, every character in Jonson's plays attempts in some manner, and we might look briefly at the efforts of "projection" in *The Alchemist*. Abel Drugger, "A miserable rogue, and lives with cheese, / And has the worms" (11.6.81–2), wants to be changed into a rich merchant, a man of importance and substance. Since he lacks the imagination to effect the change himself, he turns to Face and Subtle, and the pseudo-alchemists oblige, and construct for him a sign suggesting profound meanings in him:

> He first shall have a bell, that's *Abel;*
> And, by it, standing one, whose name is Dee,
> In a rugg gowne; there's D. and *Rug*, that's *Drug:*
> And, right anenst him, a Dog snarling *Er;*
> There's *Drugger, Abel Drugger.* That's his signe.
> And here's now *mysterie* and *hieroglyphick!*
>
> (11.6.19–24)

The rustic gentleman Kastril is essentially no more than,

> a gentleman newly warme in' his land, sir,
> Scarse cold in' his one and twentie; that do's governe
> His sister, here: and is a man himselfe
> Of some three thousand a yeere, and is come up
> To learne to quarrell, and to live by his wits,
> And will goe downe againe, and dye i'the countrey.
>
> (11.6.57–62)

This fortunate booby, however, wants to be translated into a fashionable swaggerer and a dangerous duelist:

> I have heard some speech
> Of the angrie Boyes, and seene 'hem take *tabacco;*
> And in his shop: and I can take it too.
> And I would faine be one of 'hem, and goe downe
> And practise i'the countrey.
>
> (III.4.21–5)

The simple-minded clerk Dapper wants to become a successful gambler; Dame Pliant, the country widow, wants to be a lady of fashion; and Sir Epicure Mammon, who is ordinarily "a grave sir, a rich, that has no need, / A wise sir, too" (II.3.279–80), desires to be the new messiah of wealth and joy, the man who pronounces to the world "Be Rich!" who will "firk nature up, in her own centre," who will confer "honour, love, respect, long life" on man, and "make an old man of fourscore, a childe."

All of the gulls are momentarily transformed by the rogues who prey on them: Face, Subtle, and Dol Common. These creatures, in turn, do seem in fact to have the true stone for changing base metal into gold in an almost literal sense, for they manage to convert all of the fools and their foolishness into pure gold. The cellar of their house is filled with the money, jewels, and valuable merchandise of which the fools have been bilked. The stone which Face, Subtle, and Dol possess is knowledge of man's greed, egoism, and gullibility, and they turn this knowledge into profit. But the rogues, enormously successful though they are, are finally themselves imposters whose magnificent command of language and supreme ability to shift from disguise to disguise, making themselves in each case just what the gulls desire them to be, are only covers and overlays on their unregenerate animal natures. Dol Common may pretend to be Queen of the Fairies and the mad sister of a great nobleman—and significantly enough she may be taken for such by the gulls—but she remains always no more than a "smock rampant." Subtle may appear most reverent, grave,

wise, and stuffed with erudition and arcane knowledge, but
he remains no more than the poor creature described by
Face:

> at *pie-corner,*
> Taking your meale of steeme in, from cookes stalls,
> Where, like the father of hunger, you did walke
> Piteously costive, with your pinch'd-horne-nose,
> And your complexion, of the *romane* wash,
> Stuck full of black, and melancholique wormes,
> Like poulder-cornes, shot, at th'*artillerie-yard.*
>
> (1.1.25–31)

And Face, though the most cunning of the lot, for all of his
masks of the gorgeous and magniloquent Captain, or the
humble Lungs, the alchemist's assistant, is still no more
than Jeremy the butler with his petty schemes for getting a
few pounds by selling "the dole-beere to *aqua-vitae* men,"
and "letting out of counters" (1.1.51–6).

The characters of Jonson's other plays are also involved
in similar attempts to raise themselves from the poor things
which they essentially are into something magnificent and
important. Each desires to be "the sole sir of the world"—
Cleopatra's description of Octavius—and the limits of aspiration are set only by the limits of the imagination of each
character. A Bartholomew Cokes wants only to see all the
strange sights of the fair, and a Littlewit wants only to have
his puppet show admired and acclaimed, but a Fitzdottrell
wants to raise devils and drain the English Fens. Morose
wants to silence all the noise and bustle of human activity
and empty the world of all sounds save that of his own voice.
Sir Epicure Mammon reaches out for all knowledge, all
power, all pleasure:

> For I doe meane
> To have a list of wives, and concubines,
> Equal with *Salomon;* who had the *stone*

Alike, with me: and I will make me, a back
With the *elixir,* that shall be as tough
As *Hercules,* to encounter fiftie a night.

.   .   .   .   .

I will have all my beds, blowne up; not stuft:
Downe is too hard. And then, mine oval roome,
Fill'd with such pictures, as *Tiberius* tooke
From *Elephantis:*

.   .   .   .   .

I'll ha' no bawds,
But fathers, and mothers. They will doe it best.
Best of all others. And, my flatterers
Shall be the pure, and gravest of Divines,
That I can get for money.

(II.2.34–61)

Volpone stretches out his hand toward absolute sensuality and freedom from the limitations of shape, place,
and time imposed on all mortals by their very nature. He
is speaking here to Celia and creating for her the world in
which he proposes that they shall live:

Thy bathes shall be the juyce of july-flowres,
Spirit of roses, and of violets,
The milke of unicornes, and panthers breath
Gather'd in bagges, and mixt with *cretan* wines.

.   .   .   .   .

my dwarf shall dance,
My eunuch sing, my foole make up the antique.
Whil'st, we, in changed shapes, act *Ovids* tales,
Thou, like *Europa* now, and I like *Jove,*
Then I like *Mars,* and thou like *Erycine,*
So, of the rest, till we have quite run through
And weary'd all the fables of the gods.
Then will I have thee in more moderne formes,
Attired like some sprightly dame of *France,*

Brave *Tuscan* lady, or proud Spanish beauty;
Sometimes, unto the *Persian Sophies* wife;
Or the grand-*Signiors* mistresse.

(III.7.213–30)

Where Volpone only hopes that he will have this alchemical freedom to pass through all shapes and forms, Mosca believes that he has achieved it, for he thinks of himself as a

fine, elegant rascall, that can rise,
And stoope (almost together) like an arrow;
Shoot through the aire, as nimbly as a starre;
Turne short, as doth a swallow; and be here,
And there, and here, and yonder, all at once;
Present to any humour, all occasion;
And change a visor, swifter, then a thought!

(III.1.23–9)

Jonson's characters are all satiric portraits of Renaissance aspiration, of the belief that man can make anything he will of himself and of his world, that he can storm heaven and become one with the gods, or make of earth a new paradise. Human nature and "remote matter" are considered by Jonson's characters—as they are by the characters of Elizabethan tragedy—as endlessly plastic and therefore subject to the alchemical process. Their dream of life is as spacious and as free of any limiting concept of reality as that of a modern Madison Avenue advertising copywriter who with a flash of the pen and a few colors changes toilet paper into mink, an internal combustion engine into the winged horse Pegasus, a rubber girdle into beauty, and a deodorant into popularity. But in Jonson's plays these dreams are never allowed to float entirely free of earth; they remain always solidly anchored to reality. And the reality is that dense substratum of primal matter, the materia liquida, which is everywhere present in the plays and constantly provides an ironic comment on these men who would soar out of their humanity. This is not to say, of course, that Jonson shows man as potentially no more than beast, or suggests that he must always remain no more than a collection of "haire o' the head, burnt clouts, chalke, merds, and clay." Alchemy remains a possibility, but a possibility with very definite limits. The trick lies in getting hold of the right stone, the true elixir.

In *The Alchemist* there are several references to the ancient tradition that the stone can only be discovered by the truly moral man,

> *homo frugi,*
> A pious, holy, and religious man,
> One free from mortall sinne, a very virgin.
>
> (II.2.97–9)

The stone itself is described, in accordance with the traditional lore of alchemy, as,

> The art of *Angels,* Natures miracle,
> The *divine secret,* that doth flye in clouds,
> From *east to west:* and whose tradition
> Is not from men, but spirits.
>
> (III.2.103–6)

These lines are Subtle's, and he is, of course, simply pouring out alchemical jargon, but the lines have a significance of which he is totally unaware. They point to a different conception of alchemy and the nature of the stone than that held by the characters of the play. The stone is immanent in the world "from east to west," it is resident in "nature," and it is insubstantial for it belongs to angels, flies in the clouds, and comes from spirits. All of this suggests that the true stone is moral and spiritual, and that man can only be made from beast by the exercise of his moral nature. But the fools with whom Jonson has stuffed his scene are all gross materialists tied so closely to the world of solid substantial things that they can conceive of nothing that is not either a thing or a sensation. This heavy realism finds brilliant expression from time to time in such expressions as Volpone's satisfied remark after drinking a cup of wine, "This heate is life," or Sir Epicure's invitation to Dol Common to "enjoy a perpetuitie of life, and lust."

The determined literalism and single-minded sensuality of Jonson's characters is the source of an ever widening series of ironies which provides both the humor of the plays and ultimately the moral comment on the characters and their activities. On the simplest level it is, of course, the willingness of the various characters to accept the apparent for the real that makes them immediately ridiculous. Just as they believe that the stone will "really" turn iron to gold, so they will accept Subtle as a genuine alchemist, Dol Common as Queen of the Fairies, the parasite Mosca as a true friend, or the Bible-quoting Zeal-of-the-Land Busy as a genuine saint. What the fools will do for others they will, of course, do for themselves, and so the young fop believes that he only has to dress in the latest styles to become a gentleman of fashion, the lady that she only has to be seen in the right company and at the right places to be distinguished and honorable, the pedant that he only has to spout enough inkhorn terms and drop the names of enough Latin authors to be learned.

This ready acceptance of what seems for what is leads inevitably to a fantastic mangling of language, and the fools usually reveal most tellingly the inadequacy of their views of reality by their insensitivity to words. Thus Sir John Daw includes among the list of authors with whom he claims to be familiar *Syntagma Iuris civilis, Corpus Iuris civilis, Corpus Iuris canonici,* the King of *Spaines* bible" (*Silent Woman,* II.3.81–2). Clearly, Sir John takes any words appearing on the title page of a book to be authors' names. The punning of John Littlewit in *Bartholomew Fair* is intended to show his cleverness, but reveals his plodding mind: "One o' the pretty wits o' *Pauls*, the *Little wit* of London (so thou art call'd) and some thing beside. When a quirk, or a *quiblin* do's scape thee, and thou dost not watch, and apprehend it, and bring it afore the Constable of conceit: (there now, I speake *quib* too) let 'hem carry thee out o' the Archdeacons Court, into his Kitchin, and make a *Jack* of thee, in stead of a John. (There I am againe la!)" (1.1.12–18). This kind of earthbound nonsense has more serious overtones when it appears in the speech of one of the more important characters. For example, the opening speech of *Volpone* is a mock aubade in which Volpone greets not the day but his "sacred gold" and praises it in this manner:

> Well did wise Poets, by thy glorious name,
> Title that age, which they would have the best.

The reference is, of course, to the Golden Age, but Volpone in his literal-mindedness has completely missed the fact that "Golden" has a metaphorical and spiritual value, not a literal one. The Golden Age was, in fact, so titled because, in this primitive Eden existence, men had no gold or precious metals. In each of his plays, Jonson uses this technique of revealing the limitations of his characters' views of reality through the limitations of their literal and purely denotative use of language. By and large his fools, both great and small, are men who cannot understand metaphor.

This verbal literalness from which much of the plays' humor derives ultimately provides an implicit evaluation of all the frantic human activity in them. If the characteristic action of Jonson's characters is "to become a god," or "to transmit base metal into gold," then the fundamental irony is that each of the characters in striving to be more than man always reduces himself to less than man. Because he can conceive of alchemy—i.e. "progress"—in no other than literal terms, because he can measure value only by gold and by physical sensation, a Volpone, a Sir Epicure, or a Fitzdottrell always by his very efforts to rise above himself drives himself down the scale of being and back into the world of process, mere organism, and mechanics. Every fop who places an ostrich feather in his hat, thinking thereby to become a fine man, announces his return to the world of the ostrich, and every lady who paints over her natural face to become beautiful succeeds only in manifesting that she is no more than the cosmetics she applies and that her "life" is mere chemistry. In the passage quoted earlier, in which Captain Otter describes his wife and all her aids to beauty as amounting to no more than "a great Germane clocke," we can see a creature who in her attempt to become a great beauty has reduced herself to mere mechanism. And in Sir Epicure Mammon's description of the jewels with which he will surround himself, the fantastic and exotic animals he will consume, the rich stuffs and skins in which he will be clothed, we see a man slipping back into the same "remote matter" out of which he thinks he is hoisting himself. Every mask or disguise, whether of language or vizard, becomes in this way a revelation of true character, and the commenting function of the satirist in formal verse satire is performed by the language of the fools themselves. Where he describes them as animals and machines they now, unawares, present themselves as such.

Just as the moral commentary is provided in Jonson's plays by this indirect method, so the "ideal" is stated in the same manner. There are a few instances of virtue in Jonson's plays, a few characters who seem to represent something approaching a humane ideal, standing isolated in the middle of the satiric scene. But each of these characters is suspect in some way. Celia and Bonario, the virtuous wife and virtuous son in *Volpone*, are a bit too good to be true in their pristine morality and their wooden speeches. Here

is Bonario after his father has just accused him in court of
being a liar, a thief, and an intended murderer:

> Sir, I will sit downe,
> And rather wish my innocence should suffer,
> Then I resist the authority of a father.
>
> (IV.5.112–14)

Characters such as Bonario form a pleasant contrast to the
depraved world in which they find themselves, and occasionally a line like Celia's heartbroken exclamation at the
villainy she has seen, "I would I could forget, I were a
creature" (IV.5.102) rings true; but on the whole these examples of virtue are too placid and lifeless to save themselves or make us very concerned about whether they are
saved. Their virtue is as mechanical as the villainy and
foolishness of the corrupt characters. Jonson often presents
another and more effective type of virtue, the "Truewit,"
and while it is clear that these witty and intelligent characters who are not too depraved often serve as "heroes" in
the plays, it is equally clear that wit alone is not held up as
a moral ideal and the hope of the world. Lovewit in *The
Alchemist,* Dauphine and Clerimont in *The Silent Woman,*
Quarlous in *Bartholomew Fair,* and Wittipol in *The Devil
is an Ass* are all attractive and far preferable to either the
complete fools or the clever schemers around them. Life
might at least continue if the world were made up of these
Truewits—as it would not if the world were given over to
the monsters and fools—but it would never achieve the
status of a civilization.

The absence of any truly reputable hero combining both
wit and moral virtue in Jonson's plays suggests that while
the alchemical miracle of transforming man into saint
might be accomplished by *homo frugi,* the man "free from
mortal sin," such men do not exist. At his best, Jonson's

man, like Shakespeare's, gets "a little soil'd in th' working." But if man in himself and by his own virtue lacks the stone in these satirical comedies, he does not entirely lack the means to raise himself above the level of mere thing. The ideal, the true stone available to man, is—as in Shakespeare's comedies—compliance with the dictates of Nature as they are manifested in society with its customs, institutions, and traditions. The plays, of course, present us with a spectacle of the breakdown of society and a near return to primitive chaos. The husband sells his wife to a hideous, dying man for hope of gold; the father accuses a son of plotting his murder; judges are more interested in the position and wealth of a man before them than in the justice of his case; the lawyer pleads for his own gain; a wife is locked away from the world and the "bawdy light"; wives beat their husbands and maintain separate establishments where they can entertain lovers, and avoid the consequences by employing drugs and abortionists. Jonson, like all great satirists, concentrates on the sensitive areas of social life, both public and private, and shows the distortion and infection produced in each place and relationship by the desire to be the "sole sir of the world."

The opening speech of *Volpone* is a masterful example of Jonson's indirect method of establishing the ideals of nature and society as moral reference points, while at the same time revealing their present state of corruption. Volpone hails his gold as "the worlds soule, and mine"; says he is more glad to see it than "the teeming earth, to see the long'd-for sunne"; joyfully remarks that gold darkens the sun by comparison, and that it is like "the day strooke out of *chaos*"; refers to it as a "saint" and a "relique"; and joyfully exclaims that possession of gold is a pleasure

> far transcending
> All stile of joy, in children, parents, friends,
> Or any other waking dreame on earth.

Every detail here, every metaphor that Volpone uses literally and without comprehending its meaning, cuts in the opposite direction and advises us of the vital sources of meaningful existence which he and his gold have perverted: the soul, the sun bringing life to the world, the order of civilization, religion, and human relationships.

The restoration of these values, the return to reality from illusion, is the business of the plot, and it is in his management of the plot that Jonson reveals his leanings toward comedy. The satiric elements in Jonson's comical satires—and those of Middleton, Marston, and other authors of this type of play—are concentrated in the portraits of the fools and the scenes in which they display their various brands of idiocy and vice. But for all their numbers as they pour down on London at Michaelmas Term, swirl about at Bartholomew Fair, or congregate to discuss some grandiose schemes such as draining the English Fens or turning all the base metal of the world into gold, the foolish and vicious never prevent the continuation of civilized life. They do, of course, by their greed, their lust, their waste, their intolerant zeal, and their sheer stupidity interfere with the operation of those virtues and social forms which are both the subject matter and the ideals of comedy and satire: marriage, procreation, education of the young, tolerance of others, and provision of the necessaries of life for all. But in these comical satires social health and the balance of nature are always restored, not by the heroic activities of a scourging satirist, but by a natural process. Just as there are always enough redheaded woodpeckers who have a taste for downy caterpillars, so there are always just enough sharpers to prey on the fools and render them harmless; and the fools because they are fools attract their natural enemies and feed them fat. In turn these sharpers can be counted on to eat up one another, for in the comic world every Volpone has his Mosca and every Subtle his Face.

But while it is true that Jonson's plots tend toward the comic, it is equally true that in some cases at least there is a lingering suggestion of the satiric in them, as if Jonson were unwilling to provide his material with a fully triumphant comic conclusion. Northrop Frye describes the basic comic plot in this way: "In the first place, the movement of comedy is usually a movement from one kind of society to another. At the beginning of the play the obstructing characters are in charge of the play's society, and the audience recognizes that they are usurpers. At the end of the play the device in the plot that brings hero and heroine together causes a new society to crystallize around the hero, and the moment when this crystallization occurs is the point of resolution in the action, the comic discovery, *anagnorisis* or *cognitio*." [9] A large number of Jonson's plays lack the romantic hero and heroine referred to in this passage, but I take it that comedy may employ as an image of its values other types of plots than the ultimate reunion of two lovers who have been separated by some unnatural force in the form of either an individual or social custom. Thus, in *The Silent Woman* comic values find expression in the failure of old Morose in his related attempts to prevent his young nephew Dauphine from inheriting his money and to silence all the noise of a busy world. It would seem that the basic comic ideals of growth, development, change, and vitality can be stated in a wide variety of terms in the comic plot and that the romantic love affair is only one of these terms, though certainly the most common one in English comedy.

Once we recognize that comedy employs a large number of plot situations, we can make use of Frye's description of the standard comic plot to test the degree of the comic in Jonson's plays. The essential point of Frye's theory is that comedy moves inevitably toward the elimination of the unhealthy, the disabling, the sterile elements in society, and

9. *Anatomy of Criticism*, p. 163.

that this movement culminates in the creation of a new and healthier society serving the realistic needs of its people. Elsewhere Frye adds that "the tendency of comedy is to include as many people as possible in its final society: the blocking characters are more often reconciled or converted than simply repudiated." [1] This sounds very much like Jonson's own early comic formula, Every Man Out of His Humour, and a large number of Jonson's plays have plots of this kind. In *The Silent Woman,* for example, Morose, with his antisocial passion for absolute quiet and his equally antisocial refusal to allow his nephew to have any money, is so badgered and tricked that by the end of the play he is driven out of his humor—along with the other fools—and a new society forms around Dauphine. Here, and in *Bartholomew Fair* and the plays following it there is something approaching a tone of reconciliation at the end, though the various fools are always scourged and cursed in a harsh manner more reminiscent of satire than comedy.

But in *Volpone* and *The Alchemist,* though the plot moves toward the purging of society, and the usual satiric stasis is not allowed to prevail, there is no final reconciliation. In *Volpone* the disturbing or sick characters, rather than being incorporated in the new society, are either driven out or imprisoned. Mosca is whipped and sent to the galleys for life, Volpone is loaded with irons and sent to the hospital for the *Incurabili,* Voltore is disbarred and banished, Corbaccio is stripped of his wealth and confined to a monastery, and Corvino is forced to send his wife home to her father while he himself is rowed about the canals, with a pair of horns pinned on him, to be pelted with rotten fruit by the citizens. Such a conclusion is both appropriate and satisfying, for in each case these villains and fools have finally, despite their slipperiness and their protean ability to change shape at will, been forced into their

1. Ibid., p. 165.

true forms: a slave, an incurably sick man (in a metaphorical sense), an outlaw without a profession or city, a pauper, and a civic joke. But there is in this conclusion none of the secure pleasure, none of the feeling that vitality and good sense have triumphed once again, that we usually find in comedy. That the victory is in some ways a sterile one is suggested by the fate of Celia. In a true comedy she would marry some younger, more vital member of the society; and her marriage would signalize the restoration of the city to a condition of healthy vitality. But in *Volpone* this potential comic heroine is returned to the home of her father and her vital possibilities are thwarted. Similarly, the enormous energy and braininess of figures such as Volpone and Mosca are wasted, for the city can find no way to turn these powers into useful channels. Nor can even the less sinister fools be recovered. Viciousness and idiocy, the play states through its plot, are incorrigible and can only be chained up, for, once loose, such is their energy that they will soon control the city again. *The Alchemist* moves toward a similar conclusion, for, in the end, while fool after fool is tricked and shamed and sent away with a verbal whipping, there is no sense of a better and more stable society having evolved. The master trickster, Face, has simply combined with his equally tricky master, Lovewit, to outwit the greedy idiots and carry off the spoils; and one of the spoils is the vapid Dame Pliant, the wealthy widow who, ironically enough, fills the part of the comic heroine.

Neither *Volpone* nor *The Alchemist* contains that savage despair and sense of utter frustration expressed in the plots of the blackest kinds of satire, for willy-nilly Jonson's world does right itself each time, not through any virtue immanent in man, not by the clever activity and opportunism of a single hero, not through the intervention of a beneficent, supernatural Nature,[2] not through the effectiveness

2. The nature referred to here is that mystical healing power which so

of society and its laws—the usual restorative forces in comedy—but merely by a defect inherent in vice and folly which leads them to overreach themselves. If the plots of these plays do not fit the satiric formula of an endless round of purpose and passion, neither do they quite fit the comic formula of an irresistible and joyous triumph of vitality and reality over death and illusion in which the perverted elements of society are salvaged and included in the brave new world. In *The Alchemist* and *Volpone* Jonson came very close to creating pure satire of the Menippean kind, and, once again, it is perhaps not very profitable to try to decide whether these plays are either satire or comedy in an absolute and exclusive sense.

Jonson's practice in his plays after 1604 set the pattern for comical satire for a generation to come. Marston, Middleton, Shirley, Beaumont and Fletcher, and Brome all seized upon Jonson's methods of construction and his solution of the problem of presenting satiric comment on the follies of the age without trying to manage the unruly satyr satirist. While Jonson was solving this problem in comical satire, other dramatists were attempting to fit the same difficult satirist into satiric plays expressing a darker view of human vice and folly, and it is to this "tragical satire" that we must now turn to complete our history of the career of the satyr satirist.

---

often operates in the comic world, not the nature of physical law and mechanical operation. The Nature which moves through Shakespeare's *The Winter's Tale* is a good example of the first meaning of the word, while the concluding moral of *Volpone,* spoken by one of the corrupt judges, expresses very clearly the second meaning:

Mischiefes feed
Like beasts, till they be fat, and then they bleed.

Both of these "natures" are present in Jonson's plays, but the first Nature never interferes with the acts of men. It is present in man and the world to be utilized and realized, but it remains a potentiality for men to strive for. For an interesting dramatic treatment of this idea see *The Alchemist,* II.3.121 ff., where Surly and Subtle debate whether alchemy is natural.

CHAPTER 5

TRAGICAL SATIRE

After a particularly elevated passage describing the Roman matron's habit of poisoning a husband with whom she becomes bored, Juvenal's satirist pauses to remark that while Satire may now appear to be wearing the tragic boot and declaiming a grand theme in Sophoclean tones, murder has become so commonplace in Rome that it is a fitting subject for a genre which ordinarily deals with fools rather than villains and with follies rather than crimes.[1] Though the lines are clearly ironic, they also provide a justification for the Juvenalian type of satire in which the satirist seems always on the verge of stepping over onto tragic ground. If the world is totally depraved and such great crimes as murder and incest are ordinary practice, then the follies with which satire usually sports are mere foibles unworthy of serious discussion. In this potentially tragic world the satirist will be required to show sterner virtues and employ more vicious methods of correction than are needed by the satirist who works in less dangerous surroundings.

The Elizabethans were well aware of the close relation of satire to tragedy. Some critics thought that satire had its origins in tragedy, and John Milton could remind his readers that "a Satyr as it was borne out of a *Tragedy,* so ought to resemble his parentage, to strike high, and adventure

1. Satire vi, lines 634–40.

dangerously at the most eminent vices among the greatest persons, and not to creepe into every blinde Taphouse that fears a Constable more then a Satyr." [2] John Marston, probably taking his cue from Juvenal, could warn his Muse after an attack on a Machiavel not to venture on tragic ground:

> Bold-faced Satire, strain not over-high,
> But laugh and chuck at meaner gullery.
> (*Pigmalion*, II, 105–6)

The attraction of the tragic for the Elizabethan authors of formal satire is evident in their choice of sensational subject matter, their use of certain features of the high style, and their frequent references to the "high flight" of their satires or to the fact that their Muse stalks "a loftier gate than Satyres use." This interest in the tragic aspects of satire found full expression in the satiric scene, the satirist, and the plots of some of the new satiric plays.

The same types of fools are usually present in these plays: the dissolute courtier, the rack-rent landlord, the cuckold, the fop, the epicure, and the empty-headed, gullible, immoral ladies of fashion who care only for new lovers, new clothes, and new gossip. But these characters are given a sinister turn, and mixed among them are more dangerous types: the flatterer, the Machiavel, the parasite, the traitor, and men whose lust and greed are cast in a heroic mold. The fools become the instruments of the villains, and the stakes of the struggle are now life, thrones, honor, power. The scene is no longer the London street or the houses of the well-to-do, but more perilous and mysterious places. The fools and villains now crowd in threatening masses on the plains of Troy, or press in on the remnants of virtue in the palace of Tiberius. The satirist finds himself isolated in the symbolic setting of the desert after he has banished

2. "An Apology for Smectymnuus," p. 329.

himself from Athens, or he makes his way about the dark "Italian lascivious palace." Our surest method of finding our way into this world of tragic satire is, again, to follow the fortunes of the satirist.

Although Thersites, the satirist of Shakespeare's *Troilus and Cressida* (1601), is a joke to Agamemnon, he is at the same time the most intense image of the satiric character in all Elizabethan literature. He is composed only of those fundamental energies that drive the satirist, energies which in him are allowed to go unchecked until they arrive at absolute pride in self and absolute loathing of all other creatures. To Thersites the Trojan War is a simple matter: "All the argument is a whore and cuckold." [3] Human love and suffering are no more than "Lechery, lechery, still wars and lechery." Troilus is a "young Trojan ass that loves the whore"; Diomedes, a "Greekish whoremasterly villain"; Cressida, a "dissembling, luxurious drab"; Nestor, an "old-mouse-eaten dry cheese"; Ulysses, a "dog-fox." Thersites' most common criticism of other men is that they are stupid: Agamemnon "has not so much brain as ear-wax," Ajax is "beef-witted," all who hold power are either young fools or old ones who have so little wit that they cannot "deliver a fly from a spider without drawing the massy irons and cutting the web." By contrast, Thersites regards himself as subtle and intelligent, though his scheming has no other end but self-glorification and gets him nothing but beatings. Thus, his conception of the scene before the gates of Troy is identical to the setting of formal satire: a single sane and sensible man stands isolated before a totally depraved world ruled by ignorance. His reactions to this situation are typical of the satirist. He moves frantically from one victim to the next "lost in the labyrinth of . . . fury," railing at anyone and everyone he encounters. His speeches are a cascade of venom in which epithet is piled on epithet

3. II.3.77–8.

to the point where language seems insufficient to convey his
hatred. He seems always to be straining for some final in-
sult, some phrase which will obliterate his victims and completely express his hatred. He uses the usual satiric images
of disease, decay, bodily functions, and animals in such a
concentrated manner that they form the body and substance
of his speeches. Men are peacocks, ticks, sheep, bulls, goats,
water flies, asses, oxen. They have, or should have if Thersites had his way, the bone-ache, leprosy, sore eyes, itch,
scabs, red murrain. His speeches are larded with references
to fustiness, decay and moldering; and he concentrates his
attention on the bones, the belly, the guts, the bowels, the
sinews, the blood. The world is no more than a dungheap
to Thersites, and the intensity with which he describes its
decay suggests the satirist's usual compulsive hatred, mixed
with an unhealthy fascination, for the degenerating body.
When we first meet Thersites he is lovingly exploring the
possible diseases that Agamemnon might have. So lost is
he in his own weak puns and rapt visions of the particulars
and course of a disease, that he is not aware of Ajax until
that dullard strikes him:

> *Ajax.* Thersites!
> *Ther.* Agamemnon—how if he had biles—full, all
> over, generally?
> *Ajax.* Thersites!
> *Ther.* And those biles did run?—say so? Did not the
> general run then? Were not that a botchy core?
> *Ajax.* Dog!
> *Ther.* Then would come some matter from him. I see
> none now.
>
> (II.1.1–10)

On one occasion only does Thersites attempt to justify
his poisonous attacks by explaining, in the accepted satiric
fashion, that he is the surgeon using strong means to treat

a violent disease. Speaking of how Achilles and Patroclus may run mad with "too much blood and too little brain" he says, "but if with too much brain and too little blood they do [run mad], I'll be a curer of madmen" (v.1.52–6). But this formula is tossed off in a moment and no more is heard of it. Other characters attribute his virulence to envy, another standard motive, and Thersites admits to being envious (ii.3.21–2). But these conventional motives are no more than rationalizations for Thersites, and the true source of his satire appears to lie in some dark complex of pride, frustration, and loathing. In some ways it is as futile to try to explain why Thersites rails as it is to search for the logical reasons why Iago, who resembles him in many ways, intrigues. Thersites is a malevolent force, a type of primal hatred and pride, and what Shakespeare has done is to take the conventional character of the satirist and strip away his pretensions to being a moral healer and intensify his basic loathing of all mankind. In Thersites we are very close to those basic drives and outlook which give rise to satire, and which in this case are not redirected by any extraneous moral considerations or glossed over by any pretension to justice and honesty. Where other satirists use metaphors of disease to describe the moral infirmities of their age, Thersites often works in the mode of the primitive satirist who, using sympathetic magic, called down infections on men and blasted parts of the body by naming them. He invokes the "bone-ache" on men "who war for a placket," and curses Patroclus in the formulaic manner of earlier enchanter satirists, "Now the rotten diseases of the South, the guts-griping ruptures, catarrhs, loads o' gravel i' th' back, lethargies, cold palsies, raw eyes . . . take and take again such preposterous discoveries!" (v.1.20–8).

Thersites' view of the world as a writhing mass of decaying flesh where power is no more than muscle moved by stupidity, his proud exemption of himself from this muddle, and his railing and curses are all extreme forms of typical satiric points of view and activities; but in *Troilus and Cressida* they are but one perspective on, and one way of dealing with, a confusing and turbulent world. Despite certain structural and tonal similarities to the new dramatic satires, *Troilus and Cressida* is not finally a satiric play. That is, very simply, it is not in the end an attack on any specific attitudes or modes of conduct. It is rather an exploration, a deeply pessimistic one, of the validity of certain attitudes and modes of conduct, those connected with the very human activities of love and war. Many of these attitudes are revealed as illogical, brutal, or unrealistic, but they are not derided and judged by any implicit or explicit moral standard. Instead, they are presented as various human attempts to deal with and identify the titanic forces of history and passion—woven together here in the rape of Helen and the Trojan War—which involve men and carry them forward to their fates. The men and women thus caught up are not very attractive: they are schemers, panderers, whores, weaklings, braggarts, dunces, politicians. But there is nothing they can do about it, and their ruins are no mere satiric object lessons, as are the falls of Jonson's Sejanus and Catiline, but a pitiful demonstration of human weakness and ineffectuality.

Thersites' realistic perspective—"all the argument is a whore and a cuckold"—his evaluation of man as no more than a stupid animal, and his curses are in the long run no more efficacious in diagnosing and treating the sickness of the world than is the professional-soldier approach of Hector, the death-before-dishonor approach of Troilus, or the philosopher-statesman approach of Ulysses. But the latter are superior to the satirist's way in several respects. They are at least serious attempts to understand the world and meet it squarely, and not the projections of an infected mind; and they permit their adherents to preserve some honor, courage, and dignity in defeat and death, while the satirist Thersites turns coward and acknowledges himself a "bastard"—i.e. an unnatural man—to save his miserable life in the confused melee that concludes the play and destroys all virtues and values except courage. This world is more terrible than any ever pictured by a satirist, and in its dark and mysterious depths the small-souled satirist with his comparatively simple perspective is inadequate in every way.

In *Timon of Athens* (c. 1605) Shakespeare again turned his attention to the satiric sense of life and the satiric character developed in the new satire. But *Timon* takes quite a different direction than does *Troilus,* for here the satiric character occupies the center of the stage and the play is primarily a search for the causes of this diseased outlook. Where Thersites is simply a given, a dark energy who has no final explanation, Timon the satirist is a mutation, a distortion of a nature which was originally one of love and generosity. The play is the most penetrating analysis ever made of the satiric sense of life, and so is of interest to us not only because of its place in the history of the satirist in Elizabethan and Jacobean drama, but because of its bearing on our general argument, the nature of satire.

Timon is written in a symbolic or allegorical mode. There are realistic incidents and occasional speeches which ring true to life in the most immediate sense, but on the whole the characters change attitudes so rapidly and are such pure expressions of love or hate or greed, without subtle nuances and shadings, that they seem to be more symbols than men. Similarly, the situations and scenes are so obviously contrived and arranged as to suggest a morality play. When we first see Timon he is surrounded by wealth, by pleasure, and by joy. "We are lost in a riot of display, a gold-mist of romance and pleasures of the senses. The setting is brilliant, the wealth apparently inexhaustible, the pleasures free. We can imagine the rich food and wine, the blare and clash of music, embraces, laughter, and passages of glancing love; the coursing of blood, the flushed cheek, the mask of fair dancers and Cupid." [4] Presiding over this feast of pleasure is Timon whose generosity brings it into existence. He ransoms a friend from prison, is the patron of the arts, raises a faithful servant to a position where he can marry, showers his friends with rich gifts. His bounty has preserved the Athenian state and every citizen has at one time received favors from him. The banquet itself sums up the situation in symbolic terms: Timon is host and all Athens is his guest. The banquet is the feast of earthly love, of generosity, of human society, and Timon is the incarnate spirit of love itself, the divine energy that makes society possible by raising man above the level of beast. He expresses the ideal which he embodies with striking simplicity, "We are born to do benefits" (1.2.105).

This golden world cannot last. Timon has, to borrow his own image, tried to give man love in the symbolic form of gold as generously as the moon floods the dark with light; but unlike the moon he has no sun to replenish his stores. When his money is gone, mankind turns on him; for them his gifts have been not symbols of love but simply hard cash, and, acting according to the dictates of "policy," they reject him. His reaction is violent, and his hate now becomes as powerful as his love has been. He is transformed into a railing satirist who curses the world as indiscriminately as he once blessed it. After giving a mock feast, a feast of hate which expresses his new attitude, he turns on his "mouth-friends" and denounces them in true satiric fashion:

> Live loath'd, and long,
> Most smiling smooth, detested parasites,

4. G. Wilson Knight, *The Wheel of Fire* (New York, Meridian, 1957), p. 209.

Courteous destroyers, affable wolves, meek bears,
You fools of fortune, trencher friends, time's flies,
Cap-and-knee slaves, vapours, and minute-jacks!
Of man and beast the infinite malady
Crust you quite o'er!

.   .   .   .   .

Burn house! Sink Athens! Henceforth hated be
Of Timon man and all humanity!

(III.6.103–15)

In his rage for truth and his desire to escape hypocrisy,
Timon tears off his clothes and leaves Athens and society
for the wilderness, where he subsists on roots, berries, and
anger. He is now the true image of man as the satirist perceives him, and he becomes the heroic denouncer of vice.
His war against mankind is not a war of correction, for
he does not believe correction possible since man is entirely
bestial. He hopes only to strip away pretensions, to destroy
hypocrisy. When he discovers gold again he uses it to urge
the men who flock to him once more to wage open warfare
on their fellows. The women are paid to become absolute
whores to sow consumptions "in hollow bones of man,"
and by giving man the bodily pox make evident the in-
visible moral infection of the mind. The soldier Alcibiades
is paid to destroy all Athenians, who are entitled, Timon
says, to no pity because in reality they are all bawds, usurers,
and bastards. The thieves are paid to "do villainy . . .
like workmen" because all men are no more than thieves
who work "in holier shape."

No profession, no station escapes Timon's scathing tongue,
but his boundless hatred transcends mere man and extends
to nature itself:

The sun's a thief, and with his great attraction
Robs the vast sea. The moon's an arrant thief,

And her pale fire she snatches from the sun.
The sea's a thief, whose liquid surge resolves
The moon into salt tears. The earth's a thief,
That feeds and breeds by a composture stol'n
From gen'ral excrement. Each thing's a thief.

(IV.3.439–45)

This is saeva indignatio raised to heroic proportions,
and in Timon's titanic loathing of the world there is a
romantic grandeur which is emphasized by contrast with
two other satirists in the play. The Poet is one of the mouth-
friends who returns to Timon on hearing that he once
again has gold. Earlier the sycophantic Poet wrote elaborate
allegories, but now that Timon has turned misanthrope,
he suits his work to the patron's mood and proposes to
write "a satire against the softness of prosperity, with a
discovery of the infinite flatteries that follow youth and
opulency" (v.1.36–8). This is the basest kind of satirist, one
who writes only for money, and no doubt many of the
satiric poems and plays we have discussed were written for
this reason only. Apemantus, the second satirist, is a bitter
cynic who sees through all pretensions and rails at all he
encounters. His world is the usual satiric scene:

Who lives that's not depraved or depraves?
Who dies that bears not one spurn to their graves
Of their friends' gift?

(1.2.145–7)

His view of human history is the usual one of steady degeneration to the animal state, "The strain of man's bred
out into baboon and monkey" (1.1.259–60). Yet he goes
out among the men he loathes "to see meat fill knaves and
wine heat fools," and to curse those he watches because
he enjoys cursing. He seeks Timon out in the wilderness,
and when asked why, Apemantus replies, "To vex thee."
Timon then asks him, "Dost please thyself in it?" and

Apemantus answers directly, "Ay" (IV.3.236–8). Apemantus'
pleasure in railing is obvious, but this is a rare moment of
honesty, and elsewhere he offers the conventional reasons
for his bitter attacks: when Timon tries to soften him early
in the play by offering gifts, Apemantus snarls, "No, I'll
nothing; for if I should be brib'd too, there would be none
left to rail upon thee, and then thou wouldst sin the faster"
(1.2.244–6).

After Timon has turned satirist, he and Apemantus are
brought together (IV.3). In part the scene is a *coup de theâtre*
in which two railers are brought face to face to pit their
invective skills against one another; but the scene has more
profound implications, for, with their intense knowledge
of themselves and of satire, Timon and Apemantus seek
out the weak points in one another. To Apemantus, Timon
is a madman turned fool. He possessed the goods of the
world and threw them away on the patently unworthy.
Timon's present misanthropy and retirement from society
are to Apemantus no more than "A poor unmanly melancholy sprung from change of fortune." He is completely
incapable of understanding the intensity of Timon's vision,
which seems to him only the "putting on the cunning of
a carper," and believes that Timon would be a rich and
favored man again if he could. In contrast Apemantus believes himself to live in "willing misery," not enforced, and
takes pride in his own contented discontent.

But to Timon, Apemantus' disgust with the world is
meaningless, for it is forced on him rather than accepted
with knowledge. Apemantus, Timon tells us, was born "a
slave, whom Fortune's tender arm / With favour never
clasp'd, but bred a dog." Had he had the opportunity he
would have plunged himself into "general riot" and followed pleasure. Therefore, Timon concludes, Apemantus'
railing has no virtue in it:

> Why shouldst thou hate men?
> They never flatter'd thee. What hast thou given?
> If thou wilt curse, thy father (that poor rag)
> Must be thy subject, who in spite put stuff
> To some she-beggar and compounded thee.
>
> (IV.3.269–73)

In short, Apemantus is no true satirist, only a freak of nature, the malcontent who rails and curses for the same reason that a dog barks or a snake bites. Timon proves this when he gets Apemantus to admit that if he had control of the world he would "give it to the beasts, to be rid of the men," and that he himself would "fall in the confusion of men, and remain a beast with the beasts" (IV.3.321–7). Apemantus would see no loss in this change for he is already a beast, but Timon who has been favored by fortune and blessed by nature has glimpsed the human potential, the possibility of being fully a man: "We are born to do benefits." Thus his satire has a moral force behind it, and its intensity is no mere rhetorical trick or the inborn envy of a poor creature for his betters, but the expression of agony of a man who fully perceives the "loss in transformation."

There is a Learlike grandeur to Timon, and his situation and speeches often resemble Lear's, but where Lear passes through satiric outrage with the world to tragic perception, Timon persists in his unyielding hatred. He is offered chances for redemption but rejects them. His steward Flavius remains faithful and follows him into the waste, the thieves vow to reform, and Alcibiades, who has also been rejected by Athens, offers the example of mercy after he takes the city. But Timon fails to see in these particulars what Lear sees in Cordelia, a principle of hope for all mankind. His hatred only deepens until he reaches the point where he can enumerate with feeling the terrors men are subject to, "their griefs / Their fear of hostile strokes, their aches, losses," and then callously propose that men prevent these trials by taking advantage of a tree in his "close" to hang themselves. Here is the final failure of the satiric sense of life when carried to the extreme. It refuses to accept any evidence of good in man, and it fails in pity toward "nature's fragile vessel," which is subject to such buffeting in life. There is no question in the play that the Athenians are despicable; they are, in fact, greed and selfishness personified. Shakespeare comes very close to granting the satirist his fundamental premise that the world is totally depraved, but the satiric reaction to such a world is brought into question. Do not a few signs of a human tendency to goodness qualify a total judgment? Is not some modicum of pity necessary?

The final judgment of Timon is made by the plot. In formal satire action is always arrested before it leads to change, and the satirist, inflexibly locked in an attitude of hostility to the evil world, stands always facing unregenerate fools and villains. So powerful is Timon's rage, however, that it demands an outlet and breaks through the satiric stasis, but since the world is adamant and Timon cannot obliterate mankind, his anger must vent itself on the only available object, himself. The subject becomes the object of hatred, and Timon kills himself. There is, as Shakespeare saw, a form of death wish lurking in satire, a compulsive urge to destruction and nothingness. He also saw that the titanic fury of a great satirist is not innate but rather the perversion, the twisting, of a desire for goodness and for love.

Timon of Athens is the culmination of one particular line of development of the satirist in the theater. Once he was transferred to the stage, the changed perspective and enlarged scene denied the satirist a controlling position in the satiric work, and he became in the lesser plays a figure who merely provided amusement with his railing and inconsistencies, in the better an object of appraisal. In those plays of Shakespeare, *Troilus* and *Timon,* in which a character clearly and directly connected with the traditional satyr appears,[5] the criticizing functions for which the figure was designed have become of secondary importance, and the satirist now is used as the representative of a particular view of life and a particular reaction to the ills of the world. The satiric sense of life and the characteristic satiric attitude are thus brought under examination. In *Timon* the purest variety of satiric impulse is explored by allowing it its full extension and following it to its inevitable end of self-destruction in the endless and unperturbed roll of the ocean. In *Troilus* the meanest but most effective variety of satirist is placed in a wider context than he usually operates in, and his vision of the dark and travailing world is silently contrasted with more meaningful views.

The tendency to analyze the satiric character in the drama is equally evident in a large number of plays which we have not discussed, but in these plays we can best approach the problem of the satirist from another direction. In the plays dealt with so far the failure of the dramatists to incorporate the satirists into their plots is most noticeable. By and large the satirist, except when he is the subject of the play as in *Timon,* has a tendency to stand outside the action as a commentator on it, or at best to be only loosely attached to it in some perfunctory and unconvincing manner. In part this is doubtless a carry-over from non-dramatic satire, but in drama a plot of some kind is required, and there is evidence in the satiric drama from the

---

5. There are, of course, a number of characters in Shakespeare's plays who are related to the satirist, e.g. Hamlet, Iago, and the Duke in *Measure for Measure.* But each of these is a considerably more complex character than the satirist, and I am attempting here to deal with only those characters who are unmistakably instances of the type figure. For a description of Shakespeare's satiric work see O. J. Campbell, *Shakespeare's Satire,* New York, 1943.

years 1599 to 1603 or 1604 of a considerable attempt to
find some way to integrate the satirist and his activities
with the forward movement of the play. I shall not re-
count the details here but rather concentrate on one play
which very clearly shows the problem, and another play
which illustrates the solution.

John Marston introduced satirists in his plays with greater
regularity than any other satiric dramatist, including Ben
Jonson. Between the years 1599 and 1606 he probably
wrote eight plays,[6] each of which has a satirist of some sort.
The plays written before 1604 are a series of experiments
in which the satirist is included, unsuccessfully, in very
nearly every popular type of drama: morality play, revenge
tragedy, Plautine comedy, and romantic comedy. The very
variety of dramatic forms suggests the restless search of the
playwright for a suitable vehicle for his satirist, and in one
play *Antonio and Mellida* (1599) the problem is brought
into the open.

Even by Elizabethan standards, *Antonio and Mellida*
is a truly remarkable hodge-podge of separated lovers, song
and dance, rhetorical fire works, Stoic heroism, Machiavellian villainy, fools, and a railing satirist. All of this sensational material is loosely held together by a plot which
advances by leaps and bounds when the author remembers
it, but is forgotten whenever he wants to work all the
changes on a particular emotional situation or expand some
dazzling piece of rhetoric.

Andrugio, Duke of Genoa, is defeated by Piero Sforza,
Duke of Venice, in a sea battle. Andrugio is presumably
drowned, but his son Antonio reaches shore and lives in
Piero's court disguised as an Amazon! He falls in love with

6. The word "probably" is used because the assignment of *Histriomastix*
(1599?) and *Jack Drum's Entertainment* (1600) to Marston is still open to
question. The eight plays do not include *Eastward Ho* (1605), written in
collaboration with Chapman and Jonson.

Mellida, Piero's daughter, and finally escapes with her. In his wanderings he discovers that Andrugio lives. But the two lovers are pursued by the completely evil Piero who recaptures Mellida and offers a reward for the head of Andrugio. In a trick ending, Andrugio enters the court, bringing his head with him of course, and claims the reward. Piero, overcome by Andrugio's virtue and bearing, forgives and reforms. Immediately afterward the supposedly lifeless body of Antonio is brought in, but when the general lamentation is over he rises and claims Mellida. The subplot is composed of a series of episodes designed to display the familiar fools of formal satire: Alberto, the ridiculously unfortunate lover; Balurdo, the wealthy fool chasing fashion; Forobosco, the parasite; Matzagente, the braggart soldier with a Tamburlainish vocabulary; Galeatzo, a proud courtier; Castilio Balthazar, the courtier-fop; and Rossaline, the vain court lady flitting from lover to lover. Among this group walks the satirist, Feliche, commenting on the depravity and idiocy he sees around him.

Feliche is the usual twisted and contradictory satirist, and the actor who is to play the part expresses some bewilderment about his strange role: "But I have a part allotted me, which I have neither able apprehension to conceit, nor what I conceit gracious ability to utter." [7] He then goes on to describe the character he must play:

> 'Tis steady and must seem so impregnably fortressed with his own content that no envious thought could ever invade his spirit; never surveying any man so unmeasuredly happy, whom I thought not justly hateful for some true impoverishment; never beholding any favour of Madam Felicity gracing another, which his well-bounded content persuaded not to hang in the front of his own fortune; and therefore as far from

7. "Induction," lines 108–10.

envying any man, as he valued all men infinitely distant from accomplished beatitude. These native ad-
juncts appropriate to me the name of Feliche.

(lines 113–23.)

This is the public personality of the satirist, and it would
seem to require no great "apprehension to conceit" the
part. But the difficulty comes, as always, when the satirist
begins to get down to the vicious work of actual satire.
Feliche's vaunted calm and dispassionateness fade away
whenever he breaks into the characteristic vile and intemperate denunciation of one of the depraved fools
around him:

> Oh how I hate that same Egyptian louse,
> A rotten maggot, that lives by stinking filth
> Of tainted spirits! vengeance to such dogs,
> That sprout by gnawing senseless carrion!
>
> (II.1.131–4)

After a particularly revolting scene in which one of the
court ladies, Rossaline, spits on the floor and the foolish
courtier Castilio hastens to do her command and rub it up
with his shoe, Feliche fulminates in this manner:

> O that the stomach of this queasy age
> Digests, or brooks such raw unseasoned gobs,
> And vomits not them forth! O! slavish sots!
> Servant, quoth you? faugh! if a dog should crave
> And beg her service, he should have it straight:
> She'd give him favours too, to lick her feet,
> Or fetch her fan, or some such drudgery:
> A good dog's office, which these amorists
> Triumph of: 'tis rare, well give her more ass,
> More sot, as long as dropping of her nose
> Is sworn rich pearl by such low slaves as those.
>
> (II.1.94–104)

These are the accents and metaphors of Kinsayder, and they clash violently with the Stoic calm of which Feliche boasts.

Now, where in verse satire the contrast between these intemperate ranting speeches and the professions of Stoic content are not immediately apparent, they are perfectly clear in the play; and the distance between what Feliche is and what he says he is, appears again and again. He amuses himself by tricking the courtier Castilio into showing him a letter purportedly from Rossaline but actually a tailor's dun. Feliche then takes sadistic delight in exposing him and viciously beating him from the stage. Elsewhere, he passes an idle moment by trying to persuade the melancholy lover Alberto to hang himself. He confesses sadly to his own lack of success in love and betrays his prurient interest in sexual matters.[8] No matter how often Feliche may piously exclaim, "I hate not man, but man's lewd qualities," his actions on stage betray him. At one point he gives himself away completely. Having strutted up and down the stage and pointed out in a long, ornate speech how he envies no man and is completely happy with his simple life, he reacts like an envious and most un-Stoic fool when it is suggested that the love of the court ladies has been bestowed on one of the courtiers, but not on him:

> Confusion seize me, but I think thou liest.
> Why should I not be sought to then as well?
> Fut, methinks I am as like a man.
> Troth, I have a good head of hair, a cheek
> Not as yet wan'd, a leg, 'faith, in the full.
> I ha' not a red beard, take not tobacco much:
> And 'slid, for other parts of manliness—
>
> (III.2.69–75)

8. III.2.81 ff. and II.1.241–61.

The actor's confusion about the contradictory nature of
the character he is to play and doubts about his ability
to handle the strange language of the satirist are perfectly
understandable, the more so since his difficulty parallels
exactly that of the modern critics in "conceiting" the satirist.

In *Antonio and Mellida,* Feliche wanders loose about the
palace doing whatever odd jobs come his way and man-
aging to deliver only a few ranting speeches. There isn't
time for him to do any more. Certain lines from the "Induction" make it clear that Marston was acutely aware of
his failure to find a way to give Feliche more opportunity
to rail. After a number of characters have presented themselves and described their "humors," Feliche comments,
"I fear it is not possible to limn so many persons in so
small a tablet as the compass of our plays afford" (lines
145–7). Antonio answers, "Right! therefore I have heard
that those persons, as . . . you, Feliche, that are but
slightly drawn in this comedy, should receive more exact
accomplishment in a second part; which, if this obtain
gracious acceptance, means to try his fortune." But Feliche
is even more unfortunate in the promised second part of
Antonio and Mellida. In the interests of the blood-revenge
plot he is hanged at the outset of the play, and the satiric
work is taken over by his venerable father, Pandulfo, a
more judicious but less interesting character.[9]

9. Marston, like the majority of his contemporaries, held no Aristotelian
notions about unity of action being the sine qua non of playwriting, and
in his various prologues, inductions, and epilogues he frequently mentions
that entertainment is his only aim. So the fact that his satirist Feliche was
no more than a dramatic excrescence probably never occurred to him. But,
as the lines quoted from the "Induction" show, it did occur to him that he
was not getting the fullest theatrical advantage from his satirist. And
curiously enough the only way in which the satirist could be freed for
unlimited railing was to fit him into the play by making him an integral
part of the plot. So the playwright who was interested only in creating
entertainment was inevitably forced into solving structural problems in

We have seen that in formal satire the satirist has a tendency to play the tempter. He leads his victims on and encourages them in their foolishness only to reveal them for what they are and scourge them. In his three early comical satires Jonson made use of this trait of the satirist to bring his plays to a conclusion. It simply remained for some playwright to perceive that the satirist could be made an intriguer throughout a play, not just at the conclusion, and that the plot of the play, either serious or comic, could be the satirist's attempts to expose the fools and villains. The chief advantage of such a method would be that the satirist could be given relatively unlimited time to rail, since the railing would now become the chief motive force in the plot. Marston's *The Malcontent* (1604) is perhaps the most interesting of the many Jacobean plays constructed on this principle.

Briefly, *The Malcontent* tells the story of Altofronto, former Duke of Genoa, who has been deposed by Pietro with the aid of the citizenry and the Duke of Florence. At the point the play begins, Altofronto disguised as Malevole, a malcontent, returns to Genoa and undertakes a series of intrigues which first place Mendoza, a Machiavellian schemer, in the ducal palace and finally bring about his overthrow and the return of Altofronto to his rightful throne, once again with the aid of the fickle mob.

Malevole is the satirist of the play, and a few examples of his language and activities will establish his conventional character. When asked for news by Ferrardo, Malevole responds in the usual snarling tone: "Common news! why, common words are, God save ye, fare ye well; common actions, flattery and cozenage; common things, women and cuckolds" (1.1.60–2). On other occasions he employs

---

order to make the most of his ranting satirist. Ironically, only a well-constructed play could contain the disparate materials of his drama without limiting their theatrical effectiveness.

the typical soaring rhetoric and displays his profound pessimism. "World! 'tis the only region of death, the greatest shop of the devil; the cruelest prison of men, out of the which none pass without paying their dearest breath for a fee; there's nothing perfect in it but extreme, extreme calamity" (IV.2.25–9). Act I, scene 1, where Malevole greets each member of the court in turn and makes scathing comments on their appearances and morals, is, with the exception of a few bits of dialogue, in the exact pattern of formal verse satire where the satirist stands in a crowded place and describes the passersby. Finally, Pietro describes Malevole in terms which specifically identify him as the traditional satirist:

> This Malevole is one of the most prodigious affections that ever conversed with nature: a man, or rather a monster; more discontent than Lucifer when he was thrust out of the presence. His appetite is unsatiable as the grave; as far from any content as from heaven: his highest delight is to procure others vexation, and therein he thinks he truly serves heaven; for 'tis his position, whosoever in this earth can be contented is a slave and damned; therefore does he afflict all in that to which they are most affected. The elements struggle within him; his own soul is at variance within herself; his speech is halter-worthy at all hours. . . . See, he comes. Now shall you hear the extremity of a malcontent: he is as free as air; he blows over every man.
>
> (1.1.26–42)

Malevole never lets an opportunity pass to anatomize and flay any villain or fool he sees, and his railing now has an added function: it not only opens up moral infection but becomes the instrument which Altofronto uses to regain his dukedom. The two functions of satirist and in-

triguer are neatly combined in the following speech in
which Malevole tells Pietro that his Duchess is having an
affair with Mendoza, the scheming Machiavel of the play:

> *Pietro.* Death and damnation!
> *Mal.* Lightning and thunder!
> *Pietro.* Vengeance and torture!
> *Mal.* Catso!
> *Pietro.* O, revenge!
> *Mal.* Nay, to select among ten thousand fairs
> A lady far inferior to the most,
> In fair proportion both of limb and soul;
>
>   .   .   .   .   .
>
> To meet her spirit in a nimble kiss,
> Distilling panting ardour to her heart;
> True to her sheets, nay, diets strong his blood,
> To give her height of hymeneal sweets,—
> *Pietro.* O God!
> *Mal.* Whilst she lisps, and gives him some court-
> *quelquechose,*
> Made only to provoke, not satiate:
> And yet even then the thaw of her delight
> Flows from lewd heat of apprehension,
> Only from strange imagination's rankness,
> That forms the adulterer's presence in her soul,
> And makes her think she clips the foul knave's loins.
> *Pietro.* Affliction to my blood's root!
>
>   (1.1.144–68)

Malevole plays his part here with extreme shrewdness. He
is on the surface playing the traditional role of the satirist
who uncovers hidden vice without regard for personal danger. His subject is a favorite one with the satirist, the lewdness of woman, and in order to render vice ugly he describes
it in exact and vivid terms. At the same time there is a certain lip-smacking interest in the elaboration on the details

of the sexual act which suggests the usual prurience of the satirist. But, while the speech may be an excellent piece of satire, it is simultaneously a fine bit of intrigue. Every word is carefully chosen to inflame the imagination of the jealous husband, and his anger is carefully fed bit by bit to bring him to visualize the act itself. So thoroughly does Malevole control Pietro by the end of these lines that he can go on to a final piece of impudence in which he describes how Mendoza may beget a bastard son on the Duchess who may in the course of time marry an acknowledged child of Mendoza. Pietro is properly shocked and exclaims "Hideous imagination!" But then Malevole thoroughly bewilders him by proceeding to show that adultery, though a terrible sin, is not so bad as simony! The satirist is playing with his victim, and the results are all he could desire. Pietro breaks with Mendoza. Mendoza soon recovers, however, and Malevole uses the same technique of simultaneously satirizing and setting the villains at odds again, and encourages Mendoza to murder Pietro. In this way satire becomes a potent political weapon, and Malevole describes his technique in this way:

> Discord to malcontents is very manna:
> When the ranks are burst, then scuffle, Altofront.
>
> (1.1.250–1)

Malevole's efforts are successful, and the play ends with the overthrow of Mendoza, the banishment of the fools, and Malevole's restoration to power as Altofronto. Pietro and Aurelia, the usurpers, are brought through Malevole's satire to recognition of what their lives have been, and when Malevole effects the cure by telling Pietro bitter, harsh truths, he employs the medical imagery of the satirist and justifies his methods with the conventional explanation:

Pietro. Thou pinchest too deep; art too keen upon
me.

Mal. Tut, a pitiful surgeon makes a dangerous sore:
I'll tent thee to the ground. Thinkest I'll sustain myself by flattering thee, because thou art a prince? I had
rather follow a drunkard, and live by licking up his
vomit, than by servile flattery.

(IV.2.93–99)

The Malcontent is filled with satiric speeches and incidents of the kind discussed above, and Marston lavished
more attention on satiric utterances and situations here
than in any of his other plays. We might conclude then,
as many have, that the play is merely a vehicle for popular
satirical rant and lurid scenes of debauchery in an Italian
palace, and that the disguise of Altofronto as Malevole is
no more than a successful way of coupling an exciting intrigue pattern with a large amount of railing. While *The
Malcontent* is certainly this, it is something more as well.
We can best understand its additional dimensions by exploring the relationship between the disguise and the character, Malevole and Altofronto.

Altofronto was originally a Duke of a most free and open
nature. He describes his former state in this manner:

Behold forever-banish'd Altofront,
This Genoa's last year's duke. O truly noble!
I wanted those old instruments of state,
Dissemblance and suspect: I could not time it, Celso;
My throne stood like a point midst of a circle,
To all of equal nearness; bore with none;
Rein'd all alike; so slept in fearless virtue,
Suspectless, too suspectless.

(I.1.219–26)

Like Timon, Altofronto once idealized man, and traces of
this attitude linger in his malcontent speeches. For example,

in speaking of the evil of Pietro's Duchess, Aurelia, Malevole argues that a man makes a woman "commandress of
a better essence / Than is the gorgeous world, even of a
man" (1.1.151–2). Disillusionment overtook him however,
when Pietro, Aurelia, and Mendoza banded together with
the citizenry, "Still lickorous of untried novelties," and
overthrew and banished him. His Duchess, Maria, was imprisoned, and the court became a nest of Machiavellian intrigues for power, sexual corruption, and plain idiocy,
where villain and fool strove only to gratify their lusts.
To say that "it became" this is not quite correct, for since
the characters of the play were the courtiers during Altofronto's reign as well, and the citizenry he ruled and the
mob which overthrew him were one and the same, the implication is that the state of Genoa and the world which
it mirrors, were always the same. What has changed is Altofronto's point of view. He now sees the palace and city as
a banished Duke who has been treated to a full view of
human depravity. So Altofronto becomes Malevole.

Malevole is not only a disguise assumed for the political
purpose of cleansing the state, but a facet of Altofronto's
character as well. He, like other satirists and other men,
has been disenchanted: having thought man a god and
justice the rule of the world, he has discovered that Fortune
and chance play a large part in human affairs, that men
follow their selfish desires rather than right, and that virtue can be defeated by cunning. When Altofronto speaks
in his own person to those few who know him, or in an
aside, he reflects on the world's depravity in deeply pessimistic but restrained terms:

> How smooth to him that is in state of grace,
> How servile is the rugged'st courtier's face!
> What profit, nay, what nature would keep down,
> Are heav'd to them are minions to a crown.

> Envious ambition never sates his thirst,
> Till sucking all, he swells and swells, and burst.
>
> (I.1.288–93)

But in the role of Malevole the satirist, Altofronto gives full and violent expression to the despair and loathing of man which he feels because of his misfortunes. He can go the extreme of declaring all life to be nothing but corruption and rottenness:

> Think this:—this earth is the only grave and Golgotha wherein all things that live must rot; 'tis but the draught wherein the heavenly bodies discharge their corruption; the very muck-hill on which the sublunary orbs cast their excrements: man is the slime of this dung-pit, and princes are the governors of these men.
>
> (IV.2.141–7)

Or, using the license of the satirist, he can abandon all restraint in dealing with the fools, as he does in this greeting of the white-haired rake Bilioso: "And how does my old muckhill, overspread with fresh snow? thou half a man, half a goat, all a beast! how does thy young wife, old huddle?" (I.1.76–9).

But the satirist's view of the world and his reaction to it are not allowed to stand unchallenged. Malevole's "scuffling" methods do bring about the overthrow of the usurpers, and his savage descriptions of the fools and villains are accurate, but they are shown to be excessive. By the end of the play he has "cured" Pietro and Aurelia, and he discovers that no enticements can force his own imprisoned wife, Maria, to yield to Mendoza, who is now Duke. Maquerelle, the old bawd who has accompanied Malevole to tempt Maria, expresses a view of womankind to which he would have acquiesced at the beginning of the play, "Why, are ye ignorant that 'tis said a squeamish affected niceness is natural to women, and that the excuse of their yielding is only, forsooth, the difficult obtaining? You must put her to't: women are flax, and will fire in a moment" (v.2.144–8). But Maria's steadfastness has convinced Malevole that though some women are bad, all are not depraved:

> now I see,
> Sooner earth's fire heaven itself shall waste,
> Than all with heat can melt a mind that's chaste.
>
> (v.2.155–7)

Under the impact of repeated demonstrations of virtue he arrives slowly at a more balanced view of the world. The process continues, and when he finds out that "the castle's captain stands for me, the people pray for me," he can add, "and the great leader of the just stands for me" (v.2.281–3). In the concluding scene he sums up the transition he has undergone:

> O, I have seen strange accidents of state!
> The flatterer, like the ivy, clip the oak,
> And waste it to the heart; lust so confirm'd,
> That the black act of sin itself not sham'd
> To be term'd courtship.
> O, they that are as great as be their sins,
> Let them remember that th' inconstant people
> Love many princes merely for their faces
> And outward shows; and they do covet more
> To have a sight of these than of their virtues.
> Yet thus much let the great ones still conceive,
> When they observe not heaven's impos'd conditions,
> They are no kings, but forfeit their commissions.
>
> (v.3.180–92)

The speech sums up the progress of the satirist who happens in this case also to be a Duke. Having looked at the world and found it dirt rather than fire, he falls into an extreme pessimism which finds relief in railing. But having seen evidence of virtue in a few, he returns to belief

in the ultimate necessity of moral conduct, with the quali-
fying knowledge, however, that most men are base. The
response of the satirist to the world's evils is clearly shown
to be an exaggerated view, and here we see in another way
that the satirist was not conceived of by Marston as an absolute extension of his own personality, but as a creature with
an overly intense and unwarranted reaction to what is,
nevertheless, very real and powerful evil.

The fusion of the satirist and intriguer in the person of
Malevole solved many of the dramaturgical problems connected with the satirist, and became during the following
years the standard method of handling the satirist. Middleton used it in *The Phoenix* (1603/4) where the disguised
Prince Phoenix roams among a group of villains and fools,
sees their plots, comments on them, and finally exposes
them to bring the play to a conclusion. *Measure for Measure*
(1603–4) casts Duke Vincentio in the same role, although
his criticism of humankind is more restrained than that of
Malevole as he moves through the debauchery of Vienna
marking the sins he sees around him. Marston's *The Fawn,*
Middleton's *Your Five Gallants,* Tourneur's *The Revenger's Tragedy* and *The Atheist's Tragedy,* Sharpham's
The Fleire, Webster's *The White Devil* and *The Duchess of
Malfi* all contain characters who are at least partially satirists
who combine their satiric activities with an intrigue of
some kind.

No discussion of the Elizabethan satirist would be complete without reference to the manner in which he was fitted
into the tragedy of blood-revenge. We have already noted
that Juvenalian satire has a tendency toward the tragic and
that, conversely, most tragic heroes have pronounced satiric
qualities; but the Elizabethan blood-revenger is a special
instance of the tragic hero and similar to the satirist in
many ways.[1] Both figures, for example, find themselves in

1. There is a certain appropriateness in the union of the Juvenalian

a world where virtue has been dispossessed by vice and in a once healthy society now become morally sick. Both are unable to hold their tongues but discover in themselves an agonized compulsion to reveal the truth by speaking out, and to unmask the world's pretenses to virtue by clever arrangement of events and scene. Both find it necessary, though for somewhat different reasons, to probe to the very source of infection in the state and cut it out of the body politic. The traditional metaphorical tools employed for this work by the satirist, the surgical probe and caustic medicine, blend readily with the actual tools of the revenger, the sword and the cup of poison.

Hamlet is, of course, the greatest instance of the combination of the two roles. He is not only the Prince of Denmark called on to revenge his father's foul murder and clear the throne of the usurper, but is also the surgeon satirist, the "scourge and minister," who finds the time "out of joint," and feels that he must "set it right." When he enters reading from that "satirical rogue"—Juvenal,[2] no doubt—who says that "old men have grey beards . . . and . . . a plentiful lack of wit"; when he holds up the picture of Old Hamlet and Claudius to Gertrude for comparison; when he catalogues the miseries of existence for the honest and sensitive man, "the law's delay, the insolence of office"; or when he mockingly comments in the graveyard on the

---

satirist and the hero of the blood-revenge tragedy, for both figures were originally closely allied. Seneca's plays, the source of Elizabethan revenge tragedy, and Juvenal's satires were both literary products of the post-Augustan Roman Empire, and in both, despite the differences of genre, we find similar "heroes" dealing with amoral, corrupt societies. The Senecan tragic hero has as little ability to change his ideas through suffering as the rocklike satirist of Juvenal. The former maintains his virtue by enduring without change whatever miseries the world loads on him, while the latter maintains his virtue by never ceasing to speak out and tell the world the truth about itself.

2. Gilbert Highet, *Juvenal the Satirist* (New York, 1954), p. 213, suggests that Hamlet is here reading from Juvenal's Satire x.

dusty end of the great lawyer, the splendid courtier, and the cunning politician, Hamlet is very close to the satirist in subject, style, tone, and method. But the Hamlet whose will is "puzzled," who can wonder, "What should such fellows as I do crawling between earth and heaven?" has a complexity, a depth, and a speculative turn of mind which carry him far beyond the limited vision of the satirist, and, for that matter, of the blood-revenger. And the world in which he must move, for all its surface resemblance to the satiric scene, has a corresponding complexity and mystery about it which force him constantly to ponder and revise his earlier ideas. A discussion of *Hamlet* would for these reasons lead us away from satire and into the tragic world.

But in Tourneur's *The Revenger's Tragedy* (1607), the satiric qualities of the scene, hero, and plot are not absorbed by the tragic, though they are ultimately modified by something like a tragic view of character and action. The story of the play is simple: some years before the action begins the Duke of a nameless Italian state has caused the deaths of Vendici's betrothed, Gloriana, and his father. Disguised as Piato, a malcontent, Vendici makes his way into the court, where he serves as royal pander, sows mischief, and arranges the death of the Duke. Then shifting to his own person he contrives the death of the Duke's heir, Lussurioso. At the end of the play Vendici, after proudly admitting his hand in these murders, is ordered executed, along with his brother Hippolito, by the new Duke, a just and honest man who has suffered much under the old regime.

The setting for this action is an Italian ducal palace populated with the usual villains and fools. The Duke is no more than a doddering, but still dangerous, old lecher continually searching for new objects for his lust. His legitimate son Lussurioso is equally lustful and clever, while his bastard Spurio plots against his brother and sleeps with his stepmother, the Duke's second wife. Her three sons by

a previous marriage, Ambitioso, Supervacuo, and "Junior,"
are no more than vain, vicious young brutes. From this corrupted throne and family evil spreads out over the entire
court and kingdom. Junior, surrounded by his cronies,
rapes a young wife in the middle of a masquerade ball when
her cries will be drowned by the music. The corruption of
justice is revealed in his trial where he escapes death by
the pleadings of the Duchess and the command of the Duke.
The officers of state are mere toadies who hasten to do any
bidding of those in power. Vendici's own family catches the
general disease when he is sent by Lussurioso to buy his
sister, Castiza, and persuade his mother to become a bawd.
Castiza resists, but Gratiana, the mother, gives in to the
lure of gold. Behind these specific events of the play, the
language, primarily that of Vendici, brings into being the
kingdom itself through which the infection spreads:

Now tis full sea a bed over the world;
Theres iugling of all sides; some that were Maides
E'en at Sun set are now perhaps ith Toale-booke;
This woman in immodest thin apparell
Lets in her friend by water, here a Dame
Cunning, nayles lether-hindges to a dore,
To avoide proclamation.
Now Cuckolds are a quoyning, apace, apace, apace, apace.
And carefull sisters spinne that thread ith night,
That does maintaine them and their bawdes ith daie! [3]

This apocalyptic vision of the world outside the court being
enfolded in the night of lust and self-interest is kept before
us throughout the play by frequent references to the usual
targets of Elizabethan satire, the yeomen's sons who "wash
their hands, and come up Gentlemen" (II.1.242), the trades-
men who take advantage of these fools and buy their land,

3. II.2.152–61. All citations of *The Revenger's Tragedy* are to *The Works
of Cyril Tourneur*, ed. Allardyce Nicoll, London, Franfrolico Press, 1930.

the lady who bathes "in sinfull baths of milke,—when many an infant starves." [4] In short, this kingdom is the dense world of "three-pilde flesh," of hurried but aimless movement, casual carnality, and animal savagery usually created in satire, though here given a more sinister turn than is customary.

But if the details with which the scenes are fleshed out derive from Renaissance Italy—and Renaissance England —the supporting skeleton derives from another age. Still perceptible under the contemporary details are the old morality play structure and conception of character. [5] The ducal family—who, incidentally, are seven in number—retain their type names, Spurio, Ambitioso, Lussurioso. But the relationship of these characters to the morality play is suggested more by their woodenness, their lack of complexity, their single-mindedness, than by the use of devices such as type names. Each of them seems to be only a living vice, a personification of a single characteristic, and each of them moves in a mechanical, uncomplicated fashion toward satisfaction of his particular lust. It was Tourneur's genius to perceive, in an age when "realistic" dramatic characters had become the fashion and could be created by any fairly competent writer, that the only way of satisfactorily imaging

4. III.5.89. This speech of Vendici's extending from line 47 through line 119 provides an excellent example of the manner in which the Jacobean dramatist managed to extend the range of his satire. Rather than restricting his satiric voices to comments on the vices actually portrayed in the action, the playwright provided his satirists with speeches in which they describe a variety of fools and villains who seem to exist in a world just beyond the limits of the stage proper. In this speech, for example, Vendici attacks the swearer, the drunkard, the usurer, the proud courtesan, the noble who sells land to maintain her, the thief, the judge, the epicure; and he enlivens his attacks in the manner of verse satire by creating little scenes in which the sins are brought to life momentarily, e.g. a "selfe-affecting Dame" bathing in milk, and a riotous party in a brothel.

5. For a fuller discussion of this aspect of the play see L. G. Salingar, "*The Revenger's Tragedy* and the Morality Tradition," *Scrutiny*, 6 (1938), 402–24.

a personality given over to vice is to portray it in the "flat" single-dimensional manner of the morality tradition. For characters of this kind have lost their complexity and the "reality" which comes from being fully alive. *The Revenger's Tragedy,* despite the exotic nature of some of the vice displayed in it and its blood-revenge plot, is conceptually very close to the world of the morality play in which the Seven Deadly Sins struggle with and very nearly succeed in overcoming such characters as Justice, Chastity, Honor, Love, Faithful Service, and Truth, who are represented in Tourneur's play, in a superficially realistic manner, by the courtiers, the judges, and the members of Vendici's family. As a result of this reduction of character to single vices and virtues, the satiric qualities of the scene are intensified, while the tragic qualities are diminished. For, as we have seen, characters in the satiric world are usually sketched in clear-cut blacks and whites. Neither satire nor Tourneur's play has any place for such bewilderingly complex and contradictory characters as Shakespeare's Gertrude, Claudius, Laertes, or even Polonius.

In keeping with the satiric tendencies of the scene, the hero of the play, Vendici, resembles the satirist more than he does the tragic hero. In his first appearance on stage he is placed in the same position in relation to the scene that the satirist in Juvenalian verse satire occupies. The stage is dark and over it passes a procession made up of the Duke, members of his family, and a train of court attendants carrying torches. As they pass silently, Vendici stands to one side unobserved and comments on them:

> Duke: royall letcher; goe, gray hayrde adultery,
> And thou his sonne, as impious steept as hee:
> And thou his bastard true-begott in evill:
> And thou his Dutchesse that will doe with Divill,
> Foure exlent Characters—O that marrow-lesse age,

Would stuffe the hollow Bones with dambd desires,
And stead of heate kindle infernall fires,
Within the spend-thrift veynes of a drye Duke,
A parcht and iucelesse luxur. O God! one
That has scarce bloud inough to live upon.
And hee to ryot it like a sonne and heyre?
O the thought of that
Turnes my abused heart-strings into fret.

(1.1.4–16)

The use of the word "Characters," i.e. set satirical portraits,
suggests the close relationship of this scene and speech to the
satiric tradition.

This initial scene establishes the perspective of the play.
Seen from the outside, from the point of view of the
audience, the *mise en scène* is that of formal satire with
Vendici as satirist standing in the foreground and commenting on the activities and characters of the play
proper, the world of the ducal court. This scenic effect is
achieved in a number of ways during the course of *The Revenger's Tragedy*. Vendici may stand aside as he does in
the first scene and simply address the audience directly
while a dumb-show takes place on the stage proper; or he
may appear alone on stage, or with his brother Hippolito,
and deliver a long railing speech on human iniquity; or he
may position himself in the foreground by employing irony,
i.e. his speech may seem flattery to the self-blinded character to whom it is specifically addressed, while the audience
understands that it is bitter sarcasm; or, finally, he may take
advantage of the aside as he does in v.1.109 ff., where, as
each obsequious courtier addresses some particular piece
of outrageous flattery to the new Duke, Lussurioso, Vendici
steps forward and delivers a withering comment to the
audience.

But where the satirist in formal verse satire remains always outside the scene he describes, Vendici steps into it

from time to time and becomes an actor in the world he loathes. Each time he does so, however, he puts on a disguise; first he assumes the person of the pander Piato, and then he uses his own name but a false character, that of a malcontent ready for any gainful employment. Whenever Vendici stands outside the scene he uses the standard tools of the satirist, words, to achieve his purpose of unmasking and punishing the villainy of the world; but when he steps into the play proper, intrigue and malicious meddling become his chief methods of operation. He tells Lussurioso that Spurio is in bed with the Duchess and sends him off to kill them; he tempts his mother with gold to become a bawd for her own daughter; he arranges an assignation for the old Duke, tricks him into kissing the poison-smeared lips of the skull of Gloriana, then treats him to the sight of Spurio embracing the Duchess; and at the end of the play he contrives a masque in which the dancers fall on Lussurioso and his party and kill them. Each of these activities, except the temptation of the mother, seems at first glance to be solely a function of Vendici's role as blood-revenger, for they are all retributions for what his family has suffered. But each of these events also achieves the satiric aim, it unmasks pretense and clears away illusion to reveal the truth.

This is plain enough in the scenes in which the Duchess is revealed as a whore, Lussurioso as a murderer, and Gratiana as a corruptible bawd, but in order to see how the murders of the old Duke and Lussurioso are achievements of the satiric end of unmasking villainy we must look briefly at what Vendici takes for reality. The majority of satirists are morally and socially oriented. That is, they trace the personal and social corruption they describe to the loss of certain ethical and social virtues, and they hope —in a hopeless way—to drive man back to these virtues by showing him how idiotic and depraved he has become. So they cut away the layers of pretense with which men cover

themselves and reveal that underneath they are fools, animals, machines. But Vendici cuts a little deeper and discovers a further reality, the skull.[6] Perceiving that "lust is
death" and that therefore the characters of the play who are
no more than ambulant sexual appetites are in reality dead,
his satiric business of cutting away pretense can be realized
only by cutting away the bodies of his enemies and reducing
them to the reality of the skeleton. In this way the actions
of the blood-revenger and the satirist are perfectly fused,
and the pessimism and cruel methods of the Elizabethan
satirist are given their ultimate expression.

The skull, that "terror to fat folkes," is Vendici's touchstone, the "steele glass" which he holds up to life to reflect
its true image. Contemplating Gloriana's skull which he
carries around as a memento mori, he asks it,

> Do's the Silke-worme expend her yellow labours
> For thee? for thee does she undoe herselfe?
> Are Lord-ships sold to maintaine Lady-ships
> For the poore benefit of a bewitching minute?
> Why dos yon fellow falsify hie-waies
> And put his life betweene the Judges lippes,
> To refine such a thing, keepes horse and men
> To beate their valours for her?
> Surely wee're all mad people. . . .
>
> (III.5.75–83)

The skull here reduces all artificial beauty and all fancy
dress to nonsense, and Vendici applies it with equal effec-

6. Despite the traces of medieval otherworldliness present in this attitude,
in a Renaissance context this somber vision of the world seems most immediately to be related to Calvinism. For a discussion of Tourneur's connections with this philosophy, see Michael Higgins, "The Influence of
Calvinistic Thought in Tourneur's *Atheist's Tragedie*," *Review of English
Studies*, *19* (1943), 255–62. The idea, already suggested in Ch. 3, that
Juvenalian satire and the Calvinist view of the world and man are basically
congenial is borne out to some degree by an interesting fact. John Calvin
wrote only one poem, as far as we know, during his life, and that one poem
contains an imitation of Juvenal. See Highet, *Juvenal the Satirist*, p. 212.

tiveness to most of the usual forms of human vanity during
the course of the play, proving again and again that you can
"deceive men, but cannot deceive wormes." But his master-
piece, which combines both his functions as revenger and
satirist, is the scene of revelation he arranges for the old
Duke. Vendici's betrothed has some years earlier killed herself rather than submit to the Duke, and when the Duke
commissions Vendici, now disguised as Piato, to find a
young girl for him, Vendici dresses the skull in rich, hang-
ing silks, veils it and smears its lips with poison. Revenge is
accomplished by leading the Duke to this "bony lady" and
allowing him to kiss her in the belief that she is beautiful.
This is more than revenge, for the scene that Vendici arranges here is the true image of lust. In his view of life,
beauty is no more than a skull dressed in gorgeous cover-
ings, the luxurious embrace is not life clasping life but
death touching death, and the lecherous kiss is the seal on
the death warrant.

The Duke does not die immediately of the poison, and
Vendici arranges another scene of truth before finally dis-
patching him with the dagger. While his tongue is being
eaten away by the poison, the Duke is forced to be a spec-
tator at a meeting of his Duchess and his bastard, Spurio, in
which they reveal their incestuous love for one another and
their common hatred of the Duke. The first of Vendici's
arranged scenes exposes in symbolic terms the true nature
of the Duke's entire life and of lust in general, while the
second scene restates the same truth in more realistic terms.

We have seen many times already that the satirist for all
his attempts to present himself as merely honest in his
evaluation of the world, no matter how grotesque his vision
may be, inevitably reveals that he too is morally sick. This
is as true of the satirist-revenger Vendici as it is of such
obviously culpable creatures as Thersites or Macilente. In
his reaction to the vicious, depraved world of the palace,

his imagination has become infected, and, with the satirist's characteristic pessimism and lack of balance, he can see *only* rottenness, lust, and animality in the world. This narrowed and unhealthy view of life appears most clearly in the speeches in which he addresses the skull of Gloriana. When he reflects on her once living beauty, he can recall that,

> 'twas a face
> So farre beyond the artificiall shine
> Of any womans bought complexion
> That the uprightest man, (if such there be,
> That sinne but seaven times a day) broke custome
> And made up eight with looking after her.
> Oh she was able to ha made a Usurers sonne
> Melt all his patrimony in a kisse.
>
> (I.1.23–30)

Even in thinking of the woman he loved he is unable to separate her beauty and virtue from the fleshly attraction it exerted in the sinful world. So obsessed does he become with the reality of the skull and the consequent meaninglessness of life and love that after a long discussion of how all living things come to the grave he can turn to Gloriana's skull and exclaim,

> And now me thinkes I cold e'en chide my selfe,
> For doating on her beauty.
>
> (III.5.72–3)

The agonized conviction that all that lives is loathsome, forces him to believe that any person not yet corrupted requires only the opportunity to become so. He tests this theory on his mother and sister when he is sent to them to persuade his sister, Castiza, to yield to Lussurioso. Castiza rejects the offer, but the mother after some urging gives in. The scene (II.1) is an excellent dramatization of the agonized and divided mind of the satirist. On one hand Vendici the son wants desperately to believe that his mother

would not sell her own daughter, and this side of his nature
is expressed in a series of asides such as, "I e'en quake to
proceede, my spirit turnes edge" (line 122). On the other
hand Vendici the satirist, scenting hidden corruption and
unable to cease until he has uncovered it, can paint for
Gratiana a tempting picture of the riches she will enjoy if
she persuades her daughter, and can explain to her with oily
plausibility,

> You tooke great paines for her [Castiza] . . . ,
> Let her requite it now, tho it be but some;
> You brought her forth, she may well bring you home.
>   (lines 113–15)

The sadistic delight with which the satirist in formal satire wields his whip and applies his burning medicines is
translated in *The Revenger's Tragedy* to the blood lust of
the revenger. Vendici not only sees his work of killing as
necessary to reveal the truth about the world, but he comes
to enjoy it and executes his victims with fiendish ingenuity
and unnecessary cruelty. When he murders the old Duke he
nails down his tongue with a dagger, threatens to tear up
his eyelids "and make his eyes like Comets shine through
bloud." He can exclaim with savage excitement—and bad
critical judgment—"When the bad bleedes, then is the
Tragedie good" (III.5.216). Vendici also resembles the satirist in his pride in his own ingenuity and his rhetorical
skill. His brother Hippolito, who has a more practical turn
of mind, can admire Vendici's long, railing speeches—"You
flow well brother"—but again and again he is forced to
break in on Vendici's excited explanations of elaborate
schemes and sonorous speeches on human vanity to remind
him of the workaday necessities of the situation.

Vendici also has the satirist's usual double nature, for he
is at once the inspired prophet who sees that the depraved
palace world is no more than a charnel house, and at the

same time the very spirit of death itself. The play is thus a
danse macabre in which one skeleton leads other skeletons
to the grave. Vendici himself seems partially aware of his
close relationship to the corruption he attacks so determinedly, for he remarks musingly,

> My life's unnaturally to me, e'en compeld
> As if I liv'd now when I should be dead.
>
> (1.1.134-5)

By the end of *The Revenger's Tragedy* the traditional
aims of both the blood revenger and the satirist have been
achieved. The members of the viperish ducal family, the
"nest of Dukes," who have destroyed Vendici's family and
vitiated the kingdom have either been killed or banished—
though there is some doubt about what happens to Supervacuo who simply disappears from the play after v.3.74.
Antonio, the elderly noble whose wife was ravished by
Spurio, is proclaimed the new duke; and Vendici's pun on
Antonio's gray hair identifies his assumption of the throne
with the return of the older and better society for which the
satirist always strives:

> Your hayre will make the silver age agen,
> When there was fewer but more honest men.
>
> (v.3.126-7)

At this point a satire could end—though it would be more
optimistic than is usual—but Tourneur carries the action
on to its logical conclusion. When the new Duke Antonio
remarks on the strange manner in which the old Duke was
murdered, Vendici, blinded by the satirist's usual delight
with his own skill, cannot resist revealing that he and Hippolito were the murderers, and cannot help adding, with
true craftsman's pride, "Twas some-what witty carried tho
we say it." When Antonio expresses surprise, "You two?",
Vendici preens himself a bit more, "None else ifaith my
Lord nay twas well managde" (v.3.142). Antonio's reaction

is immediate: "Lay hands upon those villaines. . . . Beare 'em to speedy execution." His explanation for this action, that the brothers who found it so easy to murder one duke would find it equally easy to murder another, is a final judgment on the satirist-revenger. Except in certain rare moments of self-analysis Vendici, like other satirists, proudly exempts himself from his scene. He may move *in* a world of corruption, but he is not *of* it. Antonio, like the Elizabethan and Jacobean dramatists, sees, however, that the satirist-revenger is one with his world, one symptom of a generalized infection. Ironically, a thorough healing of the world then requires that the chief means for accomplishing that goal, the satirist-revenger, should himself be destroyed after his work is finished. Vendici in his last speech is half aware of this bitter necessity and can state the grim paradox which has been revealed:

> Tis time to die, when we are our selves our foes.
>
> (v.3.154)

These words, constituting as they do an attenuated tragic recognition, could never be spoken by the satirist, who always remains steadfast in his belief in his own righteousness. But Tourneur, like the other dramatists of his age, was unwilling to allow the tensions of the satiric character to remain unresolved or the narrow satiric view of the world to pass for reality unquestioned.

In the "satiric tragedies" we have looked at, the scene has always been more complex than it is in Juvenalian formal satire. Human nature has been sufficiently ambiguous, or there have been enough good men, or the world itself has shown enough evidence of a moral tendency, to challenge the satirist's simplified image of the human scene. But in *The Duchess of Malfi* (1613) the almost totally depraved and decaying world which the satirist postulates is brought to life in the ducal palace at Amalfi and in the episcopal

palace at Milan. The Duchess and Antonio are surrounded
by men and women whose lives are no more than a struggle
for power, for gold, for satisfaction of lust. The metaphors
which the satirist traditionally uses to describe the filthiness
and idiocy of mankind now become literal realities before
our eyes. Ferdinand stalking the Duchess in her chambers is
more wolf than man, and he contracts lycanthropia before
the play is ended and becomes a wolf in all but outward
form. Julia demanding immediate sexual satisfaction from
Bosola is no longer woman but a rutting bitch. The images
of insanity which the satirist uses as metaphors for man's
lack of reason are translated here to the dance of the madmen, the frenzies of Ferdinand, and the mad vision of the
Cardinal. Disease is everywhere, and the rotting flesh and
physical functions which so fascinate the satirist pervade the
play. Even the Duchess cannot escape carnal involvement
and the continuing process of corruption in which all life
is caught up:

> our Duchesse
> Is sick a dayes, she puykes, her stomacke seethes,
> The fins of her eie-lids looke most teeming blew,
> She waines i'th' cheeke, and waxes fat i'th' flanke.
> (II.1.65–8)[7]

This world is the natural habitat of the satirist, and
Webster provides one, Bosola, who is a textbook model. He
has every peculiarity of the satiric character, every trick of
speech, every trait which had become traditional in the
preceding years. Here, very near the end of the satirist's
appearance in the theater, we find the "ideal" Elizabethan
satirist, the pure satyr, and it will be worth while to catalogue his traits before going on to see what use Webster
made of him in his tragic scheme.

7. All citations of *The Duchess of Malfi* are to *The Works of John Webster*, ed. F. L. Lucas (London, Chatto and Windus, 1927), Vol. 2.

"Sometimes the Divell doth preach," says Bosola (1.1.317), when in one of those flickering moments of revelation the satirist is prone to, he, like Kinsayder commenting on his "squint-eyed sight," recognizes his own twisted nature while attempting to justify his railing at the world's deformities. But ordinarily Bosola keeps such knowledge to himself, or forgets it, and attempts to keep to the world the face which the satirist traditionally claims to be the true image of his character, the face of an honest, fearless, straightforward man who calls "a spade a spade" because his moral uprightness and zeal for truth will not allow him to flatter and pretend that villainy is virtue. "Let me be simply honest," he cries; advises his Duchess when she appears to be angry with Antonio that this alone was "an honest states-man to a Prince" among a rout of parasites and rogues; and still playing the part of the honest counsellor tells the savagely dangerous Ferdinand, who has boasted of his unfathomable policy, "You are your owne Chronicle too much: and grosly flatter your selfe." On the world at large Bosola rails with true satiric disgust and with equally true satiric facility for finding the vivid phrase and the repellent metaphor. The first scene of Act II provides a good example of his railing. Here he attacks, in what he calls his "rough-caste phrase," a number of standard targets: the courtier, the judge, women and their painting. His description of a woman's cosmetic closet is in the old style: "One would suspect it for a shop of witch-craft, to finde in it the fat of Serpents; spawne of Snakes, Jewes Spittle, and their yong children['s] ordures—and all these for the face: I would sooner eate a dead pidgeon, taken from the soles of the feete of one sicke of the plague, then kisse one of you fasting . . . I do wonder you doe not loath yourselves" (lines 37–45). Aware that he is putting on a first-rate performance, Bosola proudly advises his auditors, "observe my meditation now," and turns from attacking specific follies to a rousing general denunciation of the human animal:

What thing is in this outward forme of man
To be belov'd? we account it ominous,
If Nature doe produce a Colt, or Lambe,
A Fawne, or Goate, in any limbe resembling
A Man; and flye from't as a prodegy.
Man stands amaz'd to see his deformity,
In any other Creature but himselfe.
But in our owne flesh, though we beare diseases
Which have their true names onely tane from beasts,
As the most ulcerous Woolfe, and swinish Meazeall;
Though we are eaten up of lice, and wormes,
And though continually we beare about us
A rotten and dead body, we delight
To hide it in rich tissew.

(lines 47–60)

All of the satirist's rhetorical tricks, his typical language and imagery, and his attitudes are in these lines, and this is but one of the many star performances which Bosola provides.

While Bosola is aware from time to time of his own unpleasant and twisted nature, on the whole he is enchanted by his own words and deceives himself into believing that he is the Tamburlaine of Vice acting from the purest motives. For example, he discovers that the Duchess has secretly had a child, and callously informs on her, for profit, to her mad brothers. This act is the basest kind of betrayal, but Bosola exultantly presents it as a praiseworthy example of the satirist's heroic quest for hidden sin, and smugly characterizes the Duchess' "failing" in a sententious manner:

Though Lust doe masque in ne['e]r so strange disguise,
She's oft found witty, but is never wise.

(II.3.92–3)

The other characters of the play, however, are not taken in by Bosola's mask of honest piety; they understand him as

we have, with the authors' help, understood other satirists.
Their comments seek out the traditional ambiguities of the
character, find the tensions, and assign other motives to the
railing than saeva indignatio. Antonio observes that Bosola's

> rayling
> Is not for simple love of Piety:
> Indeede he rayles at those things which he wants,
> Would be as leacherous, covetous, or proud,
> Bloody, or envious, as any man,
> If he had meanes to be so.
>
> (I.1.24–9)

Envy, which is mentioned several times, is, however, only
one of the usual complex of twisted motives attributed to
Bosola. His "old garbe of melencholly" is spoken of by
Ferdinand, and Antonio fears that Bosola's "foul mellan-
cholly will poyson all his goodnesse." His diseased state of
mind compounded of envy and melancholy is thought to
arise from two conventional sources: lack of suitable employment and too curious study as a young man. "Want of
action," Antonio tells us with reference to Bosola,

> Breeds all blacke male-contents, and their close rearing
> (Like mothes in cloath) doe hurt for want of wearing.
>
> (I.1.82–3)

At Padua Bosola was as much "a fantasticall scholler" as
Chrisoganus, Lampatho Doria, and similar pedants,

> who studdy to know how many knots
> Was in *Hercules* club, of what colour *Achilles* beard was,
> Or whether Hector were not troubled with the tooth-ach—
> He hath studied himselfe halfe bleare-ei'd, to know
> The true semitry of *Caesars* nose by a shooing-horne.
>
> (III.3.51–6)

And all this he did, Delio explains, not for love of learning
but "to gaine the name of a speculative man."

But melancholy, envy, lack of employment, and fantastic studies are in themselves fairly conventional explanations for the satiric character. Bosola, like other satirists, has darker and more twisted forces at work in the deeps of his character which appear only obliquely in his language and actions, and are glimpsed by the other characters only in moments of crisis. The Duchess sees him truly for an instant when he is berating Antonio in a pious fashion and wishes she could "beat that counterfeit face, into thy other" (III.5.142), but she breaks off without describing the darkness into which she has looked. Antonio too perceives that beneath the mask of "Let me be simply honest" Bosola has a monstrous pride, is "puff'd up with . . . preferment" (II.1.88), and tells him bluntly, "I do understand your inside." And at the conclusion of the play when death has washed away all disguises, one of the courtiers characterizes the dying Bosola as "Thou wretched thing of blood" (V.5.116). These brief lines are no more than half-formed insights into Bosola's characteristic satiric pride, his loathing of man and his works, his psychotic hatred of the flesh which is mixed with fascination, his sick concentration on disease and the bodily processes, and his sadistic joy in torturing others. All of these qualities float to the surface in his language and find partial expression in his delight in tormenting his victims, particularly the Duchess who in her purity and determination to remain "human" resists his persistent attempts to involve her in the general madness, bestiality, and decay of flesh which he believes to be the normal state of the world. Although a modern psychiatrist would not be completely satisfied with his explanation, Webster provides a source for Bosola's perverted nature. He has been betrayed and brutalized by the world. At some time in the past he has committed a murder for the Cardinal, who then abandoned him. As a result Bosola was sentenced to the bestial life of a galley slave. His only comment on the experience is the laconic "for two yeares together, I wore two Towells in stead of a shirt," but he has been marked. He has seen the world from the under side, and his life of brutality, treachery, and disappointment has permanently warped a character that was none too straight in the beginning, for he had been the Cardinal's bravo before being chained to a galley bench.

Bosola combines in himself, and gives full expression to, all the peculiarities of the Elizabethan satyr, but Webster does not employ him in a conventional manner. The other dramatic satirists no matter how tainted their natures and how suspect their motives have not willingly and actively engaged in evil, though the end effect of their railing may be further to infect an already sick world. But Bosola, who is an intriguer like Malevole, becomes the villain of the play by selling his talents to Ferdinand and the Cardinal, and knowingly using his railing to do their business and ultimately line his own pockets. His intrigues, which result in the exposure of the secret marriage of the Duchess and Antonio and put them in the power of her mad "Aragonian" brothers, need no recounting, and one example will show the way he works. After the Duchess has been captured, Ferdinand wants to drive her insane, so he and Bosola arrange a series of macabre scenes—each of which is an emblem of the play as a whole—in which Bosola appears disguised as a tomb-maker. Ironically, the intended disguise reveals his true nature which is concealed by his normal "face." Satire is Bosola's weapon, and he attempts with all the satirist's rhetorical skill to force on the Duchess the extreme satiric sense of life, to make her see herself and the world through his eyes as no more than slimy bestiality:

> Thou art a box of worme-seede, at best, but a salvatory
> of greene mummey: what's this flesh? a little cruded

milke, phantasticall puffe-paste: our bodies are weaker
then those paper prisons boyes use to keepe 'flies in:
more contemptible: since ours is to preserve earth-
wormes: didst thou ever see a Larke in a cage? such is
the soule in the body: this world is like her little turfe
of grasse, and the Heaven ore our heades, like her looking glasse, onely gives us a miserable knowledge of the
small compasse of our prison.

(IV.2.123–31)

Even in this fantastic scene Bosola does not abandon his
sanctimoniousness, but despite the reference to the soul and
the obvious relation of the speech to the tradition of Christian asceticism, the emphasis here is on despair, and it is on
this aspect of the satiric character that Webster capitalized
in constructing his play.

Bosola has despaired of man and of honesty at the beginning of *The Duchess of Malfi*. The world is no more than a
hospital "where this mans head lies at that mans foote, and
so lower, and lower." Since every man is an arrant knave,
why not become a flattering pander and "hang on the eares"
of the great "like a horse-leach" until full of blood, and
"then drop offe?" The despair inherent in the satiric sense
of life, not saeva indignatio, thus becomes Bosola's principal motive, although the mask of righteous indignation
is still worn and the pretense of working a cure is maintained.

But *The Duchess of Malfi* is not finally a satiric play existing only as a vehicle for Bosola and his criticisms of humanity. The satiric scene may have become the dramatic
scene, but there remains in Webster's scheme the possibility
of tragic dignity for individuals caught in a mad and bestial
world. The Duchess cannot deny or conquer in any material sense the evil which destroys her family and her body,
but she can refuse to submit to it, to become a Bosola herself, and she can maintain simply that she is "Duchesse of

Malfy still." And the "Duchesse of Malfy" is not only a nobly born woman, but, as language and scenes reveal, the very spirit of love, life, joy, and society. Bosola stands in direct contrast to the Duchess. He too has felt the dark, blasting power of hatred and unchained individualism, the killing forces embodied in Ferdinand and the Cardinal. But his reaction has been despair, cynicism, and railing. In this way the tragic reaction to an undisputedly mad world is counterpointed with a satiric reaction,[8] and the sinister aspects of the latter are underscored by allowing the satirist to follow his baser instincts and become the mere creature of those forces which have destroyed him once and bring him at last to his confused and miserable death, which contrasts so strongly with the quiet and dignified manner in which the Duchess faces her death at the hands of the strangler.

The conflict between the tragic and satiric attitudes is the ground of the play, and it is manifested not only outwardly in the struggle between the Duchess and Bosola, but inwardly in the soul of the satirist. His conflict is neither so intricate nor so deep as Hamlet's, but somewhat like Hamlet, Bosola combines in himself a cynical acceptance of the vicious world and a nagging conscience which demands that he resist in some way what he feels to be wrong. Acceptance is his way for the most part. His acquiescence with Ferdinand's plan to use him as a spy, "I am your creature," is as simple and straightforward as the tragic statement, "I am the Duchesse of *Malfy* still." But when he is paid off with the job of master of the stables he can cynically note that his corruption "grew out of horse doong." After the death of the Duchess, in which he has been chief agent, Bosola's conscience urges him even more strongly, and his

8. Webster's characteristic mixture of tragedy and satire has recently been discussed by Travis Bogard, *The Tragic Satire of John Webster*, Berkeley, 1955.

attempts to cope with it while still keeping his feet on the "slippery yce-pavements" of the court result in the sudden reversals of his character which have long troubled critics. His final decision to kill the Cardinal remains appropriately ambiguous, springing partly from a desire to help Antonio and partly from a desire to save himself from the vicious Cardinal, who after employing him to kill Antonio has now decided to be rid of his agent. In the confused and bloody melee of the concluding scene Bosola kills Antonio *by mistake* and then destroys Ferdinand and the Cardinal at the cost of his own life. The ending is a typical blood-revenge conclusion emblematic of the savage and disordered life of the principals, and Bosola's state of mind at this point is particularly interesting since it is the final judgment of the Jacobean theater on the satirist and the satiric sense of life. Webster having made his point through Bosola's activities that satire is essentially a negative and selfish approach to an undisputedly rotten world, an approach which denies man's "owne good nature," attempts in Bosola's last speeches to show the confusion and darkness of the satiric mind. Bosola ends with a platitudinous warning to mankind,

> Let worthy minds nere stagger in distrust
> To suffer death, or shame, for what is just.
>
> (v.5.127–8)

But his language suggests that he himself is lost in a world and in a death which he has not understood. He killed, he tells us, "in a mist" and "unwittingly," and speaks of the world as "gloomy," "a shadow," and a "deepe pit of darkenesse." His own life, and those of the other villains, leaves no mark on the world but is like "dead wals, or vaulted graves, / That ruin'd, yeildes no eccho." He can describe his dying as no more than holding his "weary soule" in his teeth, and his only cause for exultation is that he has accomplished the destruction of the Cardinal. The emptiness and sterility of the satirist's way is made clear even in this, the most pessimistic Jacobean play, and Webster's rejection of the extreme satiric view of the world is in keeping with the general Elizabethan and Jacobean attitude.

About 1615 the satyr satirist in his purest form disappeared from the theater. There remained, of course, characters, usually villains, who shared the satirist's despairing view of the world and who occasionally described human depravity in tones reminiscent of the satirists of Nashe, Marston, and Hall. Satiric drama continued to flourish in the hands of Jonson, Middleton, and Massinger, but it now was Menippean in form, and the satiric end of scourging the fools was achieved by allowing them to reveal their fundamental ridiculousness in their own speeches and actions. But the old satiric commentator, guilty himself of all the sins he attacks, torn by psychic disorders, and ready in an instant either to describe some particular fool in foul but striking terms or deliver a gorgeous and elaborate tirade on the dirtiness of mankind and the present Age of Iron, was no longer employed by the dramatists. In a theater where sensational characters came and went the satirist had no doubt become passé by this time—he had held the stage for fifteen years or more—but the real reason for his disappearance must be sought outside the fickle tastes of the audience.

While the discussion to this point has been focused on the conventions of satire, and particularly the satirist, the reader must have noted that at several points satire has intersected with a number of the most important movements in late Elizabethan and early Jacobean thought and literature. Stylistically it is related by its emphasis on harshness, ellipsis, and colloquialism to the Metaphysical style in poetry and the Senecan style in prose. In its concern for "realism," its avowed purpose of speaking "truth," and its scorn for the traditional poetic modes as mere fables, it is a part of the new realistic movement in poetry and drama of the 1590's and 1600's. Through its use of the somber Latin poets of the Silver Age as models, and its involvement in such stern philosophies as Calvinism, neo-Stoicism, and Cynicism, it is connected to the increasing pessimism of the age. The satirist himself resembles, and often blends with, tragic heroes of the period such as Lear, Hamlet, and Chapman's "Senecal Man," heroes whose deep disillusionment with life often finds expression in railing satiric attacks on the world. The satirist also shares a low estimation of the human animal with such Machiavellian villains as Iago, Edmund, and Sejanus, and often, as in the case of Bosola, merges with this type.

This list of literary relationships could be extended over several pages, but the point is clear that Elizabethan satire and its satirist were but one part of a larger complex of philosophies, styles, reading tastes, and literary forms which had as their common center a renewed and increasingly pessimistic concern about such vital issues as the nature of man and the status of evil in the universal scheme.[9] The new formal satire on the Juvenalian model was but one form, and not always an entirely serious one, in which these doubts and anxieties found expression, and it is perfectly natural that it should coincide in many ways with the styles, philosophies, characters, and other forms expressing these same concerns.

9. This shift in thought to which I am referring is that which has aptly been called "the Counter-Renaissance," by Hiram Haydn in his book *The Counter-Renaissance*, New York, 1950. Although Haydn reads the formal satires and satiric plays in a straightforward manner, i.e. as a direct report of the author's atttiudes without allowance for the ironic use of the satirist, the regularity with which he turns to works of this type for illustrations of his general argument that the age was one of progressive disillusionment provides striking proof of the involvement of Elizabethan and Jacobean satire with the darkest and most difficult problems of the time.

Once Marston, Hall, Nashe, and other authors of formal satire had localized the universal satiric scene and satirist by giving them an English setting and English manners, the satirist very quickly hardened into a symbol for a gloomy, exaggerated view of the sickness of the world. Though he had been specifically forged for attacks on vice and villainy, his satiric functions began to drop away, and he became in the plays the representative of a pessimistic attitude and an advocate for extreme methods of dealing with the ills of society. If we can leave aside the satiric works of such theatrical entrepreneurs as Dekker, Sharpham, and Middleton, who were willing to capitalize on any theatrical convention without concern for its possible serious implications, and look only at those works in which the authors seem to be trying to follow their material to its necessary conclusion, we can perhaps make some statement about why the satirist was treated as he was.

It is a notable fact that the satirist always operates most comfortably in a limited context, a rigorously circumscribed world. His chosen battleground is an exact, literal, and uncomplicated here and now. For him virtue is virtue and vice is vice, and he carefully avoids any airy speculations about human complexity or the mysterious nature of the universe. The ways of his fathers are good enough for him, and a healthy society, not ultimate knowledge or personal salvation, is his stated goal. The satirist, then, tries to create and live in what has been called a "pure" poem, a poem that "tries to be pure by excluding, more or less rigidly, certain elements which might qualify or contradict its original impulse." [1] The author behind the satirist may, of course, be aware of many elements which do contradict the original impulse of the satirist, particularly the imperfections of the satirist himself, and may purposely complicate

1. Robert Penn Warren, "Pure and Impure Poetry," in *Criticism, The Foundations of Modern Literary Judgment*, ed. Mark Schorer, Josephine Miles, and Gordon McKenzie (New York, Harcourt Brace, 1948), p. 372.

his satire by including such elements. This is the case in the Elizabethan formal satire where impurities are allowed to creep into the poems via an ironic treatment of the satirist.

This process of complication was intensified by the transference of formal satire to the stage, for the dramatic mode by its very nature tends away from the pure and towards the impure. Each character must endure comparison with other characters, and his theories and actions are objectively tested by being followed out to their conclusions. But the nature of the dramatic mode was not the only force working for the complication of satire, for the Elizabethan poets, even some of the inferior ones, had a habit of placing every act, attitude, and point of view in the widest possible perspective. Heaven and Hell appear to have been their spatial boundaries, and Creation and Judgment their temporal limits. Seen in these vast perspectives men and their problems appear quite different from what they seem to be in the narrow perspective of the satirist, and the satirist himself with his typical statements about the world's ills and his prescriptions for its cure is reduced to something considerably less than the heroic proportions he assumes in formal satire.

The all-inclusive question which in one form or another is regularly posed in late Elizabethan and Jacobean drama is, "Who am I?" Lear asks it in a number of ways and receives different answers from men and from the elements at various times; but each answer is only provisional, and as he encounters new complications he is forced to modify his definition. This is the tragic process, one of inquiry, progression, and dialectic. But when the Duchess of Malfi, nearly maddened by the changes she has undergone, begins searching for her identity she asks her question "Who am I?" (v.2.122) of Bosola and receives the satirist's final answer: "Thou art a box of worme-seede, at best, but a salvatory of greene mummey." He goes on to remind her that "Heaven ore our heades . . . onely gives us a miserable knowledge of the small compasse of our prison," and reads her a lecture on the error of her past ways, "Thou art some great woman sure, for riot begins to sit on thy fore-head (clad in grey haires) twenty yeares sooner, then on a merry milkemaydes." The Duchess, however, refuses to accept the identification thrust on her by the "plaine" satirist, and her simple answer, "I am Duchesse of *Malfy* still," is a rejection of Bosola's attempt to define her as no more than a piece of rotting, sinful flesh, lost in an impenetrable cosmos. Her refusal to accept the satirist's viewpoint is but one statement of the refusal of her age, for the dramatists, no matter how willing they may have been to admit that the world is very nearly as debased as the satirist says it is, would not agree that man is no more than the slime of the sublunary dung-hill. This is, they show again and again, but one way of looking at the world, and an imperfect one. They did not rest content with contrasting the satirist's way with more dignified and heroic ways as in *Troilus* and *The Duchess of Malfi*, but probed back into his past to discover in his psychic history the sources of his misanthropy, and carried him forward, as in *Timon*, to show that his scourge is no effective instrument for dealing with a mad world. Even Ben Jonson, a dramatist with a distinct satiric bent, found pure satire too limited to contain his vision of the world, and after a few experiments he subdued his satire to a semicomic scheme in which the sterile satiric combat of satirist and fools was broken up and the health of the society was restored through the operation of the laws of nature.

Satire appears to have had too narrow a range for the more gifted dramatists, and they turned their "satiric" plays into examinations of the credentials of satire itself and explorations of the validity of the satiric sense of life. In doing so they inevitably subordinated satire to tragedy or comedy, and left it to the next age to become the great period of English satire.

CHAPTER 6

CONCLUSION

Taking the character of the satirist as the key term in the Elizabethan satiric formula, I have attempted in the preceding chapters to trace the course of satire during the late English Renaissance by following the fortunes of the satirist from his genesis in the critical theory which associated satire with satyrs to his final appearance as a distinct type in Jacobean tragedy. My most immediate purpose has been to demonstrate that the Elizabethan and Jacobean satirists are best understood as conventional figures designed for a specific function in satire, not as spokesmen for the authors' views or direct reflections of their own characters. The evidence for this understanding of the satirists appears, to me at least, to be overwhelming. First of all, we have the continuity of the tradition itself. From Nashe's Pierce Penilesse to Webster's Bosola, the satirist remains basically the same unpleasant, exaggerated critic railing against the sins of the world in a lurid style, and guilty of many of the failings for which he attacks others. Furthermore, once we abandon the notion that the satirist equals the author, it becomes apparent that in both formal satire and satiric drama the authors treat their satirists in a highly ironic manner by stressing their peculiarities and by placing them in contexts and situations which bring their motives and attitudes into question. Both of these facts make clear the separation that exists between an Elizabethan author and

247

his satirist, for it seems impossible that all the authors of satire had nearly identical characters and that they were all so unsophisticated, as men and artists, that they were unable to conceal the glaring weaknesses of this character.

But we have other forms of evidence as well. Whenever such professional critics as Lodge and Puttenham or the satiric authors themselves discuss satire, they always speak of playing a part and employing an appropriate style. The particular part and style are decided on not by reference to the personality of the author but in terms of the supposed ancient origins of the satiric genre, its purpose, and the correct manner for writing in this form as established by the practice of the classical authors of satire. The orthodoxy and degree of acceptance of these prescriptions for writing satire are attested to by the regular attempts of the authors, and particularly the less gifted ones, to create the required scourging satyr and stuttering style, and the various caricatures of this figure and parodies of his style. Finally, Ben Jonson's *Every Man Out of His Humor,* which is practically a dramatic diagram of formal satire as the Elizabethans understood it, makes clear the fundamental distinction between the author's feelings of outrage at the world's follies and the character employed to do the actual work of scourging the fools and bringing them to their senses.

Wherever we have looked at the English satire of the late Renaissance we have found traces not of romantic self-expression but of self-conscious art, of traditions, conventions, consideration of poetic means in terms of poetic ends, and concern for the suitability of one part of a satiric poem to the other parts. If looking at satirists did not become such a tedious and unrewarding matter after a time, many times as much evidence could be adduced, but the principal grounds for my argument have been stated and the piling up of further details would in no way prove my case. The immediate practical value of understanding the distinction between satirist and author is, of course, an improved reading of various Elizabethan satiric works which have been distorted by the assumption that the satirist speaks for the author and that his speeches are therefore intended to be taken at face value. This view has been particularly influential in the reading of Marston's plays, which have been regularly declared to be unsatisfactory and wildly inconsistent because the satirist is at times ridiculous and inconsistent. In one case, *Histriomastix,* the theory that the satirist equals Marston and that he writes *only* as the satirist has even affected bibliographical matters and led to the assertion that *Histriomastix* as we have it is a reworking of an older play to which Marston added only those parts in which Chrisoganus speaks as a satirist. No matter how they are read, Marston's plays, with the possible exception of *The Malcontent,* are not masterpieces, but if we accept his satirists as fully dramatic and independent characters, the plays do make sense at least, and Marston himself ceases to be the psychiatric case which the biographical type of criticism has made of him.

Although it has not been seriously proposed in recent years that Thersites and Timon speak for Shakespeare, or Bosola for Webster, a realization that these and other Jacobean satirists are elaborations of a stock figure associated with an exaggerated and pessimistic approach to the problems of the world does have a bearing on our reading of the satiric tragedies of this period. In the plays in which such satirists as Thersites, Vendici, and Bosola appear, theirs is the most despairing voice. They take the view that man is no more than a selfish animal, that life is a process of rotting, that society has become a syndicate of thieves and bullies, and that human history is a record of degeneration. Their answer to this situation is to heap curses on beastly man; or to attempt to tear away the masks that cover his corruptness and reveal him for what he truly is; or to accept the state of things cynically and "scuffle" with the rest or hang to the great like leeches until full of blood. These satirists and their melancholy views of the human condition are the darkest parts of the somber world of Jacobean tragedy and tragical satire, but it is well to remember that the standard role of the Elizabethan satirist is that of the extreme pessimist. His views are never to be taken entirely seriously, for he is by custom a sick and disappointed man, who, while he may hit the mark from time to time, looks at the world askew. As such, his words are always to be taken as the extreme statement of the pessimistic point of view, the absolute worst that can be said of the world, and not as the final view of the author, who uses the satirist as no more than one form of statement about how the world goes. Recognition of this fact not only tends to weaken arguments about the hopeless tone of Jacobean drama in general and the "dark periods" of the dramatists, but it prepares us to respond to the ironic treatment of such satiric characters as Malevole, Timon and Vendici who have often been accepted uncritically.

The illumination of certain satiric poems and plays has not, however, been the only purpose of the foregoing chapters, for they have been designed to provide at the same time an illustration of the general theory of satire advanced in Chapter 1. Most obviously, Elizabethan satiric theory and practice support my basic contention: that satire is not a form of biography or social history but an artistic construct, the parts of which—scene, satirist, and plot—are to be understood in terms of their function in the satiric poem. But more specifically, these satiric works, Roman and medieval as well as Elizabethan, lend support to my argument that despite variations resulting from changes in ethos and differences in particulars, the basic components of satire, scene, satirist, and plot remain fairly constant in all ages because they are always the expression of an unchanging sense of life.

The Elizabethan satiric scene has not been discussed as thoroughly as the satirist for the reasons that the Elizabethans concentrated their attention on the satirist, and that most modern critics have taken it more or less for granted that the worlds created by such writers as Marston and Jonson are symbolic rather than literal approximations of reality. But wherever we have looked at the satiric scene it has shown the standard configurations: massive amounts of foolishness and villainy, and a jumble of material things pressing in a disorderly fashion upon, and threatening to obliterate, the remnants of sanity and decency. Whether the scene is Juvenal's Rome, the medieval "felde ful of folke," the streets of Tudor London, or the "Italian lascivious palace," vice and idiocy appear in the same distorted faces, the grotesque flesh, and the obscene acts which manifest moral ugliness and total involvement in bestial carnality. These figures move among the shambles they have made of the state, the city, the palace of the prince, the family, those visible expressions of the humane ideals of reason, order, love, and control.

The satirist who stands before this scene commenting on it has in every instance the same basic character deriving from his function in the poem, though the medieval plowman plays down one side of his personality by weakening his attack and retreating into the scene. The Elizabethan satyr satirist, however, provides a particularly striking example of the way in which the satiric character is shaped by the requirements of the satiric poem. The face he turns toward the world, his public personality, is a rough one, that of an honest, straightforward, and thoroughly indignant man, but it satisfies the requirement of satire that the speaker should be a man of probity. His private personality—which, in fact, becomes fairly public in Elizabethan satire—is made up of the usual tensions incumbent on practicing the satiric trade. He is prurient, sadistic, sick in mind, proud, pessimistic, envious, and downright untruthful. The satiric authors make no attempt to conceal these deficiencies, and they recognize that this twisted character is inevitably created by a vigorous attack on vice. The choice of the satyr as a model for the satirist expresses their belief that satire is an activity only for the character who finds swinging the lash a congenial occupation, and they explicitly ground the distorted point of view of their satirists on the necessities of satire itself, e.g. "squint-eyed sight" is necessary to "catch the world aright."

The plot of Elizabethan formal satire is the usual stasis, but the most interesting comment on the satiric plot is provided by those Elizabethan and Jacobean plays which include a satirist. The study of the "satiric" drama undertaken in Chapters 4 and 5 had as its first object a demonstration of the continuity of the tradition of the satyr satirist, but these plays, it developed, are not so much satires as they are themselves, at least in part, investigations of the nature of satire, investigations conducted in dramatic rather than critical terms. As such, they direct our attention to some of the peculiarities of satire, particularly the curiously truncated satiric plot. By seeing the satirist operating in a "normal" plot in which conflict leads to change and resolution we are made aware of the fact that in pure satire he usually works in a world where there is no true change and where he is not, therefore, ever judged by the effect of his railing on the course of events. In the same fashion these Elizabethan and Jacobean plays reveal indirectly the restricted, "pure" qualities of the usual satiric scene by showing the inadequacy of the typical satirist's understanding of and ability to deal with a more complex world than that created in formal verse satire.

In the long run, of course, a demonstration of what the

Elizabethans believed about satire *proves* nothing except that the Elizabethans believed it. I am not arguing that because John Marston, Ben Jonson, and Thomas Lodge understood satire in a certain way their theory is therefore correct for all time, but their way does seem to provide a much more satisfactory approach to the satires of their own age, and to those of other ages as well, than do the historical and biographical methods which have been so much in favor. Thus, the Elizabethan understanding of the nature of satire is offered not as proof positive—a very rare thing in literary criticism—that satire is a form of poetry made up of interlocking symbolic parts, but as a critical approach which resolves the various dilemmas created by historical and biographical criticism, and permits us to read satiric poems as dramatic and coherent works of art.

One final word is necessary. Although the Elizabethan and Jacobean dramatists largely rejected satire, their rejection should not be taken as final proof that the genre is inferior to tragedy and comedy or a less adequate mirror of ultimate reality. Satire is disqualified in Renaissance drama by placing the satirist in either an essentially tragic or an essentially comic scene where he is made to appear shortsighted and wrongheaded. But the satirist was designed for satire and the satiric scene, he is but one part of a larger organism, and it was inevitable that he should be inadequate in a scene of a different order. A hero from one genre is always a failure in another: Satan would make an excellent tragic hero but in the epic world of *Paradise Lost* he becomes both villain and fool; Gregers Werle has all the attributes of the tragic hero but in the bitterly comic world of Ibsen's *The Wild Duck* he is only a trouble maker; and Falstaff, the comic hero, is finally found seriously lacking in the predominantly tragic world of *2 Henry IV*.

INDEX

YALE STUDIES IN ENGLISH

This volume is the one hundred and forty-second of the Yale Studies in English, founded by Albert Stanburrough Cook in 1898 and edited by him until his death in 1927. Tucker Brooke succeeded him as editor, and served until 1941, when Benjamin C. Nangle succeeded him.

The following volumes are still in print. Orders should be addressed to YALE UNIVERSITY PRESS, New Haven, Connecticut.

87. OSBORN, L. B. The Life, Letters, and Writings of John Hoskyns. $3.50.

90. BERNARD, J. E., JR. The Prosody of the Tudor Interlude. $3.00.

92. RICH, T. Harrington and Ariosto: A Study in English Verse Translation. $2.00.

102. WORTHINGTON, JANE. Wordsworth's Reading of Roman Prose. $2.50.

108. HAMMOND, LANSING VAN DER HEYDEN. Laurence Sterne's *Sermons of Mr. Yorick*. $2.75.

109. BORST, WILLIAM A. Lord Byron's First Pilgrimage. $3.75.

110. MICHEL, LAURENCE (editor). *The Tragedy of Philotas*. By Samuel Daniel. $3.75.

112. CALDER, GRACE J. The Writing of *Past and Present*. A Study of Carlyle's Manuscripts. $3.75.

113. DONALDSON, E. TALBOT. *Piers Plowman:* The C-Text and Its Poet. $5.00.

114. LYON, JUDSON STANLEY. *The Excursion*. A Study. $3.75.

116. SEYBOLD, ETHEL. Thoreau: The Quest and the Classics. $3.00.

117. KNIGHT, DOUGLAS. Pope and the Heroic Tradition. A Critical Study of His *Iliad*. $3.00.

119. DAVIS, MERRELL R. Melville's *Mardi*. A Chartless Voyage. $4.00.

120. WAITH, EUGENE M. The Pattern of Tragicomedy in Beaumont and Fletcher. $4.00.

122. IRVING, E. B., JR. (editor). The Old English *Exodus*. $5.00.

124. QUIRK, RANDOLPH. The Concessive Relation in Old English Poetry. $4.00.